CHICANA WAYS

Chicana Ways

Conversations with Ten Chicana Writers

KARIN ROSA IKAS

University of Nevada Press
Reno & Las Vegas

University of Nevada Press, Reno, Nevada 89557 USA
Copyright © 2002 by University of Nevada Press
Photos © Dr. Karin Ikas unless otherwise noted
All rights reserved
Manufactured in the United States of America

Designed by Omega Clay

Library of Congress Cataloging-in-Publication Data
  Chicana ways : conversations with ten Chicana writers / Karin Rosa Ikas.
    p. cm.
  Includes bibliographical references and index.
ISBN 0-87417-492-9 (alk. paper)—ISBN 0-87417-493-7 (pbk. : alk. paper)
1. Mexican American authors—Interviews. 2. American literature—Mexican American
authors—History and criticism—Theory, etc. 3. American literature—Women authors—
History and criticism—Theory, etc. 4. American literature—20th century—History and
criticism—Theory, etc. 5. Women and literature—United States—History—20th century.
6. Authors, American—20th century—Interviews. 7. Women authors, American—Interviews. 8. Mexican American women—Interviews. 9. Mexican American women in literature. 10. Mexican Americans in literature. I. Ikas, Karin.
PS153.M4 C455 2001
810.9'9287'0896872—dc21   2001002289

The paper used in this book meets the requirements of American National Standard for
Information Sciences—Permanence of Paper for Printed Library Materials, ANSI z39.48-
1984. Binding materials were selected for strength and durability.

11 10 09 08 07 06 05 04 03 02   5 4 3 2

For my family
and all dear friends
in Germany and
all over the world

CONTENTS

ILLUSTRATIONS

PREFACE

ALL OF the author interviews were tape-recorded except those with Estela Portillo-Trambley (conducted by phone and mail) and Demetria Martínez (videotaped). In editing the interviews, I had to reorganize some material and shorten some sentences; however, I neither censored nor fundamentally changed what the writers said. If I felt explanations were needed, I inserted additional information in brackets. The edited texts were then shown to the writers, who occasionally clarified words and suggested slight changes but did not substantially alter the interview.

All of the photographs were taken by Dr. Karin Ikas except those of Denise Chávez (by Marion Ettlinger), Jamie Lujan (by Lois Tema), Demetria Martínez (by Jeff Smith), Cherríe Moraga (by Jean Weisinger), and Estela Portillo-Trambley (by Achilles Studio).

I would like to thank all of the individuals and institutions that made this book possible. Without their belief in its significance and their subsequent support, this project would not have been realizable. My sincere thanks go to Professor Rüdiger Ahrens of the University of Würzburg, Professor Heiner Bus from the University of Bamberg, and my friends and colleagues at the University of New Mexico at Albuquerque (Rudolfo Anaya, Maria Teresa Márquez, and Professors Héctor Torres, Erlinda Gonzales-Berry, and Tey Diana Rebolledo), the University of California at Berkeley (Lillian Castillo-Speed, Head of the Ethnic Studies Library; and Professors Norma Alarcón and Genaro Padilla), and the University of California at Santa Barbara (Professor Francisco A. Lomelí, Chair of the Chicano Studies Department; Professor Luis Leal, and all of the people at the Colección Tloque Nahuaque, particularly Raquel Quiroz González).

My deepest appreciation goes to the writers who took the time to talk with me and share their thoughts, ideas, and concerns. I enjoyed their humor and intelligence, their seriousness about writing, and their lack of pretentiousness. Above all, I am grateful for their cordiality and hospitality.

Finally, I would like to thank my friends and family who were there with their love and support when the going got rough.

INTRODUCTION

I N 1931 the American historian James Truslow Adams coined the term "the American Dream" to specify "America's distinctive and unique gift to mankind" as "a dream of a land in which life should be better and richer and fuller for every man, with opportunity for each according to his ability or achievement. . . . It is not a dream of motor cars and high wages merely, but a dream of a social order in which each man and each woman shall be able to attain the fullest stature of which they are innately capable, and be recognized by others for what they are, regardless of the fortuitous circumstances of birth or position."[1] However, for many Mexican American men and women, also known as Chicanos and Chicanas, "the American Dream" often remains an unfulfilled promise.[2] Sometimes it even turns into an American Nightmare, as several sociological studies and statistics show. Nevertheless, despite the failures and frustrations, a vision of "a better and fuller [life] for every man and woman" in the Americas endures as Chicanos and Chicanas struggle to overcome the tensions between a faulty present and a deeply ingrained faith in a better tomorrow.

Part of that struggle involves defining an identity, which, given their bicultural heritage, has always been a complex challenge for Mexican Americans. Living in multiple realities that require a variety of survival techniques, they often rely on a dynamic concept of identity. As Ramón Saldívar notes in *Chicano Narrative: The Dialectics of Difference*, the Chicano/a experience cannot be captured within concepts that regard reality as fixed.[3] This is particularly true for Mexican American women who are struggling to seize subjectivity despite pressure to conform to traditional concepts of femaleness and guarantee cultural perseverance by living their lives as obedient wives, tortilla makers, cooks, and servants to their husbands and families.

Many modern Chicanas, no longer willing to be victims or accept subordination in a patriarchal setting, are daring to speak out and tackle the multiple forms of discrimination within Mexican American culture and society in general. As writer and feminist Gloria Anzaldúa states: "We are beginning to realize that we are not wholly at the mercy of circumstance, nor are our lives completely out of our hands. That if we posture as victims we will be victims, that hopelessness is suicide, that self-attacks stop us in our tracks. We are slowly moving past the resistance within, leaving behind the defeated images."[4]

This movement toward a self-defined Chicana identity is decisively characterized by an ongoing transgression of borders. As such it challenges essentialist notions of identity and shapes a new way of being, as Anzaldúa elaborates in her programmatic essay "La Conciencia de la Mestiza: Towards a New Consciousness," published in *Borderlands/La Frontera* in 1987: "En unas pocas centurias, the future will belong to the mestiza. Because the future depends on the breaking down of paradigms, it depends on the straddling of two or more cultures. By creating a new mythos—that is, a change in the way we perceive reality, the way we see ourselves and the ways we behave—la mestiza creates a new consciousness, a mestiza consciousness."[5]

In the struggle for a self-defined identity and a less discriminatory society, art and literature are particularly important. As Yvonne Yarbro-Bejarano notes, "the fact that Chicanas may tell stories about themselves and other Chicanas challenges the dominant male concepts of cultural ownership and literary traditions. In telling these stories, Chicanas reject the dominant culture's definition of what a Chicana is. In writing, they refuse the objectification imposed by gender roles and racial and economic exploitation.[6] Berkeley feminist critic Norma Alarcón (incorporating Julia Kristeva's concept of the symbolic contract) emphasizes that writing can therefore be seen as a way for the female "speaking subject to position herself at the margins of the system and reject the traditional definitions of 'woman' and 'man.'" It enables Chicanas to overcome a system "within which women may have a voice on the condition that they speak as future wives or mothers."[7]

Being members of several minority groups (Mexican Americans/Latinos, third-world women, women in general, and sometimes lesbians/

homosexuals), Chicanas have to confront various types of discrimination while trying to create and establish an independent identity.[8] For Chicana writers, creative acts are thus "not merely aesthetic exercises but important ways to liberate oneself from racial, socio-cultural and sexual oppression, to create a new culture and even survive,"[9] as Gloria Anzaldúa aptly puts it. In fact, many Chicana writers might even be called "political" writers if one applies Cherríe Moraga's notion of the political writer as "the ultimate optimist, believing people are capable of change and using words as one way to try and penetrate the privatism of our lives. A privatism which keeps us back and away from each other, which renders us politically useless."[10] Thus the nexus of the American Dream could provide Chicana writers with a visionary energy to pursue personal development and social transformation alike. As literary critic Francisco Lomelí points out, "Chicana writers examine their situation within both marriage and other social and economic circumstances. In so doing, they express an awareness of the need to change the roles of women in contemporary society."[11]

In addressing themselves and their roles within Chicano/a, Latino/a, and American literature from different angles, many contemporary Chicana writers call for heterogeneous approaches and border-crossing perspectives for those reading and studying their works. In the end, modern Chicana writers—such as Gloria Anzaldúa, Josefina López, Denise Chávez, Jamie Lujan and her colleagues at Latina Theatre Lab, Pat Mora, Estela Portillo-Trambley, Lucha Corpi, and many others—shape Antonia Darder's transborder experience by proving that "the transcultural dimension of biculturalism must be situated within a continually changing process of cultural identity formation, as much as within complex human negotiations for social and material survival."[12] By doing so, they reaffirm the claim of the renowned Chicano playwright and director Luis Valdez: "Art is not a question of affirmative action. It is an affirmation of one's belief in human universality [because] the world is not black and white. It is a multitude of colors."[13] Such a humanistic world would grant everyone enough freedom to pursue a dynamic journey of self-determined identity formation and a personal rendering of the American Dream.

In reflecting upon her own individualization, Josefina López provides a colorful firsthand impression of what this personal journey is likely to look like for many modern Chicanas successfully coping with their multifaceted existence:

I have been many people, many identities. I came to this country when I was five as a Mexican. Then I became a Mexican-American as a result of going to Australia to represent the United States and realizing I could no longer reject myself as Mexican. Then I became "Hispanic" because I went to New York City and I preferred it over "Spanish." Then I went to UCSD and joined MECHA and became a Chicana, . . . then a Chingóna . . . then I became human and a possibility, instead of remaining a fighter, who always acted like a victim privately. . . .

I have been on a long journey into self-discovery, yet I know this is finally the beginning. I no longer have to be anything except be.[14]

There are many reasons why in recent years female writers of Mexican American descent have become such a vital part of U.S. minority literatures and also a thriving force in developing women-of-color literature and criticism.[15] As Tey Diana Rebolledo and Eliana S. Rivero reveal in *Infinite Divisions,* "writing becomes not only a sensuous act that allows Chicanas to endure, to create their own images, and their own souls," but also a means of stimulating feminists of different colors and ethnicities to work on concepts of female identity that cross borders in many regards.[16] Many of the writers discussed here also call for less restrictive and cosmopolitan concepts of identity formation to allow all women to pursue individual happiness in a more humane world. "For finally," says Cherríe Moraga, "we write to anyone who will listen with their ears open to the currents of change around them."[17]

Chicana Ways: Conversations with Ten Chicana Writers intends to guide an international array of readers, students, scholars, and critics to these writers' work and to give witness to what more these and other Chicana authors have to say about contemporary literature as well as how they feel about themselves, their works, and their communities. It invites you to encounter and connect to Chicana ways of life.

Doing so, this book fills a void in Chicana and ethnic studies as well as American and English studies. It is the first collection of interviews exclusively with female writers of the fastest-growing minority group in the United States: Mexican Americans. Of the interview collections published in the vein of multiculturalism within the past twenty years, only a few have focused on minority subgroups such as black women writers,[18] Native American women writers,[19] and others. Until now, interviews conducted with Chicana writers could only be found in journals or magazines,[20] or as part of broader-based collections such as interviews with southwestern or Chicano writers in general, with

Latino/a writers, women writers, women-of-color writers, multicultural writers, or lesbian writers. Too often, the few Chicana writers included in these collections appeared to function more like tokens supposed to represent the Chicana voice per se. This book, in contrast, reveals the multiplicity of Chicana voices and demonstrates that it is impossible for just one or two writers to represent the whole group or, better, groups of Chicana authors. Such a limited perspective only leads to distorted and oversimplified ideas about Chicana authors and literature.

The opportunity to conduct ten interviews with quite different Chicana authors became available to me after I was awarded a U.S. traveling grant by the German Academic Exchange Service (DADD) to conduct research and collect material for my Ph.D. thesis at the University of New Mexico at Albuquerque, the University of California at Berkeley, and the University of California at Santa Barbara. I interviewed not only internationally acknowledged authors—including the lesbian feminists Gloria Anzaldúa and Cherríe Moraga; well-known poets Pat Mora, Lorna Dee Cervantes, and Lucha Corpi (also a novelist); and prose writers Mary Helen Ponce, Denise Chávez, and Estela Portillo-Trambley, one of the pioneers of modern Chicana literature—but also new and quite experimental writers, including Jamie Lujan, an actress and playwright who is also the cofounder of the Latina Theatre Lab initiative, and Demetria Martínez, the Arizona-based (but New Mexico native) poet, novelist, journalist, and activist.

The interviewed writers spent much of their lives in Texas, New Mexico, and California, but this regional aspect is given added breadth because some of them now live elsewhere. California-born Lorna Dee Cervantes, for example, now teaches at the University of Colorado at Boulder, Demetria Martínez lives in Tucson, Arizona, and Pat Mora alternates between Ohio and her native Southwest. Also, some of the writers still have very strong ties to Mexico, particularly poet and novelist Lucha Corpi, who was born and grew up in Mexico and then moved to California when she was eighteen.

I conducted the interviews in libraries, bookstores, coffee shops, restaurants, and the authors' homes. All of the writers were disarmingly frank about themselves and their work, and each interview was a delight and a revelation. One recurring topic of conversation involved these women's efforts to shatter myths and overcome borders not only by writing, but also through their whole way of living. And all of them share the belief that it is vital to create a broader, freer space for women to form their identities and for cultural development to take place, including promotion of cross-cultural and international alliances. Because they have very different approaches to these goals, each writer has a unique, powerful, and important perspective to contribute. While New Mexicans Denise Chávez and Pat Mora focus on culturally and locally specific elements and traditions, Gloria Anzaldúa and others emphasize the importance of crossing various borders participating in an international exchange of ideas in areas such as feminism, queer studies, multiculturalism, and single and multiple identity formation. Gloria Anzaldúa and Cherríe Moraga have also played major roles in the foundation, formulation, and establishment of women-of-color feminism as well as queer theory, and they reflect upon that as well. Altogether these writers cover all genres, producing poetry, novels, short stories, children's literature, autobiographies, essays, and critical writing, as well as traditional and new dramatic forms such as sitcoms, one-woman shows, and musical comedies. On all formal as well as thematic fronts these ten writers are battling the myths and stereotypes that continue to circumscribe freedom of expression and life fulfillment for Chicana women and minorities in general.

My intention in producing this collection of interviews is to present the multiplicity and diversity of Chicana voices to an international audience and to stimulate further interest in these writers and their works in the United States. The growing number and popularity of recent publications of Chicana literature in the United States demonstrate that Chicanas are gaining momentum and that their influence will continue to be felt for some time.

Welcome to their work and worlds!

NOTES

1. James Truslow Adams, *The Epic of America* (New York: Blue Ribbon Books, 1931), p. 404.

2. For detailed accounts of "the American Dream" concept, see Peter Freese, ed., *"America": Dream or Nightmare? Reflections on a Composite Image* (Essen: Blaue Eule, 1990). Freese identifies six criteria as key elements of the American Dream: (1) "the belief in PROGRESS; (2) the belief in the general attainability of SUCCESS; (3) the belief in MANIFEST DESTINY; (4) the idea of the continual challenge of respective FRONTIERS; (5) the belief in the American form of government for the people, by the people, and for the people as the sole guaran-

tor of LIBERTY and EQUALITY; and (6) the conviction expressed in the notion of the MELTING POT and its historical mutations from CULTURAL PLURALISM to MULTIETHNICITY." For further studies on the American Dream phenomenon, see also Frederic I. Carpenter, *American Literature and the Dream* (New York, 1955); Lew Smith, *The American Dream* (Glenview, N.Y., 1977); Brian Tracy and Erwin Helms (eds.), *American Dreams—American Nightmares* (München, 1981); and Gerhard Kirchner et al. (eds.), *The American Dream: Myth and Reality in Contemporary America* (Frankfurt: Peter Lang, 1982).

3. Ramón Saldívar, *Chicano Narrative: The Dialectics of Difference* (Madison: University of Wisconsin Press, 1990), pp. 205–218.

4. Gloria Anzaldúa, foreword to *Making Face, Making Soul—Haciendo Caras,* ed. Anzaldúa (San Francisco: Aunt Lute, 1990), p. iv.

5. Gloria Anzaldúa, "La Conciencia de la Mestiza: Towards a New Consciousness," in Anzaldúa (ed.), *Borderlands: La Frontera* (San Francisco: Aunt Lute, 1986), pp. 77–91, p. 80.

6. Yvonne Yarbro-Bejarano, "Chicana Literature from a Chicana Feminist Perspective," in María Herrera-Sobek and Helena María Viramontes (eds.), *Chicana Creativity and Criticism: New Frontiers in American Literature* (Albuquerque: University of New Mexico Press, 1996), pp. 213–219, p. 215.

7. Norma Alarcón, "Making Familia from Scratch," in *The Americas Review* 15/3–4 (1987): 147–149, p. 148.

8. As a very useful source of information on the situation of Mexican American women in the United States, see Teresa Córdova et al. (eds.), *Chicana Voices: Intersections of Class, Race, and Gender* (Albuquerque: University of New Mexico Press, 1990); Adelaida Del Castillo (ed.), *Between Borders: Essays on Mexicana/Chicana History* (Encino, Calif.: Floricanto, 1990); and Teresa L. Amott and Julie A. Matthaei, *Race, Gender and Work: A Multicultural History of Women in the United States* (Boston: South End Press, 1991). See also Francisco Lomelí (ed.), *Handbook of Hispanic Cultures in the United States* (Houston: Arte Público, 1993).

9. Gloria Anzaldúa (ed.), *"Making Face, Making Soul: Haciendo Caras,* una Entrada" (San Francisco: Aunt Lute, 1990), pp. 15–28, p. 24.

10. Cherríe Moraga, "Refugees of a World on Fire," in Anzaldúa, *Making Face,* p. iii.

11. Francisco Lomelí, "The Chicana in Chicano Literature," in Julio A. Martínez and Francisco Lomelí (eds.), *Chicano Literature: A Reference Guide* (Westport, Conn.: Greenwood, 1985), pp. 97–107, p. 104.

12. Antonia Darder, "The Politics of Biculturalism: Culture and Difference in the Formation of Warriors for Gringostroika and the New Mestiza," in Antonio Darder and Rodolfo D. Torres (eds.), *The Latino Studies Reader: Culture, Economy and Society* (Malden: Blackwell, 1998), pp. 129–142, p. 138.

13. Luis Valdez, "A Statement on Artistic Freedom," in *American Theatre* (November 1992): 18–19.

14. Josefina López, *"My Low Self-Esteem Days" and Other Poetic Thoughts* (Studio City, Calif.: Vinny Curto, 1997).

15. See, for example, Cordelia Chávez Candelaria, "Latina Women Writers: Chicana, Cuban American and Puerto Rican Voices," in Lomelí, *Handbook of Hispanic Cultures*, pp. 134–162; Tey Diana Rebolledo and Eliana S. Rivero (eds.), *Infinite Divisions: An Anthology of Chicana Literature* (Tucson: University of Arizona Press, 1993).

16. Rebolledo and Rivero, *Infinite Divisions*, p. 33.

17. Moraga, "Refugees," p. iii.

18. For example, Claudia Tate (ed.), *Black Women Writers at Work* (New York: Continuum, 1983).

19. For example, Laura Coltelli (ed.), *Winged Words: American Indian Writers Speak* (Lincoln: University of Nebraska Press, 1992).

20. For example, "Interview with Pat Mora Conducted by Norma Alarcón," *Third Woman* 3/1–2 (1986): 121–126; "Interview with Gloria Anzaldúa Conducted by Ann Louise Keating," *Frontiers: A Journal of Women Studies* 14/1 (1993): 105–130.

CHICANA WAYS

Gloria Anzaldúa

Writer, Editor, Critic, and Third-World Lesbian
Women-of-Color Feminist

"To me theory is a way of writing a story, a way tradition says that we should write a story."

SANTA CRUZ, CALIFORNIA, DECEMBER 20, 1996

A SELF-DESCRIBED border woman and "dyke," Gloria Anzaldúa is one of the leading third-world women-of-color feminists in the United States. She is a Chicana, Tejana, lesbian feminist, poet, writer, critic, and editor. Anzaldúa is deeply committed to political and social issues that affect the lives of all third-world women of color, in particular lesbians. Consequently, she travels throughout the United States and the world to attend conferences, to give lectures, and to read her poetry and fiction to diverse audiences.

Anzaldúa's first book, *Borderlands/La Frontera: The New Mestiza,* was published in 1987. It is an interwoven mixture of essay, *cuento,* memoir, and poetry in English, Spanish, and Tex-Mex, and it describes her concepts of the border woman and the mestiza of mixed racial and cultural background. Her second book, *This Bridge Called My Back: Writings by Radical Women of Color,* coedited with Cherríe Moraga and published in 1983, received the Before Columbus Foundation American Book Award. In 1990, she edited another anthology of women-of-color writings, *Making Face, Making Soul: Haciendo Caras,* which received the Lambda Lesbian Small Book Press Award. Among the other numerous awards her works have won are an NEA Fiction Award and the Sappho Award of Distinction. Anzaldúa was also a Rockefeller Visiting Scholar at the University of Arizona in 1991.

Her essays and stories have been published in many mainstream and alternative presses, and for the last decade she has been working in a new genre, children's literature. Her bilingual books for children include

1

Prietita Has a Friend/Prietita Tiene un Amigo (1991), *Friends from the Other Side/Amigos del Otro Lado* (1993), and *Prietita and the Ghost Woman/Prietita y La Llorona* (1995).

A seventh-generation American with Mexican roots, Gloria Anzaldúa was born on September 26, 1942, in the Valley of South Texas to Urbano and Amalia García Anzaldúa. A rebellious Chicana from an early age, Gloria refused to accept the traditional role that her mother, family, and Chicano culture tried to impose on her. Instead, she devoted most of her time to pursuing an education. In 1969 she received her B.A. in art from Pan American University in Edinburgh, Texas, and three years later, her M.A. in English and art education from the University of Texas at Austin. Her quest for an education took her to several universities around the United States. Since earning her master's degree, she has been a lecturer in creative writing, feminist studies, and Chicano studies at the University of Texas at Austin and its Mexican American Studies Center (1974–1977), the University of California at Santa Cruz (1978–1979), San Francisco State University (1979–1980), Oakes College at UC Santa Cruz (1982–1984), Vermont College, and Norwich University in Indiana. In spring 1988, Anzaldúa returned to UC Santa Cruz as a Distinguished Visiting Professor in Women's Studies. She is now working toward a Ph.D. in the History of Consciousness program at UC Santa Cruz, where she also teaches literature, creative writing, and women's studies courses. Although she continues to participate in workshops, conferences, and panels, she devotes as much time as possible to her writing, which she considers to be her "significant other."

KARIN IKAS In your life, particularly in your personal life, but also in your writing career, you had to struggle a lot because you had hardship and oppression to overcome right from the beginning. Can you tell us a bit more about that—about your childhood and how you were raised?

GLORIA ANZALDÚA I grew up on a ranch settlement called Jesus María in the Valley of South Texas. At that time there were four or five of these ranches in that area. And on each of these ranch settlements there lived between two to four families. My mother and my father, who lived on one of these ranches, met there and married while they were quite young. My mother had just turned sixteen when I was born. Both of my parents had no high school education. Until I was eleven years old, we lived in a ranching environment. All of us had to participate in the farmwork. For example, we had to work in the fields [and] raise animals like cows and chickens. Then we moved closer to a little town called Hargill, Texas. We had a little house and continued ranching there. However, until I turned ten, we were continuously changing places as we were working on different ranches and in different places as migrant workers. We had started out as migrant workers when I was about seven or eight, but I had missed so much school in the first years of elementary school that after a year my father decided he would just migrate by himself and leave us at home so that all of us children could go to school regularly.

I first went to school permanently in Hargill, and I graduated after eighth grade. After that my sister and I were bused to school in Edinburgh, Texas. Although I stopped being a migrant laborer while I was still very young, I continued working in the fields of my home valley until I earned my B.A. from Pan American University in 1969. Doing so, I learned the hardships of working in the fields and of being a migrant laborer, and that experience formed me. I have a very deep respect for all the migrant laborers, the so-called *campesinos*. That experience also reinforced me in my work with migrant kids. After I got my M.A. in English and education from the University of Texas at Austin in 1972, I became a high school teacher, and I taught a lot of migrant kids. For one summer I even traveled with the migrant families who were on their way from Texas to the Midwest. By doing so, I became a liaison between the migrant camps and the regular schoolteachers for one year. Later [the education authority] hired me to be the bilingual and migrant director of the state of Indiana. At that time I was already teaching, but I was mostly working with kids in South Texas, migrant kids, and emotionally disturbed and mentally retarded kids.

K.I. Were these kids of different ethnic or racial background, or were they mainly Chicanos and Chicanas?

G.A. Not all were Chicanos and Chicanas. It depended on the kind of class I was teaching. The migrant kids' classes I was teaching were 100 percent Mexican, but I was also teaching the so-called genius classes, ninth, tenth, eleventh, and twelfth grade. And these genius classes were about 50 percent white. The Chicano and Chicana enrollment in the schools of South Texas is, altogether, about 80 percent. Then I started teaching bilingual five-year-olds. In addition, I taught emotionally disturbed and mentally retarded students who were ages seven to thirteen. Later I moved on to high school, where I taught English and literature in the ninth, tenth, eleventh, and twelfth grades. Afterwards I lived in

Indiana for a while. After Indiana I became a Ph.D. candidate at the University of Texas at Austin [where] I was also a lecturer in Chicano studies. Thus, I was teaching while I was going to school myself. I did a keynote speech in Austin this last spring, and a former student of mine showed up, telling me, "You know we read *Borderlands* in your class back then, and you haven't changed since then. You sound just like you sounded first in *Borderlands*."

K.I. Would you agree that you haven't changed since *Borderlands*?

G.A. No, not at all. I very much feel that I have changed. My former students' interpretation of me through the writing influenced their memories, because I wasn't as political and feminist in the beginning. I was always rebellious and political when it came to the cultural stuff, but not to the same degree I was later, when I wrote *Borderlands*. So they read *Borderlands*, which was published in 1987, but most of which I wrote from 1984 to 1986. In *Borderlands* I was much more extreme, political and angry than I was before, when I was teaching at UT Austin. But what many people do is that they just take *Borderlands* as the way to figure out how I am in general and how I must have been ten years before. However, yes, I was always angry and I am still angry. And in my teaching I keep telling those Chicano kids about how women are so much considered to be inferior and how that has happened.

K.I. What motivated you in particular to edit *This Bridge Called My Back*?

G.A. One motivation for doing *This Bridge Called My Back* was that when I was at UT, I wanted to focus my dissertation on feminist studies and Chicana literature and soon realized that this seemed to be an impossible project. The adviser told me that Chicana literature was not a legitimate discipline, that it didn't exist, and that women's studies was not something that I should do. You know, this was back in 1976–1977. I felt like, if you were a Chicana at a university, all you were taught were these red, white, and blue American philosophies, systems, disciplines, ways of knowledge, et cetera. They didn't consider ethnic cultures' studies as having the impact or weight needed to enter the academy. And so in a lot of these classes I felt silenced, like I had no voice. Finally I quit the Ph.D. program at UT and left Texas for California in 1977.

When I moved to San Francisco, I participated in the Women's Writers' Union, where I got to know Susan Griffin, Karen Bromine, Nellie Wong, and Merlie Woo among others. Also I joined the Feminist Writers' Guild, which was a little bit less radical. This is where I met Cherríe

Moraga. A few months later I asked her to become my coeditor for *This Bridge Called My Back.* Anyway, I found that this little community of feminist writers in San Francisco, Oakland, and Berkeley—this Feminist Writers' Guild—was very much excluding women of color. Most of the white women I knew were part of that organization. I did meet Louisa Tish there, though. She is an Afro-American woman from Louisiana who has all those books on spirituality, and practices all that in her own life, so you can call her a *santería.* Every two weeks we would have our meetings and everybody would talk about the white problems and their white experiences. When it was my turn to talk, it was almost like they were putting words into my mouth. They interrupted me while I was still talking, or after I had finished, they interpreted what I just said according to their thoughts and ideas. They thought that all women were oppressed in the same way, and they tried to force me to accept their image of me and my experiences. They were not willing to be open to my own presentation of myself and to accept that I might be different from what they thought of me so far. Therefore, one of the messages of *This Bridge Called My Back* is that gender is not the only oppression. There is race, class, and religious orientation . . . generational and age kinds of things, all the physical stuff. . . . I mean, somehow these women were great. They were white, and a lot of them were dykes and very supportive. But they were also blacked out and blinded out about our multiple oppressions. They didn't understand what we were going through. They wanted to speak for us because they had an idea of what feminism was, and they wanted to apply their notion of feminism across all cultures. *This Bridge Called My Back,* therefore, was my sweeping back against that kind of "All of us are women so you are all included," and we were all equal. Their idea was that we all were cultureless because we were feminists; we didn't have any other culture. But they never left their whiteness at home. Their whiteness covered everything they said. However, they wanted me to give up my Chicana-ness and become part of them; I was asked to leave my race at the door.

K.I. So *This Bridge Called My Back* was your response to all that?

G.A. Yes, exactly. Some of the things that I said in "La Prieta"[1] and "El Mundo Zurdo/The left-handed world"[2] were all introductions, the foreword and the essay to what I said in "Speaking in Tongues" in *This Bridge Called My Back.* And I was the only woman of color doing that at that time—that is, speaking against this silencing from the outside by getting our work published. However, after several months of struggling with

This Bridge on my own, and trying to convince other women of color that they really have a voice worth being listened to and being published, I asked Cherríe Moraga to become a coeditor and support me with this project that had become too overwhelming for me alone.

K.I. How did Chicanas receive your next book, *Borderlands/La Frontera?*

G.A. Well, when Chicanas read *Borderlands,* when it was read by little Chicanas in particular, it somehow legitimated them. They saw that I was code switching, which is what a lot of Chicanas were doing in real life as well, and for the first time, after reading that book, they seemed to realize, "Oh, my way of writing and speaking is okay" and "Oh, she is writing about La Virgen de Guadalupe, about La Llorona, about the *corridos,* the gringos, the abusive. So if she [Gloria Anzaldúa] does it, why not me as well?" The book gave them permission to do the same thing. So they started using code switching and writing about all the issues they have to deal with in daily life. To them, it was like somebody was saying: You are just as important as a woman as anybody from another race. And the experiences that you have are worth being told and written about.

K.I. How do you feel about the critical reception of *Borderlands?*

G.A. Critics are more open towards it right now. For some reason or other I got lucky in that they still teach my book at school and university. They teach it as a way of introducing students to cultural diversity. However, some of the writing is glossed over as, particularly, white critics and teachers often pick just some parts of *Borderlands.* For example, they take the passages [where] I talk about *mestizaje* and borderlands because they can more easily apply them to their own experiences. The angrier parts of *Borderlands,* however, are often ignored as they seem to be too threatening and too confrontational. In some way, I think you could call this selective critical interpretation a kind of racism. On the other hand, I am happy that the book is read at all. For us, it is not always easy to have people read our work or deal with our art. If the work is not interesting or entertaining enough, forget it. So I have to keep all these different issues regarding the reception of my work in mind and try to compromise. For example, if I had made *Borderlands* too inaccessible to you by putting in too many Chicano terms, too many Spanish words, or if I had been more fragmented in the text than I am right now, you would have been very frustrated. So there are certain traditions in all the different genres—like autobiography, fiction, poetry, theory, criticism—and certain standards that you have to follow. Otherwise you are almost naked. It is like when you write a dissertation: there are certain rules you have to apply; otherwise they won't pass you.

My whole struggle is to change the disciplines, to change the genres, to change how people look at a poem, at theory, or at children's books. And this change is quite basic sometimes. Like when you do a book of theory, you are supposed to write in a decent body, not first of all in ways of "Here I am talking about my life." Using the "I" makes it subjective anyway. Therefore, to me theory is a way of writing a story, a way tradition says that we should write a story. And here am I pushing at the laws and rules of the genre. Every genre has a certain way to do a flaw, to do a story. So I have to struggle between how many of these rules I can break and how I can still have readers read the book without getting frustrated. These are the things that have to happen first. I need other people, who deepen my fears, like professors, critics, the students. They do have to somehow like and approve what I am writing and accept it.

K.I. The reader response is very important for you then?

G.A. Very important. And I wonder how much I can get away with these changes and still keep the reader interested. I don't want to be traditional because life is a permanent resistance against the status quo, the political climate, and against the academic standards of the different disciplines. I want to change composition, the way people write. Actually, I want to change composition rules. All these schools have told us that one has to write in a certain style and that one has to have a deductive and didactic approach to writing. These are standards . . . set already by Aristotle and Cicero, I don't know how many thousands of years ago. However, people are still teaching those methods of writing. In the introduction to *Haciendo Caras,* I therefore emphasize that there is another way of writing theory, of theory in general, and of writing anything that differs from the Euro-American traditional way of writing. And people seem to accept that, because otherwise I wouldn't be read.

K.I. The task, therefore, is to keep the traditional approaches in mind somehow, but don't stay there?

G.A. Yes, that's it. It is the same kind of struggle *mestizas* have living at the borders, living in the borderlands. How much do they assimilate to the white culture, and how much do we resist and risk becoming isolated in the culture and ghettoized? This issue applies to everything. For example, if you were working with the German Aryan culture and you were trying to make some changes in the way they looked at homosexuals, at Jews, at Germans, at their notion of Nazism, and thus were trying to make those changes in your own culture through writing poems, stories, essays, and even children's books, the question always is "How much could you criticize the German culture and still have Germans read your work?"

K.I. So do you think intercultural understanding is possible and can be enhanced by writing?

G.A. I do. I believe that both inter- and intracultural understanding can be enhanced. "Intercultural" means within the Chicano culture and Mexican culture. "Intracultural" is about how we are related with other cultures like the black culture, the Native American cultures, the white culture, and the international cultures in general. I am operating on both perspectives as I am trying to write for different audiences. On the one hand, I write for more of an international audience that came across from one world to the other and that has border people. Actually, more and more people today become border people because the pace of society has increased. Just think about multimedia, computers, and the World Wide Web, for example. By the Internet you can communicate instantly with someone in India or somewhere else in the world, like Australia, Hungary, or China. We are all living in a society where these borders are transgressed constantly.

K.I. It's like we are all living in a global village?

G.A. Right. We are all living in societies with borders on the one hand, but we are about to cross those borders permanently on the other hand. So it is like we are all living in those borderlands, you know, the ones I talk about in *Borderlands/La Frontera*.

K.I. How do you see this intercultural situation with regard to the Chicano culture and the Anglo-American influence?

G.A. In that context, one particular image comes into my mind: the banyan tree. It is a tree that is originally from India, but which I saw in Hawaii first. It looks like a solid wall. When the seeds from the tree fall, they don't take root in the ground. They take root in the branches. So the seeds fall in the branches, and it is there, above the earth, where the tree blooms and forms its fruits. And I thought, that is where *we* are getting. Instead of going to the roots of our Hispanic or Chicano culture, we are getting it from the branches, from white-dominant culture. I mean, it is not that I reject everything that has to do with white culture. I like the English language, for example, and there is a lot of Anglo ideology that I like as well. But not all of it, as not all fits with our experiences and cultural roots. And that is why it is dangerous not to know about your own cultural heritage at all, because then you don't have the chance to choose and select.

I also want Chicano kids to hear stuff about La Llorona, about the border, et cetera, as early as possible. I don't want them to wait until they're eighteen or nineteen to get that information. I think it is very important that they get to know their culture already as children. Here in California I met a lot of young Chicanos and Chicanas who didn't have a clue about their own Chicano culture. They lost it all. However, later on, when they were already twenty, twenty-five, or even thirty years old, they took classes in Chicano studies to learn more about their ancestors, their history and culture. But I want the kids to already have access to this kind of information. That is why I started writing children's books. So far I have had two bilingual books published, and I am writing the third one at the moment. This is going to be more for juvenile readers, little boys and girls who are ages eleven to twelve. Next I want to write a book for young adults who are about fifteen to sixteen years old as well. With my children's books I want to provide them with more knowledge about their roots and, by doing so, give them the chance to choose: to choose whether they want to be completely assimilated, whether they want to be border people, or whether they want to be isolationists.

K.I. How about your ties with Mexico? Do you still feel some close connections with Mexico and Mexican culture itself?

G.A. I am a seventh-generation American, and so I don't have any real "original Mexican" roots. So this is what happened to someone living at the border like me: My ancestors have always lived with the land here in Texas. My indigenous ancestors go back 20,000 to 25,000 years,[3] and that is how old I am in this country. My Spanish ancestors have been in this land since the European takeover, which pulled migration from Spain to Mexico. Texas was part of a Mexican state called Tamaulipas. And Texas, New Mexico, Arizona, and part of California and Colorado were part of the northern section of Mexico. It was almost half of Mexico that the U.S. cheated Mexico out of when they bought it by the Treaty of Guadalupe-Hidalgo. By doing so, they created the borderlands. The Anzaldúas lived right at the border. Therefore, the ones of our family who ended up north of the border, in the U.S., were the Anzaldúas with an accent, whereas the ones that still lived in Mexico dropped their accent after a while. As the generations then went by, we lost contact with each other. Nowadays the Anzaldúas in the United States no longer know the Anzaldúas in Mexico. The border split my family, so to speak.

When you ask about my ties to Mexico, I believe that the people with close ties to Mexico are just first- or second-generation Mexican Americans, and their folks came from Guadalajara or Mexico City. My folks never came from Mexico. My folks were always there in Texas. Therefore, the only tie I have to Mexico is one vacation I made in 1992 or 1993. I went to Mexico City to teach a seminar at UNAM, and I stayed there for about six weeks. As I had been sick for most of the time I was there, it is hard to say how I felt about Mexico itself back then.

K.I. If you think about the United States now and the different regions and states where Chicanos live—like Arizona, New Mexico, California, and Texas—how about the regional differences? And how did you experience that yourself, because you were born and grew up in Texas, and now you live in California?

G.A. When I moved out of Texas, I only knew Chicanos of Texas, because South Texas was about 80 percent Chicano. All the kids I went with to elementary school were Mexicans or Mexican Americans. The white kids were segregated; they had their own schools. So until I was in high school, I spent my whole life only with Chicanos/as. In high school they put me in a genius class, and there were only two Chicanos/as in that class. This high school had about three thousand students, and out of those three thousand students, the whites were the ones who were put in accelerated classes. Only two Chicanas/os, Danny Beltran and me, were put to the white students. That was my first exposure to whites; that was also when I started realizing the discrimination in the relationship with white people. You know, to be Mexican or Chicano/a was like not being respected. When I moved out of South Texas to go to the University of Texas at Austin, again I hardly did have a voice. That's when I got the idea about doing *This Bridge Called My Back.*

When I went to California later on, I found out that Chicanos in California were very different from Chicanos in Texas. The Chicanos/as in California are more open, whereas the Chicanos/as in Texas operate more from the margins, the rural ways of life. So there is the difference between Chicanos/as living in the inner city like Los Angeles versus Chicanos/as living in the country. In addition, I believe that the assimilation in California is a little bit more advanced. Not that you don't have assimilation in Texas, but we assimilate different things. The language is different, too. In South Texas we have certain words—in particular, Spanish words—which are different from Chicano Spanish in other states and regions. Chicano Spanish has a lot of variations.

K.I. What about your language? Do you consider yourself a bilingual writer?

G.A. I am bilingual; however, I use three different languages altogether. I use English, Spanish, and Navajo.4 With Spanish there are all these different registers such as working-class Spanish, Mexican Spanish, et cetera. As you know, I list all these various registers in *Borderlands*. In general, I can do all the three aforementioned languages, but I like to use Navajo in particular. From very early on I included Navajo terms in my writing. Actually, it started with poetry. When I became a writer, I first dedicated myself to the poem and began using Navajo every now and then.

K.I. You started as a writer in 1974?

G.A. Yes, I did. Earlier on I was a painter; I tried to sculpture and to do design. In addition, I took a lot of courses in art and have a degree in it; my B.A. is in art and my M.A. is in art education and literature. My mom still has some of my paintings on the walls. Nowadays, I continue to draw pictures. However, back then I had two concerns: one was that I was going to be a mediocre artist; the second was that I couldn't afford the oils, the paints, and brushes, which were all really very expensive. I could afford a tablet of paper, though. And I always wanted to do both, to be a writer and an artist. But then I thought, "Okay, I don't have enough energy and years in my life to be in an apprenticeship in two different art forms." So I picked writing.

K.I. You didn't get started by focusing on just one particular genre. You were concentrating on several. Is that right?

G.A. *Sí.* I wrote the first poem, the first story, the first creative nonfiction, and a rough draft for my first novel, all at the same time. So I didn't start writing just one genre over the years. I started out with all of them at the same time. The only thing that I have added since then is the children's literature.

K.I. Was this starting with all genres at the same time a way of trying to figure out what you like and/or master best?

G.A. Well, I think it was because I am interested in multiple projects. I have an incredible hunger to experience the world. And I can best experience the world by writing about it, thinking about it, or making little drawings about it. I always want to do a thorough job. So when I start out with an idea like *Nepantla* or border-crossing, for example, I want to be able to unravel it for different readers—for the academic professors and students as well as for children and the average person. I want to do it through different media: through poetry, fiction, and through theory because each of these genres enriches the others. For example, a lot of the adults' books I am writing have impact on the children's books and vice versa. It all provides me with this rich, rich field in which to work. Therefore, I would never accept any genre boundaries in my work. Every now and then people say to me, "Why don't you do just one thing and finish that?" Like, for example, the "La Llorona" sequel to *Borderlands*— the reading, writing, and speaking. "Why don't you just perfect one chapter and then go to the other?" And my answer always is, "I don't work that way." I am interested in taking one idea, one symbol, and trying it out as theory, as autobiography, as fiction. For example, the bridge idea I tried in anthologies, in the theoretical work, in poetry, and in fiction. So there is always the person who is a bridge to other cultures and who makes connections between different cultures, between different generations, and so on.

K.I. How do you develop your ideas?

G.A. The way that I originate my ideas is the following: First there has to be something that is bothering me—something emotional so that I will be upset, angry, or conflicted. Then I start meditating on it; sometimes I do that while I am walking. Usually I come up with something visual of what I am feeling. So then I have a visual that sometimes is like a bridge, sometimes like a person with fifty legs, one in each world; sometimes *la mano izquierda*, the left-handed world, the *rebollino*, et cetera, and I try to put that into words. So behind this feeling there is this image, this visual, and I have to figure out what the articulation of this image is. That's how I get into the theory. I start theorizing about it. But it always comes from a feeling.

K.I. So first there is the feeling, then a vision or visual, and then comes the writing?

G.A. *Sí.* For example, the feeling of not belonging to any culture at all, of being an exile in all the different cultures. You feel like there are all these gaps, these cracks in the world. In that case I would draw a crack in the world. Then I start thinking: "Okay, what does this say about my gender, my race, the discipline of writing, the U.S. society in general, and finally about the whole world?" And I start seeing all these cracks, these things that don't fit. People pass as though they were average or normal;

however, everybody is different. There is no such thing as normal or average. And your culture says: "That is reality!" Women are this way, men are this way, and white people are this way. And you start seeing behind that reality. You see the cracks and realize that there are other realities. Women can be this or that, whites can be this or that. Besides physical reality there might be a spiritual reality—a parallel world, a world of the supernatural.

After having realized all these cracks, I start articulating them, and I do this particularly in the theory. I have stories where these women, these *prietas [dark-skinned women]*—they are all *prietas*—actually have access to other worlds through these cracks. So I take these major things. I just go with it and work it out as much as I can. I bring the concept of borders and borderlands more into unraveling all that, too. And I now call it *Nepantla,* which is a Nahuatl word for the space between two bodies of water, the space between two worlds. It is a limited space, a space where you are not this or that but where you are changing. You haven't got into the new identity yet and haven't left the old identity behind either—you are in a kind of transition. And that is what *Nepantla* stands for. It is very awkward, uncomfortable, and frustrating to be in that *Nepantla* because you are in that midst of transformation.

K.I. Does it mean to be in the middle of nowhere then?

G.A. *Sí.* It's like being in a crack. You are not here anymore, but you are not over there yet, so you are in *Nepantla.* The *Nepantla* thing that I have just told you about is a strategy to show you how it is to articulate that concept. Other artists are articulating that with me. I came out with the idea for it, and these other women did the paintings. Like the one you see over there in my living room. That's a picture Lillian Wilson Grez did at the residency, and that's her idea of *Nepantla.* Everyone there did work out her version of *Nepantla,* by the way.

K.I. You're referring to the residency "Entre Américas: El Taller Nepantla," which took place from October 1 to December 2, 1995?

G.A. *Sí.* It was for five weeks, and it was sponsored by MACLA, which is the Latino Arts Center in San Jose, and the Villa Mantalvo, which is a writers' and artists' colony here in Santa Cruz. And if you read the brochure about that, it gives you more of an idea about *Nepantla.*

K.I. The *Nepantla* concept—is it somehow a sequel to *Borderlands*?

G.A. No, it is not a continuation of *Borderlands.* It is a completely new book. The title is "La Prieta: The Dark One," and I deal with the consequences of *Nepantla* as well as with the La Llorona figure in all its chapters. "La Prieta" is about my being a writer, and how I look at reality: how reality gets constructed, how knowledge gets produced, and how identities get created. The subtext is reading, writing, and speaking. So *Nepantla* is a way of reading the world. You see behind the veil, and you see these scraps. Also, it is a way of creating knowledge and writing a philosophy, a system that explains the world. *Nepantla* is a stage that women and men—and whoever is willing to change into a new person and further grow and develop—go through. The concept is articulated as a process of writing; it is one of the stages of writing, the stage where you have all these ideas, all these images, sentences and paragraphs, and where you are trying to make them into one piece, a story, plot, or whatever. It is all very chaotic, so you feel like you are living in the midst of chaos. It is also a little bit of an agony you experience. My symbol of that is Coyolxauhqui the moon goddess, who was dismembered by her brother Huitzilopochtli. The art of composition—whether you are composing a work of fiction or your life, or whether you are composing reality—always means pulling off fragmented pieces and putting them together into a whole that makes sense. A lot of my composition theories are not just about writing but about how people live their lives, construct their cultures—so actually about how people construct reality.

K.I. If you think about people and philosophies that influenced you in your writing and your writing philosophy, who or what in particular had a major influence on you?

G.A. I started out being born into a culture that philosophizes very much. All Mexicans have all these stakes in realities, and they are always very likely to start philosophizing about their lives. Then, when I was a little girl, my way of escaping through a lot of the pain I suffered was through reading. Some of my pain was cultural in origin—you know, about being Mexican—some of it was because of my gender, so about being this girl who wasn't supposed to be as important as my brothers, even though I was older. Part of this discrimination was related to the fact that I was in pain most of the time because I was born with a hormonal imbalance, which meant that I went into puberty very early on. I remember that I was always made to feel ashamed because I was having a period and had breasts when I was six years old. Then I also was this freak who was very sensitive. My way of dealing with the world was to read, to escape through reading. I would read everything. Very early on I started reading Nietzsche. Also I was reading Schopenhauer, Sartre, Kafka, and most of those heavy-duty guys. Then I turned more to the women who were philosophers, like Jeffner Allen and María Lugones, the Latina philosopher.

K.I. How would you describe your own philosophy then?

G.A. I would describe it the way I describe my spirituality. My spiritual reality I call spiritual *mestizaje*, so I think my philosophy is like a philosophical *mestizaje* where I take from all different cultures—for instance, from the cultures of Latin America, the people of color, and also the Europeans.

K.I. I would like to talk a bit more about your spiritual reality and religion in general. How does it look like exactly? Could you also tell us a bit more about your experiences with the Catholic Church, which has a very strong hold among Mexicans and Mexican Americans in general?

G.A. The grounding of my spiritual reality is based on indigenous Mexican spirituality, which is *Nahualismo*, which loosely translates as "shamanism." But the Nahual was a shape-shifter: a shaman who could shift shapes, who could become a person or an animal. The philosophy that I am now trying to unravel also goes back to Mexican indigenous times—where I use the words like *Nepantla*, like *conocimiento*—so things that come from the indigenous, the Mexican or the Chicano. And then I try to philosophize about that. With the spiritual *mestizaje* there is a component of folk Catholicism in it. But very early on—beginning with the death of my father and my *desencanto*, my disillusionment with traditional Catholicism—I rebelled. The Catholicism that Mexicans in South Texas participate in is more of a folk Catholicism, as it has a lot of indigenous elements in there. But on top of the indigenous elements are put the Catholic scenes. Therefore, underneath all those Catholic saints and the Virgin Mary there are all these Native American figures, these indigenous Mexicans like Tonantzin.

K.I. Is it more an ethnic-based problem you have with Catholicism and traditional religion, then, and not so much a gender-related issue?

G.A. Oh no, gender is an important issue, too, as in most of the major religions in the world—like Christianity, Hinduism, and Islam—women are second place and inferior. Women are regarded as nothing and often treated worse than cattle. In all these religions there is that attitude underneath. But yes, Christianity has cleaned up a lot of that. However, if you look at all the violence towards women, women are battered, molested, raped, or killed—for example, one out of every three women in this country gets molested—there is a deep hatred and fear of women. So, yeah, the white culture emphasizes that we are all equal, men and women. However, underneath all that there is this violence against women, all this negative stuff about women. So if you can see through that illusion, through those cracks, you can see to that reality—of Protestantism, Christianity, Judaism, Hinduism, Islam, and Moslem, the major religions in the world—that they still have that negative attitude towards women as they continue to regard and treat them as inferior beings.

K.I. How did you build up your spiritual reality then?

G.A. When you go through a heavy, difficult time, and you don't have the resources—you can't go to anybody in the society or in the community—you finally fall back on yourself. What I did was that I started breathing. I had to like breathing and to start meditating in order to get through the pain and that whole difficult period. And all that reconnected me with nature, from which I had gotten away. So this is why I like to live at the ocean, like I do now, here in Santa Cruz. You know, to live near the ocean means that you just go there and then get another infusion of energy. All the petty problems you have fall away because of the presence of the ocean. It therefore is a real spiritual presence for me. I feel that way with some trees, the wind, serpents, snakes—deserts, too. So in the periods that I was going through, in my very darkest times when there was nobody there for me, I realized that at least *I* had to be there for me. So I started to access that part of me, of my personality, and of something that is connected to something else—you know, like that "Antigua mi diosa" I tell about in *Borderlands*.

"Antigua mi diosa" is a figure I connected with when I was in a lot of isolation and frustration in Brooklyn, where I didn't really want to be anyway. I didn't feel comfortable in that city at all. I had to reach for something to comfort me, and "Antigua mi diosa" was both an agitator who made me suffer but also a comforter; it is like a double-edged figure. It can be turned into a goddess. Therefore, it can be incorporated in your own personality. It could become the spiritual part of you, or you can make her into a double. In my writing I call her the watcher. It is sort of like, here you are, the person writing, the author, but in the back of the head there is somebody else out there, so it is like someone else looking on the scene. One notion would be Gloria Anzaldúa as the author writing this piece. Then there is the narrator, who is also Gloria Anzaldúa, and within that there is then maybe also a character, a protagonist that is based on me. So you have three frames. And behind all these frames there is some other power that is more than just a conscious ego. That's what I call the double or the watcher. Then there is the *antigua*, somebody who is more of a greater figure, more of a divine presence. I think this is my connection with Coatlicue, the serpent woman, with La Virgen de Guadalupe, with what people call goddesses. However, I personally don't like the word "goddess." To me these are figures which embody an awareness that is divine, a divine consciousness to which people just have given different names. If you are a *santera,* there is all that *santería,* which, for example, the Orishas have, like Yamayá and Oyá [goddess of the wind]. If you are Native American, there is a figure called the White Buffalo Woman; if you are Chinese, there is Quan Yin; if you are Indian, there are other names. Therefore, people just give it different names. So what I want to do is to leave all that as an awareness or as a consciousness. Because what happens, if you give these forces a human figure and a name, is you start limiting them and their power. Therefore, I just call them cultural figures, like La Llorona, Coyolxauhqui, the moon goddess, and La Virgen. They are all cultural figures, and what's important is their consciousness and the things they are aware of. In addition, however, I believe that a rock can have awareness as well. Not like our awareness, of course. It has some kind of energy that is not like our energy, and vibration that is much lower than our vibration.

K.I. It sounds like you believe in an omnipresent life force. Would you agree with that?

G.A. Yes. However, it is a life force that is different in all of the objects. For example, the life force between a vegetable and an animal is different, just like the life force between an animal and a human is different. There are various categories of awareness. Nevertheless, I really think that everything has a presence, an awareness, a consciousness, and a place in the universe. In addition, I believe that we are interconnected, not only with all the people of the globe in a very unconscious way, but also with the animals, with the organic and the inorganic stuff. Border crossing is important in that context, too. It is not just a border crossing within a physical reality, but also a crossing of borders into a spiritual reality as well as other realities. As you can see, it is still the old theme of borders and border crossing. And I am probably going to develop that during my whole life.

K.I. How important is teaching for you?

G.A. Well, I teach very seldom now. The last time I taught a class, for one quarter, was in 1988. Since 1981 I have been teaching as a lecturer to different universities once in a while. The rest of my time, however, I spend traveling to different universities and lecturing there. Also, I go to different conferences and deliver keynote talks; sometimes I teach work-shops in writing or in reading my work. That is also how I make a living. More and more, I am asked to speak about global stuff, international subjects. It is very popular at the moment to focus on issues such as "What does it mean to be a citizen of the world?" Sometimes I am invit-ed to the "Mujer Latina Conferences," where we deal primarily with the situation of Chicanas and Latinas. I speak about issues of border cross-ing, identity, and so on. In addition, I address queer conferences. For example, I was at the "Inquiry and Theory Indeed Conference," which is a huge queer conference that took place in Iowa. Here they wanted me to address the issue of what it means to be queer, and to talk about the issues of queer theory. Sometimes I am asked to talk to anthropology departments, geography departments, modern languages departments like Spanish and Portuguese, women's studies departments. That is how I teach: I will go and be with the students, do a workshop, sign books, go to lunch with them or have dinner, do a keynote lecture. So instead of teaching 40 students or 120, like I did when I was teaching at one partic-ular high school or university, I can now address five hundred or even more people while being on tour.

K.I. You just mentioned your strong interest in international issues but also in interethnic difficulties, politics, and social issues. Do you consider yourself a teacher of the world?

G.A. *Sí*, in a way you could say so, as I do a lot of stuff on racism and the differences between cultures. A lot has to do with making people aware of different kinds of oppression and helping to overcome them.

K.I. Did you also participate in the Chicano Movement?

G.A. Yes, I did. Actually, I started out with MECHA, a Mexican Ameri-can youth organization. Also I was involved with different farmworker activities in South Texas and later in Indiana. When I became more rec-ognized as a writer, I started articulating a lot of these feminist ideas that were a kind of continuation of the Chicano Movement. But I call it "El Movimiento Macha." A *marimacha* is a woman who is very assertive. That is what they used to call dykes: *marimachas*, half-and-halfs. You were different, you were queer, not normal, you were *marimacha*. I had been witnessing all these Chicana writers, activists, artists, and profes-sors who were very strong and, therefore, very *marimacha*. So I named it "El Movimiento Macha" as the Chicano civil rights movement kind of petered out. And there were women like myself, many Chicanas, who were already questioning, having problems with the guys who were ignoring women's issues. Therefore, in the eighties and nineties, there are all these women—Chicana activists, writers, and artists—around, and I listen to them, read them, and reflect their influence on my life as well. What you could say is that in the sixties and the early seventies the Chicanos were gaining attention. They were the ones who were visible, the Chicano leaders. Then, in the eighties and nineties, the women became visible. I see a lot of Chicanas when I travel. They come up to me, and while we are talking, I ask them about their role models. They mention names like Cherríe Moraga, Gloria Anzaldúa, and other Chicana authors. It is, and will continue to be, women that they are reading, that they respect. Not the guys. So it—the Chicano Movement—has shifted into the Movimiento Macha.

K.I.   How do you feel about the contemporary relation between Chicano writers and Chicana writers on the one hand, and lesbian Chicana writers versus heterosexual Chicano/a writers on the other hand? Do you feel that these are, first of all, two separate blocks without any connections, or is border crossing happening here as well?

G.A.   Well, I agree with you in that there are different groups or categories. For example, there is the old vanguard, with old male Chicano writers like Rolando Hinojosa-Smith, Rudolfo Anaya, and all the other writers and professors who grew up during those times where they were reading the guys. They are very fearful of the women, and they feel very threatened by us because we are blasting them with their sexism, and we are questioning and challenging them. Then there is the younger generation of Chicanos. I don't know if Francisco Lomelí [University of California at Santa Barbara] is part of this; Héctor Torres [University of New Mexico at Albuquerque] certainly is. A lot of these critical writers, as well as the creative writers, are part of the younger generation. We were their models, so they are open to us. The same thing is true for the women. The older category of women who were very staunch, straight Chicanas, who supported their men, feel a little bit uncomfortable around the lesbians and the strong feminists—these older women who are only lately becoming part of the feminist ranks. But back then, during the times when I was trying to publish, they turned their backs against me. They wouldn't publish me, and no one else in the Chicano/a community would publish me either. I had to go to the Jewish and the white communities instead. Now there are these younger generations around, these kids, who are a little bit more open and who are reading us. They are in a way more broad-minded. However, you still get the traditional blocks. For example, every now and then it happens that I go to a university, and some guy says, "Oh, I love *Borderlands*," but then he realizes that I am queer. He is shocked, although he shouldn't be because if you know my other books, you already know that I am queer. Sometimes, those who find out later want to hate me, but they can't quite hate me because they have already liked me before. The queer stuff is still a problem with the guys, and it is still like a major barrier to their reading me.

K.I. What about other Chicana writers and critics? Do you feel that there might be a generational gap between established Chicana writers such as yourself, Ana Castillo, or Sandra Cisneros, who started writing in the 1980s, and the younger generation of Chicana writers who just got started in the 1990s, such as Josefina López, for example?

G.A. I don't think so. One of the things that I have noticed is how charitable, warm, and generous we are to each other. Sandra Cisneros, for example, is very supportive of my work. Then there is Antonia Castañeda, Emma Pérez, Chéla Sandoval, and Norma Alarcón. We are all dealing with each other's work. Norma Alarcón based all of her work on critiquing Chicanas. Two essays of hers in which she is writing about me came out just last year, for example. Or Tey Diana Rebolledo of the University of New Mexico in Albuquerque—she is another example. In general I would say that the professors, the academic Chicanas, are very generous. There is a little bit more rivalry with the creative writers. But I think that I am out of it because they look at me as a *gente grande*, somebody who is older, and maybe somebody who's already got more experience.

K.I. *Borderlands/La Frontera* is often regarded by critics as an example of Chicana post-colonial writing. How do you feel about that?

G.A. Well, there are two ways of spelling "post-colonial": one with the dash in between, the other one without the dash. The ones that use the term without the dash are a little bit more "us-them" based, and the ones that use the dash, of which I am one, we are more or less in each other's pockets. So it goes both ways: it is more an exchange between both sides. I have a term that is called *nos-otras,* and I put a dash between the *nos* and the *otras*. The *nos* is the subject "we"; that is, the people who were in power and colonized others. The *otras* is the "other," the colonized group. Then there is also the dash, the divide between us. However, what is happening, after years of colonization, is that all the divides disappear a little bit because the colonizer, in his or her interaction with the colonized, takes on a lot of the attributes. And, of course, the person who is colonizing leaks into our stuff. So we are neither one nor the other; we are really both. There is not a pure other; there is not a pure subject and not a pure object: We are implicated in each other's lives.

K.I. Is there one post-colonial theory you feel quite comfortable with—for example, Spivak's "Can the Subaltern Speak"? Is there a post-colonial theory that seems to express what is in your mind as well?

G.A. Actually, I think that Spivak's concept is the other way around. Spivak feels that the subaltern can't speak, but I believe that the subaltern can speak. Chicanas and other colonized people were writing and talking. Among some of the critics I read is Stuart Hall. However, with some other critics it takes me almost forever to decide what they are trying to say, like with Spivak and some of her essays, for example. About five years ago, Homi Bhabha was here at UC Santa Cruz lecturing. I had a hard time with his stuff, even though I feel like I am closer to him in philosophy than I am to the others. The critic Patricia Clough once called Trinh T. Minh-ha and me post-colonial critics, and I do agree with the way she uses this term.

K.I. How do you feel about post-colonialism in general, as the Chicana situation is quite a bit different from the post-colonial experience of the former colonies of the British Empire?

G.A. Most of the post-colonial intellectuals are writing about their being in exile from one country or the other. Some of the work I am doing now looks at us Chicanas and the way we are internal exiles within our own country. But there is a difference with regard to post-colonialism, and I am trying to articulate that in the writing. In academic circles there is prejudice against that. It is okay to listen to a black man like Homi Bhabha from Britain—import him to the United States and listen to him and his thoughts about post-coloniality—rather than take somebody from California who is a Chicano/a and who has experienced some other things. If you are very exotic—like being from Australia, Africa, India—this legitimates you more than being an internal exile. We still don't receive much attention and often aren't listened to at all.

K.I. What are you writing right now, and what future projects do you have in mind?

G.A. First I would like to finish "La Prieta: The Dark One," which will be about twenty-four stories. All characters in these stories were *prietas*—however, *prietas* that were different from each other, with different first names, different experiences, different ages. I started writing a couple of these stories as early as 1978. So this whole collection of stories went through different stages of development. About six years ago I realized that I didn't know how to write fiction. What I was writing until then was something like my memoirs, my sort of autobiography. What was keeping me back was that I was trying to stay with the truth, with the experiences that actually happened. Then I realized that to do fiction you have to be free, imagine things, exaggerate—whatever you need to do in order to convey this kind of reality that you are trying to transmit. I began to listen to people and talk about their writing and their methods. In order to learn how to write these stories, I was making notes about my process and I called the notes "Writing Outside La Prieta." It tells about my ideas for the stories, where I was having problems, how I did the research. This was very interesting for me because I ended up having two parts actually: "La Prieta" the fiction, on the one hand, and then on the other, the notes that tell about how I did it. After "La Prieta," I plan to do the sequel to *Borderlands*—theoretical pieces, a lot of which tie into the fiction.

Anyway, after "La Prieta: The Dark One" is finished, I want to focus on reading, writing, and speaking for a while. While I am in that process, I want to work on "Prietita and the Grave Robber," a middle-grade-school book for kids. Once I get all that out of the way, I am going to put out a manual, a guide for writers and artists. I am already very excited about that manual in particular; I really like doing something like that.

Then I have another series of stories, nineteen altogether, for another collection which I intend to publish. The title for that is "Fic Nineteen." It has to do with my computer and how I name my computer files. It was going to be "Fiction Nineteen" originally, but I had to cut it down to "Fic Nineteen" because you can't have big names for computer files. The stories are more experimental, more way out, more wild. They demonstrate that I can free myself a little bit more. I also am writing poetry at the moment. I'm working on two books of poems, one is called "Nightface," and the other one, "Tres Lenguas del Fuego" [Three Tongues of Fire]. In "Tres Lenguas" I deal primarily with historical women figures such as Saint Teresa of Ávila and many others. For example, one poem is about a woman alchemist; another, about a woman who went on crusades; and one is about a woman pirate who dressed as a man.

Another project I am working on is a book about myself and my relationship with my mom. It is going to be called "Myself and (m)other." Also I would like to put together all the interviews that were conducted with me in one book. And then I have a Chicana dictionary in mind. I've already started collecting entries. It is going to be like an encyclopedia that focuses on Chicanas and their culture. Among the things I have collected for it so far are terms like *quinceañera,* as well as [information on] women like Dolores Huerta and archetypes like La Llorona, La Malinche, and La Virgen.

Oh, and then I almost forgot to mention that I am writing a novel right now as well. I have already started plotting it. I don't have an exact title yet. So far I just call it "The Novel." It is going to be way down the road. The protagonist is a woman named Dolores, and I am modeling her on my sister, whose name is Hilda. She has never left home. She is like the antithesis to me in every regard. But I want to make her the protagonist, and I want to deal with Hargill, the little town in Texas where we grew up, and fictionalize it.

Finally, in addition to all these projects, at some point I want to do a fourth anthology. And the fourth anthology is going to be just Chicanas or Latinas rather than all the women of color.

K.I. So there are a lot of books and works to be expected from you in the coming years. I am looking forward to that very much.

G.A. I know it is a lot of work, and I will probably die before I have finished or realized all my plans and projects. You know, with my diabetes, you never know, because with people who suffer from diabetes, mortality is very unsure. But I hope I am lucky and get as much done as possible.

NOTES

1. In *This Bridge Called My Back,* pp. 198–209.

2. In *This Bridge Called My Back,* pp. 208–209.

3. Most archaeological evidence indicates that human occupation of the Southwest began around 10,000 B.C.

4. Navajo (also Navaho) is the language of a North American Indian people of Arizona, New Mexico, and Utah. It is also their name.

BIBLIOGRAPHY

Books

1996 *Lloronas, Women Who Howl: Autohistorias and the Production of Writing, Knowledge, and Identity.* San Francisco: Aunt Lute.

1999 *Borderlands/La Frontera: The New Mestiza.* 1987. Reprint, San Francisco: Aunt Lute Books.

Children's Books

1991 *Prietita Has a Friend/Prietita Tiene un Amigo.* San Francisco: Children's Book Press.
1993 *Friends from the Other Side/Amigos del Otro Lado.* San Francisco: Children's Book Press.
1995 *Prietita and the Ghost Woman/Prietita y la Llorona.* San Francisco: Children's Book Press.

Essays

1990 "Bridge, Drawbridge, Sandbar, or Island." In Lisa Albrecht and Rose M. Brewer (eds.), *Bridges of Power: Women's Multicultural Alliances.* Philadelphia: New Society Publishers, pp. 216–231.
"Metaphors in the Tradition of the Shaman." In James McCorkle (ed.), *Conversant Essays: Contemporary Poets on Poetry.* Detroit: Wayne State University Press, pp. 99–100.
1991 "To(o) Queer the Writer." In Betsy Warland (ed.). *InVersions: Writings by Dykes, Queers, and Lesbians.* Vancouver: Press Gang Publishers, pp. 249–263.

Edited Books

1990 *Making Face, Making Soul: Haciendo Caras: Creative and Critical Perspectives by Women of Color.* San Francisco: Aunt Lute Books.

Coedited Books

1981 With Cherríe Moraga. *This Bridge Called My Back: Writings by Radical Women of Color.* Revised and expanded edition, New York: Kitchen Table/Women of Color Press, 1983.

Forthcoming (publication date not known yet)

"Fic Nineteen."
"Myself and (m)other."
"Nightface."
"La Prieta: The Dark One."
"Prietita and the Grave Robber."
"Tres Lenguas del Fuego."
"Writing Mano: A Creative Writing Handbook." San Francisco: Aunt Lute Books.
With coeditor Francisco Alarcón. "De las Otras, de los Otros: A Collection of Art and Writings by Lesbians and Gay Chicanos."

Lorna Dee Cervantes

Poet, Educator, and Political and Feminist Writer

"Poetry is an exercise of freedom . . . freedom on all fronts."

THE UNIVERSITY OF CALIFORNIA, BERKELEY, DECEMBER 16, 1996

L ORNA DEE CERVANTES is an outstanding Mexican American poet whose poetry collections *Emplumada* (1980) and *From the Cables of Genocide: Poems on Love and Hunger* (1991) have received national and international critical acclaim and awards. She has been a leader in the Chicano and Native American literary movement by establishing MANGO Publications and editing such important journals as *Mango,* a cross-cultural literary magazine, and *Red Dirt,* a poetry journal.

Born on August 6, 1954, in the Mission District of San Francisco to an old Californian family that had settled originally in Santa Barbara, Cervantes is of Mexican and Amerindian (Chumash) ancestry. She experienced poverty firsthand as a child, and first discovered Shakespeare and the English Romantic poets among the books in the houses that her mother cleaned. When she was five, her parents separated, and she moved with her mother and brother to San Jose, California, to live with her grandmother.

Growing up during the sixties and seventies, a time of intense social upheaval, Cervantes became actively involved in the Chicano Movement as well as in the Amerindian and antinuclear movements. She began writing poetry at a very early age. When Cervantes was eighteen, she joined a *teatro* group that later toured California and participated in the Quinto Festival de los Teatros Chicanos in Mexico City in 1974. Cervantes gave her first poetry reading at the festival, and this was a turning point for her career, leading to the first publication of her work in a major paper: her poem "Refugee Ship" was printed in a Mexico City newspaper in 1974. Over the years she had several other poems published in *Revista Chicano-Riqueña* and other periodicals.

27

After graduating from high school in 1972, Cervantes began her college coursework. Most of her time and energy, however, she dedicated to her work as a poet, editor, and publisher. In 1974 she taught herself printing and founded a Chicano literary magazine and a press, both called Mango. In addition to editing and publishing *Mango* from 1976 to 1982, she edited other Chicanos' chapbooks, which she published through the Centro Cultural de la Gente of San Jose and MANGO Publications.

In 1982 Cervantes returned to college and two years later earned a B.A. in creative arts from San Jose State University. She then enrolled at the University of California at Santa Cruz and in 1990 was awarded a Ph.D. in philosophy and aesthetics. In 1994–1995, Cervantes was granted a Visiting Scholar Fellowship sponsored by the Mexican American Studies Program at the University of Houston. She now lives in Boulder, Colorado, and teaches creative writing at the University of Colorado as an associate professor.

Cervantes's well-crafted, highly lyrical poetry is direct and powerful. A central element in her writing is the tension between the desire for an ideal world, a utopia, and her awareness of a quite different reality, a world plagued by social problems, conflicts, and diseases. In *Emplumada*,[1] her first collection of poetry (1980), Cervantes presents poems that deal with cultural conflict, oppression of women and minorities, and alienation from one's roots. All of these subjects are presented from the point of view of a young women coming of age and becoming more and more disillusioned with her life and the world. *Emplumada* soon became the bestselling title in the University of Pittsburgh Press's PITT poetry series and established Cervantes as a major new voice in American poetry.

In 1991 Arte Público Press published Cervantes's second poetry collection, *From the Cables of Genocide: Poems on Love and Hunger.* Less personal and introspective than her first collection, this volume expresses more general ethnic and feminist concerns, and is a complex meditation on the nature of love, oppression, and resistance. *From the Cables of Genocide* won two important awards, the Paterson Poetry Prize and the 1993 Latino Literature Award, thus confirming Cervantes's reputation as one of America's most compelling poets.

KARIN IKAS Although you now live in Colorado, you are a native of California, born in the Mission District of San Francisco and growing up in San Jose. How did these different settings shape you as a person in general and as a writer in particular?

LORNA DEE CERVANTES Okay, let's start with the writer first. I sort of agree with the poet William Everson, who has said that "a poet especially is like a wolf and that they get attached to their territory and are part of their territory. You dwell in a place and that is were your muse comes from, that's were your writing comes from." I have always felt strongly about that in my sense of place, especially in San Jose and in this area of California in general. And I think that has definitely very much shaped me. I feel like a regional writer in that sense.

As a writer, growing up in San Jose—as opposed to growing up in San Francisco—provided a lot of advantages as San Jose does not have any kind of school of poetry and therefore is completely open. Of course, there was a lot of stimulation from Berkeley and San Francisco—you know, all this area that is very international—but yet there was also all that freedom to do and go in any direction I wanted. Plus there were a number of strong Chicano writers in that area like José Montoya from Sacramento. There was also José Antonio Burciaga from El Paso, who just passed away recently. Then there was Francisco Alarcón, Lucha Corpi, and others. So it was just a sort of hotbed of Chicano writers in the Bay Area.

I am very much tied to place. This year I was third finalist for the Poet Laureate at Colorado. I felt very bad about that, and I was hoping that I wouldn't get picked because I felt like it was false somehow. I would never be a Colorado writer; I always was and always will be a California writer instead.

K.I. Have you thought about coming back to California to live again?

L.D.C. Sometimes I think about it, and I keep that possibility in my mind. I consider myself an indigenous Californian. On my mother's side we go back five to six generations in California. So for me, as an indigenous Californian, it's like being an exile without ever having left California. When I lived in the Bay Area, there was such an influx of people—so many people coming to the area, changing it, and just taking over—it sounds like being an exile without ever having left.

K.I. You just mentioned that you are an indigenous Californian because you have Native American and also Mexican roots. Do you somehow feel obliged to these roots?

L.D.C. "Obliged" is not the word. I have always taken on the label of a "Chicana writer"; I have always accepted that label as a strategy. It is a strategy insofar as I take something that could be a negative thing, a stigma, and turn it into a positive so that it becomes a power, a force of self-definition. So in defining myself as a Chicana writer, I always felt like I can do anything I want, I can be anyone I want. However, what that implies is the consciousness that this is an occupied land and that the very fact I am writing as a Chicana writer is a political act in itself, regardless of what I am writing about. And so there is a sense of responsibility. I wouldn't call it an obligation, but a responsibility to my community or, better, to my communities.

K.I. Not all Chicano and Chicana writers have a Native American background. Do you feel that there might be a difference between you and other Chicano/a writers who have similar Indian roots and others who don't have them?

L.D.C. Well, I think it all depends on how far back they go, because most Chicanos do have an indigenous background to varying degrees, and it is just on the other side of that imaginary border, with the Mexican Indians. I grew up without any knowledge of it because the racism was so intense and genocide was such a fact here in California at that time in the 1960s and 1970s that you just didn't talk about who you were or what you were, especially not to the outsiders, to the authorities. So it's not as if I grew up on a reservation or had any other kind of cultural continuity. However, I think there is a cultural continuity, especially for indigenous people, that comes through the mothers and the generations of mothers like my mother and my mother's mother and my mother's mother's mother and so on. There is still that maternal thread. And in my case my grandmother was very influential. There is a lot of reference to that in my first book, *Emplumada*.

K.I. What about Native American writers. How influential is their writing on you?

L.D.C. Native American writers have always been a major influence on me, like Wendy Rose, Simon Ortiz, Joy Harjo, Leslie Marmon Silko, and Paula Gunn Allen, just to name a few. I used to work in an American Indian center when I was younger. But it is like what I already mentioned before regarding accepting labels. It is like a strategy. And I always felt, especially in this Western culture, that there are always the wanna-be's, the tribal wanna-be's as well. And as I didn't grow up on a reservation, I don't use the label Native American literature for my work. I grew up in the barrio, in a barrio that was 78 to 86 percent Chicano or Mexicano. So this is really my culture, these are my cultural roots. And, therefore, for example, I would never submit to an anthology of Native American literature unless I was invited.

K.I. How do you feel about African American writers then? Sometimes I get the impression that not all Mexican American and African American writers get along with each other. Could it be that there is a kind of rivalry between both groups now and then?

L.D.C. Well, I don't think so, as I never experienced that. I have working titles sometimes—you know, poems that I want to write and that are just titles at the beginning—and one of these is called "On thanking black muses." For me, poetry politicized me, and so the influence of African American writers was major, not only in my work but in my whole life. Discovering African American writers of the sixties—you know, when there was this sort of renaissance of poetry like [that of] the early Alice Walker, June Gordon, Gwendolyn Brooks, and others—was very important. About seven major black women writers were publishing in 1970; it was an incredible year. At that time I started writing in high school. And all that African American literature, particularly poetry, politicized me, as it was that which I was primarily reading and what I could identify with. It really had a major impact on my life.

As for myself and us as minority writers, I definitely see continuity. I don't see much of a separation among us, only perhaps with regard to subject matter. But even with subjects we have some common ones as we all deal to some extent with borders and the crossing of borders, et cetera.

K.I. How do you see yourself within the context of Chicano and Chicana literature? Do you consider yourself a feminist Chicana poet?

L.D.C. As you know, I have always taken on that label "Chicana" with the feminization of it. When I started writing in the seventies, it was almost all Chicano, and that was what I was studying. One of the poems in my first book, *Emplumada,* is a sort of watershed poem. It is entitled "Beneath the Shadow of the Freeway." I wrote it when I was at San Jose Community College and took Bob's classes on Tuesday nights. It took me three and a half years to write that poem. It was a direct response to my studying Chicano literature, Chicano sociology, Chicano psychology, and all of these new courses which were all Chicano, so they were all men. Men dominated, especially the literature as well. Even though there were a lot of Chicano poets I loved—like José Montoya and others—again, they were all men, and I could see all the stereotypes of women there.

Just to give you one example: There is the stereotype of the mother who never sleeps but is awake till 4 A.M. and slaps tortillas for everybody. So for me, writing that incorporated stereotypes and clichés like that presented a fantasy world. It didn't match with my reality at all, where the mothers were working in the canneries until 4 A.M. instead. They were not trying to slap tortillas but trying to put the tortillas on the table.

In discovering all that, I became increasingly aware that there was nothing in the literature that documented my history. However, for me it is very important to document my personal history, and so that is what I am doing in poetry. A lot of my poems, particularly the ones in *Emplumada*, are characterized by my strategy—that is, the personal stance, the persona, as a form of documentation—because it wasn't in the literature yet. In "Beneath the Shadow of the Freeway," for example, there is a history of these three generations of Chicanas, and that was the impetus for the whole book *Emplumada*. "Beneath the Shadow of the Freeway" is sort of the first poem in that context.

K.I. So your strategy of writing poetry implies deromanticizing and rewriting history from a woman's perspective?

L.D.C. Yes, definitely. In particular "Beneath the Shadow of the Freeway" is my direct response to all that falsified and romanticized portrayal of our history and culture. That is why I consider it as my watershed poem per se. Thinking about Chicana literature around that time, there were finally some other Chicana writers around—like Ana Castillo, Sandra Cisneros, Helena María Viramontes, Evangelina Vigil, and some others—but especially the aforementioned were writing and publishing in the late seventies. They began around 1976.

K.I. The situation of Chicana writers improved quite a bit if you think about the number of women writing in the late seventies compared to the generation of writers before, when there were just two Chicana authors out there, namely Estela Portillo-Trambley and Bernice Zamora. How do you see the differences between Chican*a* and Chican*o* literature in the seventies and early eighties?

L.D.C. At that time I saw, especially, one major difference, and that is with regard to language. The Chicano writers put their emphasis on a sort of linguistic play in the poetry. It was almost like a kind of public language they used with a lot of multiple wordplays and code switching. I don't mean the code switching in a negative sense, but clever code switching between English, Spanish, and Caló. In particular, poets like Ricardo Sánchez and Alurista were doing that. It was different from what I saw Chicanas were doing at that time. I believe this difference has to do with the real fact of what it means to be a Chicana. If I think of our generation of Chicana writers—which is in the seventies—compared to the generations that came earlier, the major difference between us is education. We are the first of the public schools; we are the first of Johnson's war on poverty and all of that. Before it was mainly writers from a certain class and a certain "judgment education." For example, if you are looking at some of these earlier writers, they came out of Catholic schools and Catholic colleges with a respectively conservative and classical education. They were very good actually. Sandra Cisneros, Ana Castillo, Evangelina Vigil, Helena María Viramontes, and myself are the first public school educated ones. In addition, we are a different class, and because of that, probably a different ethnicity, too, if you talk about the indigenous aspect of it.

But anyway—and here I also go back to your very first question—to grow up in that sort of environment is to grow up invisible, unheard, unseen, with no power and no possible envisioning of any kind of power—personal power or actual power—in the public world. What you do to survive then is to watch. You check things out and listen. There is a line in one of my new poems, which is included in my forthcoming third poetry collection, titled *Bird Ave,* that refers to that. The line goes like this: "listen, watch, be silent, was the conquest's hidden code." Here you have that "listen, watch, and be silent," and that is exactly what I saw Chicana writers, especially Chicana poets, as opposed to Chicanos, were doing. Additionally, to me, that again always comes back to this strategy I referred to before; that is, taking a negative, a stigma—for example, the aforementioned negative female stereotypes—in a way that is like making a debt into an asset and so turning it into power. Therefore, that "listen, watch, and be silent" strategy can be a power. That is what I think is informing and infusing the Chicana poetry in particular. What you see is that attention to detail and the focus on that perception is half of what being a poet is all about. Also, I believe that this is true for poets in general, female and male ones. Every poet has to take care of that perception. Then, in a next step, he or she has to put that into language. Maybe that has something to do with what some critics like to put in the camp of testimony and autobiography.

K.I. How much of your work is autobiographical?

L.D.C. Not all of it. Some is, like "Beneath the Shadow of the Freeway" and, in particular, the "Poem for the Young White Man Who Asked Me How I, an Intelligent, Well-Read Person Could Believe in the War

Between Races." The latter comes just directly out of an actual event. Other poems are not autobiographical at all, such as "Uncle's First Rabbit," which is *the* first poem in *Emplumada*. My first poetry collection, *Emplumada*, is all about a woman coming of age, and that is why I consider it to be a bildungsroman in poetry. The "Poem for the Young White Man," which is in this book, is like a sort of meeting the beast.

K.I. Is this then the same strategy Denise Chávez used for her narrative *The Last of the Menu Girls*, where she applied the bildungsroman concept in telling us in interrelated short stories, and a kind of loose novel structure, the coming-of-age of the young New Mexican adolescent Rocío Esquibel? Do you just transfer this strategy to your poetry?

L.D.C. Yes, that is exactly what it is. So if you like, you could call *Emplumada* a kind of "bildungs-poetry."

K.I. Have you ever thought about writing a prose piece, maybe your version of a bildungsroman?

L.D.C. I do that right now. Well, it is not exactly an autobiographical continuity, but I have been working on it for a long time. For me it is really hard to make that leap from poetry to prose. However, I have been working on a series of essays, to publish as a collection, with the working title "I know why the quetzals all die." The quetzals are exotic birds from the rain forest in Guatemala and Mexico. They are almost extinct now. At the time the *conquistadores* came, the people there didn't have a conception of gold. Therefore, the plumes of the quetzal, these brilliant green and turquoise plumes, were most precious to them. Montezuma's headdresses were made with all those gorgeous feathers, too. Thus, these feathers were like their gold. What made them even more precious was the fact that you couldn't cage a quetzal. The quetzals would die as soon as they were caged up and entrapped.

With my title, "I know why the quetzals all die," I commemorate these precious birds. In addition, I try to transfer their story to our situation today. So some of the essays in that new book are autobiographical; others deal more with general topics. Thus you can say that my collection is going to be kind of similar to Cherríe Moraga's work *The Last Generation*.

K.I. How do you write? Do you just write it down out of your head, or do you polish a lot? Because you mentioned before that some of your poems did take you years.

L.D.C. Well, I talk to my students about this all the time, you know, about how writers are sort of temperamentally aligned in these different phases of the process. I used to be what I call a "generational" writer, meaning that I would write, write, write, and never revise, never. It was like being sacrilegious to the process. So at that time, I would just write another poem if I wasn't satisfied with the prior one. However, I would have never thought about revising a poem. Then, all of a sudden, I did a complete flip-flop. Now I am a fanatical reviser. That is why it takes me so long between books: it is ten years between my first book and the second one, for example. And with the one I am working on right now, it will be almost another ten years.

K.I. You refer to your new poetry collection, *Bird Ave*, I suspect, not to the forthcoming essay collection, right?

L.D.C. Yes, you are right. Actually, I am working on three poetry books at the moment, and last week I had the idea that I might want to combine these three under another title. One manuscript is called "Bird Avenue" or "Bird Ave." It has a performance piece in it, which is also in an anthology. The title "Bird Ave" is a play on the words, as "Ave" is the short version of "avenue" [and also Spanish for "bird"]. I see that manuscript as a sort of continuation of *Emplumada*. The second manuscript, titled "A Gang Girl," is more of an autobiographical piece. It is a sort of continuation of "Bird Ave"; however, it has more bilingual and bicultural poems in there. Then I have another one called "How Far Is the War?" Do you remember the poem "Bananas" that I read at the poetry reading at the University of California at Berkeley a couple of days ago? It is part of that collection. So there are these three different manuscripts. Then, I do have an additional one. The working title for it is "Drive." It has a lot of poems in it from my time in Houston, Texas. The poems deal with my breaking out of California, and then with my time in Colorado. I was in Houston as a visiting scholar for one year; that is, two semesters. Part of my project there was this collection of poems that are included in "Drive." Currently, I have this major idea of collapsing all the manuscripts I just mentioned into "Drive." Maybe I take "Drive" as the title for the whole book. But that is just an idea. I am not sure yet if I am really doing it in the end.

K.I. We've already talked about the seventies, as well as the time before, with regard to the situation of Chicana writers. What about today? How would you describe this new generation of Chicana writers? Are there generational differences?

L.D.C. There is no doubt that there is a new generation of Chicana writers there. Not that long ago someone referred to me in one of the essays on Chicana literature as a kind of "Chicana writer grandmother" [laughter]. It is so funny because it was said in relation to Ana Castillo. Ana is even older than I am, plus we all—Ana Castillo, Sandra Cisneros, and me—started out the same time, which was in 1974, when Sandra was at the University of Iowa. She was getting a master's degree then and was just barely beginning to start publishing poems. So we all started out the same time, but I was like the grandmother [laughter]. But no, there definitely is a very exciting new generation of Chicana writers right now. Their literature originates from today's situation and incorporates all these issues of becoming more and more globalized, et cetera. But what I was saying about labels and identities is true for their work as well. Chicana identity can't be explained with these essentialisms of identity; if anything, it is a subversion of that. Too long we have been forced to accept subjectifications such as "you are like that because you are Indian, woman, poor," or whatever, and that goes on and on and on. But I never see it that way. This goes back to your question about African American writers, indigenous writers, and borders in general. Where are those borders? Well, they are imaginary, so "borders" can be used as a matter of strategy. I believe the thing that most of us share is life lived not under the gaze, but life lived under the gun. So what happens with our multiple identities is that they cause multiple stigmas that convert into one target. And often you are that target. It doesn't matter if you are being attacked because you are brown or a woman, or because you are poor or your car broke down, or because of your sexuality or whatever. But instead it is this strategy, this multiple strategy, to ameliorate the danger. I think the thread becomes more and more globalized, first through nuclear armaments, then through pollution, et cetera. Global destruction is a possibility in a way it wasn't fifty years ago, seventy-five years ago.

So again, the literature is coming out of that. I think that is what the outsiders—and now they are the marginalized people [laughter]—see. That's what they are getting from the literature, like when they read Sandra Cisneros's and Ana Castillo's work.

K.I. Does success change a Chicana writer and her literature? I think about Chicana writers such as Sandra Cisneros or Ana Castillo, who are sometimes criticized for becoming too mainstream in their writing on one hand, or for letting themselves and their literature too easily be used as tokenized representatives of Chicana literature, or for sacrificing quality for quantity in order to be successful and make money.

L.D.C. First of all, I don't think that Sandra and Ana really worry about it. Their only reaction on such complaints might be that they just go on to the next book. The only thing that changed with their success is that they dress better [laughter]. I'm sorry. But seriously, I think it is safe to assume though that there is a danger of being subsumed by popular culture. However, I think all that is just ironic bravado, because one of the conditions of being a Chicano poet is that you have a very keen sense of irony. Although I never talked with Sandra or Ana about that, I assume that this is true for them as well.

K.I. In "Poem for the Young White Man Who Asked Me How I, an Intelligent, Well-Read Person Could Believe in the War Between Races" [*Emplumada*], you have the lines "I'm marked by the color of my skin. / The bullets are discrete and designed to kill slowly" [p. 36]. Can you tell us a bit more about these "bullets"?

L.D.C. Again, as I have already said before, I really don't like to think in terms of essentialized notions of identities and about what it is that makes a woman like a woman, so questions like "Is there a woman's culture? Is it biological? What is it at all? What are the differences? Is it class?" There are all kinds of different classes of women, and so all women have different kinds of experiences. Therefore, essentialism does not work, and that is why I even think of essentialism in terms of danger. It is a very specific kind of danger as there is an enemy out there who hates me because of the color of my skin.

I believe there are certain experiences that go from harassment at the workplace at an upper, upper level for white businesswomen, to walking down the street to get to your car in the parking lot after hours. So it is primarily that experience of being tagged, of being targeted, because of the way someone else perceives you, as a female, a vulnerable female, as a maid, as a baby maker, as a wife, et cetera. However, I think people experience that differently.

K.I. Does some kind of "female bonding" therefore exist?

L.D.C. I wouldn't say it is a "female bonding"; it is more a kind of "danger bonding." And that has nothing to do with being a victim or with victimization—not at all. It is more related to the fact that there is a real danger. In the dominant culture—and that is what makes it dominant—there is a certain perception of power that has to do with power *over*, power over someone. And that power is expressed as repressive power. And repressive power has only one means of expression and that is force: it is violence, it is restraint, it is suffering. Not suffering on a local level, but a suffering that is like genocide. So it is a real thing. It gets exercised in very different levels in our culture. This is how people see power. What Chicana writers are doing—and especially what Chicana critics are keen on—is tackling with these other forms of power. And these other forms of power are nothing else than "power over." For example, there is the power to say no and the power to say yes. When it comes to Chicana writers, definitely on the forefront of that power concept are the lesbian and the lesbian/bisexual Chicana writers. Nowadays you become more and more into what it means to be out in the world. It is like wondering if my situation is like that because I am a woman, because I am gay, because I am a lesbian, because I am poor, et cetera.

K.I. How do you feel about the sexual differences among Chicana writers; that is, lesbian Chicana writers and heterosexual Chicana writers? Do you think lesbian Chicana writers are more politicized because they have an additional border to cross?

L.D.C. I don't feel and I don't see a real difference. I tend to think that in Chicano literature there is hardly any difference anymore today in that respect. However, in other camps this might be different.

K.I. So what about religion?

L.D.C. Well, that's exactly what I mean [laughter]. And I am no Catholic at all. . . .

K.I. Did you ever experience the Church, particularly the Catholic Church, to be repressive in particular toward women? What is your personal impression of Catholicism?

L.D.C. My indigenous background is maybe the part that really sets me apart here, or makes me at least a little bit distinct from other Chicana writers. I didn't share that heavy Catholicism most of them were confronted with. Of course, my grandmother was Catholic, I was baptized Catholic, et cetera. Actually, the mission system in California is the only reason that my family could survive back then, amidst the genocide during the earlier days of California. My grandmother's family went and hid up in the mountains in Montecito. There missionaries supported us. Montecito is a very rugged area in Santa Barbara. At that time it was quite different from the billionaire's community that it is today. But that's a different story. So my family went and hid out there for a hundred years. Thus we survived and [did not become] extinct as others of our tribal relatives. Our tribe [the Chumash] was officially extinct up until the early seventies. So in my family there is that irony: there was that Catholicism, and yet there were always those constant multiple messages. You go through all that, like in a confession, but when you come to the point, you realize all is just hypocrisy. I think "hypocrisy" was one of the first big words I ever learned.

By talking about it to you now, I realize that the fact that the Church never had real power over me and never touched me on such a deep level is what makes me different as a person and a writer from many other Chicanas.

K.I. How do you feel about the Virgin de Guadalupe?

L.D.C. Although I don't have that kind of strong connection to Catholicism, I find the Virgin de Guadalupe very interesting because of the indigenous elements that are part of her identity. Privately, I worship Yamaya, which is the goddess of water, the ocean of life force and water. She is kind of my personal deity.

K.I. So Yamaya is for your spiritual world what the Virgen de Guadalupe is for Catholicism?

L.D.C. To some extent that is the way it is. I read poems to Yamaya; I have given offerings to her. . . . But another deity who is important to me is Ishtar.[2] Thus, I am definitely a spiritual person, not a religious one. It is exercised in my muse because I really believe things speak to us. I think that is due to my indigenous roots and influence. I believe in the elements like fire, water, air, and earth, and in the four directions. Therefore, I can't accept that I am separate from water, this table, or anything else, for example. We all belong to the same planet. It is like this enormous egg, which is part of this inorganic organism of the universe. It is also part of the animal we can't hear, see, and know. To me poetry is part of that as well. Poetry definitely is a spiritual factor because it is very elemental and very personal. Therefore, poetry is spiritual practice to me.

K.I. Besides the Virgin de Guadalupe, there is another female archetype who is very important in Mexican American culture: La Malinche. How do you feel about her and the how her image is often distorted?

L.D.C. I think people who are studying and writing about La Malinche are all doing fascinating work, at least if I think about the work I have read. I have written about Malinche, too. For example, there is a reference to her in "You Really Cramp My Style Baby," a poem that is not published in my books as it is one of my earliest poems. I believe that dealing with the Malinche myth in writing is like another handle, another strategy. Malinche is a very interesting, fascinating, and important figure. She definitely is a kind of role model. To me she is like the Mexican philosopher Juana Inés de la Cruz when it comes to indigenous Latinas who use their minds.

K.I. Is Sor Juana another important role model for you and other Chicana writers?

L.D.C. Sure. How can she not be? As I said earlier, there were very few role models, especially few of those who go back that far. Sor Juana Inés de la Cruz was someone I read, admired, and got inspiration from.

K.I. What about the future projects you have in mind? Although you teach creative writing at the University of Colorado at Boulder, you still dedicate a lot of your time to your writing, too. What will be your major focus in the future: writing or teaching?

L.D.C. Well, first of all, I am on a grant right now. So I am on leave for two years. The grant is to work on my poetry. It is a three years' grant, but I am on leave for two years. Part of the grant is to organize a project that I called "Flor y Canto" in San Jose. It is going to be similar to these Flower and Songs poetry events we had in the past. There you have this strong combination of poetry and songs together with many indigenous elements. In the 1970s, there was a series of "Flor y Cantos" in different areas, like in San Antonio, in Milwaukee, Corpus Christi, and all those places. "Canto al Pueblo" was another one of these poetry events popular in the middle seventies. At that time, I actually got started as a poet myself. Therefore, I consider myself a festival poet rather than an academic poet. I didn't go to any academic writing program. As you know, my academic career came later, after I got started as a poet. In addition, I didn't get my Ph.D. in creative writing, but in the history of consciousness.

It is very exciting for me now, after more than ten years away from community work, to do community work again. That is what I am doing at the moment in Denver and around that area. I bring Chicana writers into the area—take them out into schools and into different community centers and groups. Thus, it is really about targeting youth, exposing them to the literature of these living writers, organizing festivals. Currently, I also organize the Chicano Literature Conference that we are hosting in Boulder in April 1997. And I use my grant to fund Chicana and Chicano writers to come into the area and participate in that conference. My community activism has always been a big part of my poetry. I missed that very much when I was teaching in Boulder during the past seven years. It has been really getting hard as I felt the lack tremendously. I think it adversely affected my writing. On the other hand, I love teaching. I never thought I would because I have always considered myself shy and thus I never imagined I would be a good teacher. However, I really love it. That is why I just take the two years off rather than the three years' leave. I just didn't want to be away from teaching that long. I wish there were other opportunities to work more on a community-based level than the university. But let's face it: if you are reader and writer in that culture, where do you go besides crazy [laughs] if not to university?

K.I. What would be an alternative to university for you?

L.D.C. Well, if I could have about ten times the money I am getting right now for this community interaction project, I would just do that. I would concentrate on the community work. For me, that is what feeds the writing.

K.I. How about alliances among Chicana and Chicano writers?

L.D.C. This has to do with what I mentioned about my strong interest in community work, too. My position in Boulder doesn't afford me enough contacts with Chicana and Chicano writers. You know, we get some, as I try to recruit some writers. But frankly, sometimes, when I cover off those microphones concealed to introduce new writers to the audience and enable them to give a reading, I feel like I am leading lambs to the slaughter. What is different between female and male writers, though, is our concept of poetry. For me and many other female writers, poetry is a continuum. It is not about competition. It is not about killing the father. Therefore, it is different to that male muse ideal of killing the other, the father, first, and then begin new things. But there is no new in poetry. Instead, it is a continuum. I like to think of poetry as of a sort of mothering; you mother the next generation. I know how vitally important role models work for me, like Sor Juana Inés de la Cruz or Malinche. And also, as I said before, finding black women writers who made all the difference in the world for me, then Native American writers, and finally meeting other Chicana writers. So there is a connection there. I wish I would be able to work more in that direction. For example, I would love to work more with young writers from these groups. In particular I would like to work more with young Chicanas. That is what feeds my work, and that is what I miss right now.

K.I. Currently, Affirmative Action and Proposition 209, which aims at abolishing Affirmative Action programs, are highly debated issues in California. Are you concerned about that and also about the kind of backlash that seems to go with it?

L.D.C. I am a product of Affirmative Action. I am not working class if you think about the education, et cetera, but I am welfare class. So I am a perfect example of Affirmative Action in getting all these little grants that were given to me because of these programs. When I first started, I got a $500 grant for "Beneath the Shadow of the Freeway" to write as I grew up in a neighborhood that targeted me as a disadvantaged kid. This backtracking on Affirmative Action is such a highly debated issue in California at the moment. It is very distressing for me. And you know, that is the danger of labels. It is a cultural war, and this language is one of the fronts. Although I hate to use militaristic metaphors, in that case they are most fitting. As my teacher Paul once said, "In this country there is war." They are not burning the crosses anymore; now they are burning the financial aid.

K.I. How do you feel about the future developments? Are you optimistic or more pessimistic?

L.D.C. I am always optimistic. As a strategist, you have to be optimistic to figure out how to get from here to there.

K.I. How would you sum up what poetry means for you?

L.D.C. Well, for me poetry is an exercise of freedom with implied multiplicities. Exercise implies a practice, a continuing practice, and a muscle that gets stronger with attention. It gets stronger the more you work on it, even though you start out—at least I did—as a ninety-seven-pound weakling [laughs]. So you can build up—you can build up and exercise. It is an exercise of freedom, freedom on all fronts. Language is very powerful. This is what I think I got from my family, the legacy of my family, and the legacy of genocide in my family that was done with the pen. Those billionaires are sitting up in my grandmother's land now because of power of attorney and, therefore, because of language. That's how they took our land. With this Montecito land grasp about seventy thousand acres were swept away with the pen in one day, and all that land was lost to the indigenous people. Thus the history of California was different from New Mexico. There the Anglos just came out with the guns blazing and with their thoroughbreds. By the time they came out to California, language was at the front. Here they used the pen to get what they wanted.

K.I. Are you, therefore, an angry writer?

L.D.C. Although many people say that I am writing with anger, especially when they get ahold of my "Poem for the Young White Man" I do not consider myself an angry writer at all. I am a passionate writer. But it is not anger, as I don't have time for anger. It has to do with emotion; that is what is needed. Look at the etymology of the word "emotion," for example. Emotion is like the aftereffect of an action, so it is not the pre-action, but what comes after some movement. That is why I always tell my students not to be afraid of emotion, as the emotional impact is very important.

You know, that is part of that essentializing and stereotyping strategy. People assume you should be angry. Well, sure there is some anger involved—that is just part of that process. When I first got an idea of my history, there was probably some anger there. As I told you before, poetry politicized me as it opened up my eyes. According to what we already talked about—the situation in the seventies, the time when I just felt like I am nothing—it was as if I could not do anything nor would ever be able to do anything in the near future. So for that there was some anger there in the way that I felt . . . helpless and frustrated while wondering what could be done to implement a change. But this anger never dominated, and it never will. Anyone who knows me can assure you that I am not an angry writer, and no angry person at all. For my poetry and me, a differentiation between passionate and political writing does not exist, as both merge in my work.

NOTES

1. The title *Emplumada* is a combination of the two Spanish words for "feathered" and "pen flourish."
2. Ishtar is a divinity of love, fertility, and war.

BIBLIOGRAPHY

Poetry Collections

1981 *Emplumada*. Pittsburgh: University of Pittsburgh Press.
1991 *From the Cables of Genocide: Poems on Love and Hunger*. Houston: Arte Público.
1998 *Bird Ave*. Boulder: MANGO Publications.
      Harddrive. Boulder: MANGO Publications.
      How Far Is the War? Boulder: MANGO Publications.
      Play. Boulder: MANGO Publications.
      Letters to David: An Elegiac Mass to David A. Kennedy in the Form of a Train. Boulder: MANGO Publications.

Collections of Critical Essays, and Autobiographical and Poetic Thoughts

"I Know Why the Quetzals All Die: A Portrait of an Education."
The opening section of the new work-in-progress "I Know Why the Quetzals All Die" can be found on the following web site: http://members.aol.com/ tonytweb/mangodrive.html. Lorna Dee Cervantes also placed some other poems on the web, including "Bananas," "Ten Seven-Minute Poems," "Coffee," "To a Starling Mother, July 4," and "The Journey Is Over." All can be found on the following web site: http://members.aol.com/tonytweb/lornawrit.html.
"A Gang Girl."

MARION ETTUNGER

Denise Chávez

Novelist, Playwright, and Actress

"My writing is a mirror into my culture."

LAS CRUCES, NEW MEXICO, SEPTEMBER 30, 1996

NEW MEXICO NATIVE Denise Chávez is a novelist, playwright, teacher, director, and actress whose work is very much influenced by the landscape, people, and culture of the Southwest. Although she doesn't consider herself a poet, Chávez has written some poetry as well. In her prose Chávez often explores the deeper dimensions of her past and personal life. Her plays, however, focus on a wider scope of social experience and the interrelation between the outer New Mexican landscapes of mountains and deserts and the inner worlds of her Latino characters.

Chávez was born on August 15, 1948, in Las Cruces in southern New Mexico. Her father, Epifanio Chávez, a brilliant lawyer, left the family when she was very young, and Denise and her two sisters, Faride and Margo, were raised primarily by their mother, Delfina Rede, a Spanish teacher, but also by many women from across the border who helped out while Delfina was teaching. After graduating from Madonna High School in Mesilla, New Mexico, Chávez went to college, and by 1971 she had earned a B.A. in drama from New Mexico State University. Three years later she graduated from Trinity University in San Antonio, Texas, with an M.A. in fine arts. In 1984 she received a master's degree in creative writing from the University of New Mexico in Albuquerque. She has been a playwright and actress with La Compañía de Teatro de Albuquerque and Theater-in-the-Red in Santa Fe, and has also taught playwriting at the College of Santa Fe, and English composition, literature, and drama at Northern New Mexico Community College in Española. From 1988 to 1991 she worked as an assistant professor of drama at the University of Houston. Later she taught creative writing at New Mexico

State University and at the medium-security prison Radium Springs Center for Women. She has also served as codirector of a senior-citizen workshop in creative writing and puppetry at Community Action Agency in Las Cruces, and for several years she was an assistant professor of creative writing at New Mexico State University in Las Cruces. Since its inception in 1994, she has been artistic director of the annual Border Book Festival in Las Cruces.

Chávez has had a great deal of success with her one-woman show *Women in the State of Grace,* a play about the lives of nine girls/women ranging in age from seven to seventy-eight. Her plays have also been produced at the Edinburgh Festival in Scotland and Joseph Papp's Festival Latino de Nueva York.

In 1977 Chávez taught at the American School in Paris, and she participated in an exchange of ideas on contemporary art between U.S. and Soviet artists at a two-week symposium in Moscow in 1988. Among the numerous awards she has received for her writing, acting, and community work are the 1984 Rockefeller Foundation Fellowship, the 1986 Steele Jones Fiction Award, the Lannan Foundation Fellowship, the Puerto del Sol fiction award for the story "Space Is a Solid," and in 1995, for *Face of An Angel,* the American Book Award and the Premio Aztlán for a novel written by a Chicano/Chicana, as well as the Governor's Award for Achievement in the Arts and in Literature.

Despite the more than thirty-five plays she has written and produced, Chávez is best known for her fiction. Numerous short stories have appeared in magazines, journals, and anthologies, and in 1992 Chávez's dramatic magical fable for children titled *The Woman Who Knew the Language of the Animals* was published. Chávez had earlier published a collection of seven interrelated dramatic stories titled *The Last of the Menu Girls,* whose title story appears in the *Norton Anthology of American Literature.* The stories explore the mysteries of womanhood by tracing the coming-of-age of a young New Mexican woman named Rocío Esquibel. As Rocío compares her mother's life to her own and as she meets different characters at work in the hospital and in her neighborhood, she finally formulates her own identity. Chávez's novel *Face of an Angel* (1994), winner of the American Book Award, also has a Mexican American female protagonist and incorporates many characters and elements of the Southwest. This unrestrained, humorous work chronicles three generations of women dealing with the tradition of serving husbands and God, and confronting such issues as alcoholism, religion, machismo, incest, and relationships. The main character, Soveida Dosamantes, is looking for new ways to become more complete and balanced, and in the course of writing a handbook for waitresses called "The Book of Service," Soveida looks back on her thirty years as a waitress. By doing so, she finally understands the meaning of service in her own life and becomes more aware of the impact of service with regard to the role of women in a machismo culture, as well as the interconnections between work and family life. Reviewers from the *New York Times Book Review*, *Newsweek*, *Publishers Weekly*, the *Miami Herald*, *Newsday*, and many other publications have praised *Face of an Angel*.

Currently, Chávez lives with her husband, the photographer and sculptor Daniel Zolinsky, in Las Cruces, New Mexico.

KARIN IKAS Could you tell us a bit more about yourself—your family background, how you were raised, and so on?

DENISE CHÁVEZ I grew up here in Las Cruces, New Mexico. My parents were divorced when I was about eleven years old. My mother was a teacher for forty-two years all over West Texas and then in Las Cruces. She was a career woman, and I attribute a lot of my success and my energy to her. My mother was a great role model. As she was a single parent, I used to give her gifts for Father's Day as well. She was just a really strong, wonderful, and very artistic, very talented woman. As a teacher she taught Spanish and also elementary school. She really had a love for education. A lot of my energy definitely comes from her and from all the other women in my family who helped to raise me while my mother was teaching. Everybody in my mother's family graduated from college. All of them were interested in education; they became teachers.

My father was a lawyer, and he loved education, too. During the Depression he went to Georgetown University in Washington, D.C., to get a law degree. It was really unheard of in those days that a Mexican American would leave a town like this, a dusty little town, to get a degree and become a lawyer. My father grew up being punished for speaking Spanish at school. Even though he mostly spoke English because of his childhood experience in the U.S., he spoke Spanish very well, too. I think for all of us living in the United States but belonging to different ethnic cultures means to face a contemporary dilemma: the fact that the dominant culture is English and English only. My mother always spoke to us in Spanish, and so did her relatives. When we went to visit them, we spoke to them in Spanish. My aunt refused to speak English. So we were going back and forth between a lot of Spanish. However, my father's family mostly spoke English. I think they moved towards English as a defense mechanism, something to protect them against the dominant culture. When you grow up being punished for speaking Spanish, you want to get the language of the oppressor. You want to be able to blend in and hold on to the common language. With my father mostly speaking English, and my mother mostly speaking Spanish, it was a good blend. Thus, I do use both languages in my writing.

K.I. Why do you write primarily in English, then, with just a couple of Spanish words mixed in? Why didn't you choose to write bilingually?

D.CH. I write in English because I live in an English-speaking society. However, I have written in Spanish, too. It is interesting that a lot of my poetry that I haven't had published is in Spanish. Spanish is more of a heart language, a soul language, to me. At the same time I like to think that I go back and forth between both languages. Even though I write in English, the underpinnings of the works, the basis, has to do with that linguistic ability to be able to go back and forth in English and Spanish if I choose. Thus I am able to say things in English and also throw in a Spanish word or phrase, or to deal with concepts in Spanish that are very different from English. I have also written a play in Spanish. But for some reason it just seems that most of my fiction always is in English with Spanish blended in. But I don't feel uncomfortable about that. As a matter of fact, we are just forty-two miles away from the Mexican border here in Las Cruces, and I speak Spanish every day of my life. So it is not that I have chosen English as my primary language in general. It always depends on the context, the circumstances, and to whom I am speaking. If I am talking to somebody from Mexico, of course, I use Spanish. With my neighbor and some other people, I go back and forth between both languages all the time.

K.I. So the sociolinguistic area somehow determines what language you use?

D.CH. Yes, that is correct. And it is always fluent and fluid. It changes with who you are and what the circumstances are. It's real code switching, and it works both ways. I also mix English words in when I speak primarily Spanish. Sometimes we even make up new words. For example, a few days ago I was talking to a friend of mine, and we went back and forth, and finally, before we left, I said to him, "Well, then *faxeame*." That word doesn't exist in Spanish. I had just tried to transform the English words 'fax me' into Spanish usage. It is very interesting linguistically to deal with language, as there are so many concepts and possibilities there. Some things are best said in English, and for other things you just have to use Spanish. Every language just has its own power.

K.I. Do you feel comfortable with terms like "Hispanic," "Chicana," "Mexican American," or "Latina"? Which term would you apply to yourself?

D.CH. I think all those terms are very subjective. Personally, I consider myself a Latina as opposed to a Hispanic writer. The term "Hispanic" has been invented by the "authorities" in Washington, D.C., to lump all Spanish-speaking people together.

I am not a Hispanic but a *Her*spanic, and definitely I am a Latina writer. I am also a Chicana. That term implies that you identify with the political and societal reality and responsibility of what it means to be a Chicana, which goes back to the sixties and the times of the Chicano Movement. When you say you are a Chicano or a Chicana, you take on a peculiar stance.

K.I. How would you describe your formative years as a writer? What influenced you most?

D.CH. The landscape and the places of the Southwest where I spent all my childhood and youth had, and still have, a tremendous influence on me. As I have already mentioned, I grew up in Las Cruces. Actually I was born in the back room of this very house where we are right now, and in which I am still living. My uncle built this house on this land that belonged to my aunt. This house used to be the only house on this street, and all the surrounding area used to be cotton fields. The room in the back where I was born is now the place where I work and write. However, I have a studio down the street as well. This house and its environs are my landscape. It is my inspiration, and it has a great influence upon my life and my writing.

Also, I love writers who have a lot of musicality in their work, like Federico García Lorca, the wonderful rhythm of Thomas Wolfe's work, and Eugene O'Neill, whose work I have read and studied very intensely. His play *A Long Day's Journey into Night* is one of my favorite pieces. Then there is Lillian Hellman, whose work I love a lot because she was one of the few early women playwrights. Among the Mexican writers I prefer Juan Rulfo for the wonderful mystery and magic of his writings, all those disembodied voices. I love Gabriel García Márquez and his magic realism. I like writers who play around with time and space.

When I started my artistic career, I began in theater as an actor. I think that really helped me to get an understanding of characterization. I was performing in plays of Chekhov, Shakespeare, and other playwrights from all over the world. I have done everything: Greek tragedies and plays by Aristophanes and Euripides, Restoration comedy, contemporary theater by European and American playwrights like Harold Pinter, Edward Albee, Eugene O'Neill. While working in Houston, I was incredibly lucky to work with Edward Albee. I was even sharing an office with him. Besides having attended his playwriting workshop for one semester, I was able to see him direct three plays: *Who's Afraid of Virginia Woolf?, Ohio Impromptu,* and *Krapp's Last Tape.* From Albee I learned a lot about vision, about creating things and letting them happen.

K.I. You just mentioned Harold Pinter, the modern English dramatist. Were you particularly influenced by European and American playwrights? What about Mexican American and Latin American dramatists, like Luis Valdez, for example?

D.CH. When I was growing up, there were no Chicano writers at all. I remember that when I was in high school, the first book I saw by a Chicano writer was Rudolfo Anaya's novel *Bless Me, Última.* It came out in 1971. When I looked at it, I thought, "I can't believe that this book is by a Chicano writer." I grew up in New Mexico, and I never knew Chicano writers, I never knew Hispano writers. So I had no idea that anyone was writing books about my world and my reality. Then when I saw Anaya's book, I couldn't believe that there was a writer in New Mexico who had written a novel. Anaya was a great inspiration for me. Later on he became a mentor of mine. I worked with him, and I studied with him at the University of New Mexico in Albuquerque. He continues to be a very dear friend. Prior to that there were no Ana Castillos, no Sandra Cisneroses, or Luis Rodríguezes, when I was growing up in the fifties and sixties. All I knew at that time were the little *viejitas,* the little old ladies who were writing cookbooks or memories of the family that they published themselves. Therefore, to have a book like *Bless Me, Última* was very important.

Of course, Latino writers have influenced me as well. As I said, García Lorca is one of my favorite writers. The authors who have often appealed to me have been writers of characterization and voice, whether it is Dostoyevsky, Bernard Malamud, or the Yiddish writer Isaac Bashevis Singer. It is always the writer who deals with voice and character who has a major influence upon me.

K.I. You are very good at playing with words no matter which genre you choose. There is a kind of natural flow in the language you use in your writing. To me it even seems as if words just pour out of you sometimes. With *Face of an Angel* I got the impression that this novel could have easily been a two-volume issue or so, right?

D.CH. You're right. Actually *Face of an Angel* was much longer at the beginning. When I first started, it was almost 1,500 pages long. After I mailed that manuscript to my agent in New York, we cut it down to 900 pages, and we kept working down to the 467 pages the novel consists of now. There were a lot of characters that didn't make it in the end. There is a chapter that I now think I should have kept in the book. Later on I published that chapter as a short story entitled "The Wedding." It became another reality, which is fine, too.

At the moment I don't have any plans to write a second volume and elaborate on some of the themes or subjects in *Face of an Angel*. I consider this book to be finished. That doesn't mean that the characters were not worthy of their own book. Hector and his wife, Ada, for example, definitely are. There are a lot of other characters as well who could deserve a book. At the end of *Face of an Angel* there definitely is a lot of potential for a new book there. However, I think that the world in *Face* is complete already. Therefore, I prefer to go on to another place. This book is not like *Rocky IV.* I am no Arnold Schwarzenegger doing *Terminator I, II, III* either. In the movies you have all those sequels. I am satisfied with the way the characters are right now. They are happy in their world, and I don't think I want to tamper with that.

K.I. How do you perceive your role as a writer vis-à-vis all the community work you do, including organizing and hosting the annual Border Book Festival here in Las Cruces?

D.CH. I see myself as writer who is very deeply rooted in the community. And that is why I work so hard on the Border Book Festival as the artistic director each year. In the beginning I had no idea that it was going to be so much work. We had the first Border Book Festival here in Las Cruces three years ago, but we have been working on it for five years already. At that time I got the idea that we should have a book fair in order to bring writers here, to have workshops and to take literature to people who might not have the opportunity to hear these writers otherwise. I got a grant from the New Mexico Arts Division for that project. But nothing really happened until Susan Tweit, a writer herself, and I got together. Her mission was the same as mine. She and I worked for two years on the first Border Festival. Then she had to pull back to work on another book. I didn't know that it would be so much work. But as it has been very, very rewarding, I am still quite enthusiastic about the Border Festival. I know my agent, Susan Bergholz in New York, is very worried because she feels I spend too much time on the Border Book Festival and that I should be writing instead, but I am a community activist. In that regard I am a very political writer, too. I am interested in women's issues. One of my themes is women. I am a voice for women. My voice is not the definitive voice, absolutely not, but I like to feel that I am able to tap into certain voices. It has been a struggle to balance my public life with my private writing life, my time as a teacher and my time as a solitary person working on a novel. Right now this is very difficult. But next year I am taking off just to write and devote most of my time to it.

K.I.   You have just emphasized that you write in particular for women. Do you write for women of all classes and from all ethnic backgrounds? Or predominantly for Mexican American women?

D.CH.   I don't differentiate between Mexican American, Anglo-American, Afro-American, or women of any other background. I am a Mexican American/Chicana writer writing of the Southwest, writing about the world that I know. But I think that my characters and themes are universal.

Think about the long line of mothers, and the mothers of the mothers. They want the best for their daughters and granddaughters. My old ladies, the *viejitas*, for example, could be German or Indian, Italian or Jewish. They could be from anywhere. My women characters are like all other mothers or grandmothers. They are women who struggle to find the best way, the best path, for their daughters or granddaughters and for their family. Although they are not perfect human beings, they mean well. Women have to keep in mind that they have to take care of themselves. One of the messages of *Face of an Angel* is that women need to serve themselves. They should not deny their own sexuality. It is important that they respect their own bodies and their own selves. And I hope that my writing raises an awareness here and that, like all good literature, it becomes something that reaches all people without distinction.

K.I.   Do you see yourself as a feminist? If "yes," then what type of feminist do you think you are?

D.CH.   I am a feminist writer insofar as I believe in women's freedom to be themselves and express themselves freely. Coming from a macho culture, I understand a great deal about personal freedom.

K.I.   In "Heat and Rain" you mentioned that your mother is "in her heart and soul a Mexican." What about you? How do you see Mexico? Is it more than a faraway spiritual homeland to you? What about the differences between New Mexico and Mexico?

D.CH. My heart is Mexican, as is my soul. When I am in Mexico, I blossom. I feel free in my spirit. The U.S. is a puritanical society at heart. My husband says that when I am in Mexico, I become another person. It's true.

K.I. Although you are very much influenced and shaped by the Southwest, you have traveled a lot as well. How important is traveling to you, and how does it affect you as a writer?

D.CH. I love to explore new places, and I have been to a lot of different places all over the world. I haven't been to Germany yet, unfortunately, but I would like to go to your country one day. Right after the earthquake I was visiting Mexico with a group of American women. The house another woman and I stayed at had just two rooms and one bed. The family gave us their bed, and all of them slept in the other room. There was no bathroom, just a little spigot with water outside. Going to this *colonia*, this neighborhood, that was so poverty-stricken was an incredible experience. I have never seen anything like that in my life. I have never been to India, but I can only imagine that it was something like that.

After Mexico I went to Russia, which I think has a similar ambience. I was a delegate to an international arts commission sponsored by the Forum for U.S.-Soviet Dialogue and traveled throughout the Soviet Union. I felt very comfortable with the Russian people. They are very emotional. They laugh when they are happy and cry when they are sad. And I think that this is the problem we Mexicans face here in the United States. We no longer dare to show our emotions and feelings. Here your emotions are always somehow repressed. In the Soviet Union I had no problems communicating with everyone even though my Russian was nonexistent. I found a lot of people who spoke Spanish there; thus, I was able to communicate. It was wonderful to speak Spanish in Russia.

I understand American culture and I can say that I feel comfortable in it. The job of a writer is to feel comfortable wherever you go or travel. There are kindred spirits, people that you understand, everywhere. I like to travel, I like to meet people, and I always say that I have never met a stranger. It is a privilege and also a great blessing to be a writer and to be able to communicate across borders and boundaries. Another thing that is so wonderful about literature is that it widens your horizons. It enables you to enter new places just by reading. For example, I can pick up a book and be in Germany. Then I can pick up another book and be in Italy, or on the moon, or wherever. With Anaya's *Bless Me, Última* I can be in New Mexico. That is what is so special about literature. Readers are able to inhabit the worlds.

K.I. Looking back at your youth and the beginning of your writing career, you've often emphasized that everything started at an early age with the keeping of diaries. In "Heat and Rain" you even claim that "Without my diaries, I don't think I'd ever have become a writer."[1] Why?

D.CH. Starting at the age of eight, I have always kept diaries. Just recently I was cleaning out the attic of my house. It had not been really cleaned for many years. I found a paper that listed everything that was important for me as a child. You know, when you are younger, you tend to write down all your favorite things. I had written down my name: Denise Chávez, ten years old; at the bottom of that list I had written "my secret ambition: to be a writer." I had no idea until then that I wanted to be a writer at age ten. However, writing was something I have always deeply loved. From the diaries I went on to notebooks. I used to transcribe other people's poetry. I wrote pieces myself, and I really liked that. I loved the act of writing and the physical manipulation of the pen on the paper. But I never realized—until I was going through that old material—that I really wanted to be a writer right from the beginning. However, when I think about it now, I have always loved words and people's stories.

In my childhood we would travel a lot. We spent our summers in West Texas, where it was very hot. There was nothing else to do there except read. My aunt lived in a town that had less than fifty people, a grocery store, and nothing else. Everything was just desert. You couldn't go out during the day, as it was too hot. People would come out at six or seven at night and sleep outside on cots. At that time to be a writer was more a dream than a realistic goal for me. Back then I didn't think I had the talent to become a writer.

K.I. Was there a personal encounter or a book that motivated you to become a writer yourself in the end?

D.CH. You know, writers are very special people. They always seem to be very far away, unattainable and unreachable. Like Toni Morrison, for example. You wonder "Why?" She is a human being like anyone else. I would love to meet her. But writers like her seem remote. It is almost as if they were not real. That was true with Rudolfo Anaya at the time I discovered his books. But then I did meet him. I got my master's at the University of New Mexico in creative writing. However, after I read *Bless Me, Última,* Anaya was closer than most other people. Studying with Anaya was a major awakening to me. I always thank him for his input in my life. He has been a great role model, and he influenced me a lot in my decision to finally become a writer.

K.I. What is your experience with publishers? Did you have any problems because of your ethnic background?

D.CH. I had, and still have, some problems. I have been in litigation with Arte Público Press for eight years now. I have a lawsuit pending because of a contractual dispute on *The Last of the Menu Girls.* It is a sad story. Arte Público Press first helped me a lot. I was very grateful that they published my book *The Last of the Menu Girls.* The whole issue is quite interesting as it deals with contemporary Hispano publishing, its habits, its ups and downs. However, that is another story altogether, and it would be too much to focus on here.

K.I. *The Last of the Menu Girls* was a kind of breakthrough for you then?

D.CH. Yes, definitely. Before, I had submitted a few things here and there. *The Last of the Menu Girls* had been my thesis for UNM, too. Afterwards Rudy Anaya asked me about what I wanted to do next, "just sit around or work hard to be a writer?" It was a challenge. And I said, "Yes, I am going to be a writer." The next step then was the camaraderie, the feedback from contemporary writers. People like Sandra Cisneros, who has done so much to help other writers. There is Ana Castillo and Julia Alvarez. We've been called "Las Girlfriends." Then Ben Sáenz and Dagoberto Gilb in El Paso, Texas; Gary Soto, Jim Sagel, and others all over the Southwest and the U.S. The friendship of these writers helps me a lot. There had been some earlier Chicano works, like *Pocho,* a novel that came out in 1959. But none of these earlier works really made an impact that showed that there was a great demand for Chicano literature. I think Sandra Cisneros made inroads there. Of course, there was Richard Rodríguez and his still very controversial book, *Hunger of Memory.* Sandra wasn't the earliest Chicana writer either. But she was the one who stimulated the interest in Chicano and Chicana writing. In the early eighties the publishing houses took note. The reading public wanted multicultural literature. I pay tribute to African American writers because their literature came first. We are seeing waves of multiethnic writers at present.

K.I. Do you feel that some publishers are trying to urge Chicano and Chicana writers to present particular clichés, or reinforce stereotypes of Mexican American culture in their writing because it sells?

D.CH. I think there is a lack of information and knowledge on behalf of the publishing houses because you have very few ethnic editors, number one. So very often you get an editor who simply doesn't understand what you are talking about. I know I had to explain to my editor, for example, what a piñata was. And this concerned me, as I thought, "This is a very basic cultural thing. If he doesn't know what a piñata is, how is he going to understand other cultural concepts that are very profound?" By the way a piñata is a clay pot that is decorated with animals or other figures. You use it for birthday celebrations. It is hit with a stick until all the candy you have put in it comes out. I realized that my editor from Farrar, Straus, John Glusman, was nevertheless in a way exactly the editor I needed, as he was able to be the reader I was looking for. I wanted to make my writing as clear as possible for somebody in Iowa, in California, in Vermont, or Europe as well. So, if I could clarify to my editor what a piñata was, then everything was going to be okay. It was not easy. I had to describe a piñata in one paragraph. It is pretty hard to explain something you take for granted. But you learn a lot from doing that. On the other hand, my proofreader was a Cuban woman. She was very dynamic. We got along very well, but her Spanish was different from Mexican Spanish. So there were a lot of words we had to go back and forth on. Between my editor and the Cuban proofreader, I think I got a very accurate interpretation in the end. It helped my writing because I had to be clear; I had to be precise.

K.I. What comes to mind here is the phrase "intercultural understanding." Do you think writing can help to improve intercultural understanding? And is this maybe another reason for you to write literature?

D.CH. I agree with you. My writing is a mirror into my culture. Also, my writing has a deeper message of healing, harmony, and of people trying to find a better way. My main character in *Face of an Angel,* Soveida, is trying to work against patterns of generational behavior. She wants to change the way things are done. I think we can educate and heal through writing, certainly. By doing so we can also enhance intercultural understanding.

K.I. The key word "healing" reminds me of the *curandera*, the elderly woman healer with seemingly magical power. She is one of the cultural icons of Mexican and Mexican American culture. People still pay a lot of tribute and attention to her. Earlier in the interview you mentioned the major influence of Rudolfo Anaya. As a *curandera* is the protagonist in his novel *Bless Me, Última,* I wonder if your idea of healing is very much influenced by Anaya and this book, too? What about your belief in *curanderas*?

D.CH. Well, I know people who have power and deal with herbs like *curanderas* do. I have some friends who are *curanderas*. But, on the other hand, I have been raised very Catholic, and there were certain boundaries we just didn't cross. So someone like Rudy Anaya's Última probably wouldn't have been involved in my life directly. But then again, she might have been. It is a very strange sort of thing: you have these folk beliefs, but at the same time you don't admit them easily. For example, we had a woman who worked for us. One day I burnt myself very badly, and it turned out that she was a healer. She was able to use the white of an egg to help me. Also, she had a lot of other remedies at hand that helped us later on. I knew a lot of these healers in my life. However, with regard to Última, it is different. Última and her way of life were set in the forties and fifties, and therefore it is a bit removed.

In the Chicano community nowadays there still is a deep vein of mysticism and spirituality that has nothing to do with religion. Religion is another thing. Catholicism is a religion of rituals and is thus appealing to people. There is a different influence here: It is the Native American one. If you live in that landscape of New Mexico, you have Native American blood. Our ancestors were Native Americans.

K.I. As a student you went to Madonna High School in Mesilla, a Catholic school, and you mentioned once that "religion was important then [during childhood] as spirituality is to me now."[2] Can you be a bit more specific about that? What does your spirituality look like?

D.CH. I grew up in a very traditional Catholic environment. For more than twelve years I went to Catholic school with nuns. That affected my life, of course. Additionally, my mother was very religious. She went to church at 6:30 every morning, and we used to go to confession every week. Therefore, I am still very much of a Catholic although I may not go to church regularly. But I always have my rosary with me.

We all are a *mestizaje,* a mixture of many things. I also have Native American roots, and I know that my roots are partly Jewish from Spain, the Crypto Jews or Sephardic Jews. So there is always this combination of many things. And why not have European and probably some Afro-American ancestry as well? There is that composite of different cultures, different religious concepts and beliefs that come together. However, there is also a certain kind of spirituality that permeates all that, particularly the landscape. This spirituality is unspoken, and it runs very deep.

K.I. In "Heat and Rain: Testimonio" you mentioned that as a child, "writing was a gauge of my personal life. It was a record of my physical, spiritual, and emotional ups and downs." Do you still agree with that? What is your major interest in writing right now?

D.CH. Yes, I do think that writing is a gauge of my personal life. It is just that your subjects change as you grow older. For example, in *The Last of the Menu Girls* I was growing up myself. Then, when I wrote *Face of an Angel,* it was already the voice of a more mature person and writer. I think that as you grow older, you change and evolve. Therefore, your themes change as well.

I have finished another novel now. It is called *Loving Pedro Infante.* Pedro Infante was a very famous Mexican film star who was tragically killed in a plane crash in 1957. He was an idol to many Mexican women and men. He rode a horse, had a beautiful voice, and was a movie star and a singer. As I am very much interested in the idea of machismo, to me Pedro Infante is the embodiment and epitome of the Mexican macho man. *Loving Pedro Infante* is a story about relationships and love. People love each other in that book; however, they just can't get together. It is the story of loving somebody but maybe not being able to connect with him or her at all. I don't think that these people are fated to be together in their lifetime. However, they still love each other. And Pedro Infante is the embodiment of Mexican machismo beauty, both in its positive and negative senses. When I was growing up, I—like all women—thought that Pedro Infante was very handsome. But there was no way that we could ever be really close to him. So this novel is a kind of obsessive love story. It is sad and crazy sometimes, like a *telenovela.* I am enjoying it very much. Once again, my work deals with relationships. I am a writer of voice, character, characterization, and relationships. My background and ongoing involvement in theater has helped and influenced me immensely in that regard.

K.I. What is the future of Chicano and Chicana literature: distinctiveness, or the crossing of borders towards global alliances?

D.CH. The work just keeps getting stronger and more potent. There is a great interest in Europe in Chicana and Chicano literature. It will continue to delight, empower, and bless all people with its powerful and unique vision.

NOTES

1. "Heat and Rain: Testimonio." In Asunción Horno-Delgado et al. (eds.), *Breaking Boundaries: Latina Writing and Critical Readings.* Amherst: University of Massachusetts Press, 1989, pp. 27–32.

2. Ibid., p. 29.

BIBLIOGRAPHY

Critical Essays

1986 "Our Lady of Guadalupe." *New Mexico Magazine* 64 (December 1986): 55–63.

1987 "Words of Wisdom." *New Mexico Magazine* 65 (December 1987): 73–78.

1988 "I Was Born in a Time of Extreme Heat." In Cynthia Farah (ed.), *Literature and Landscape: Writers of the Southwest.* El Paso, Texas: University of Texas at El Paso Press.

1989 "Heat and Rain: Testimonio." In Asunción Horno-Delgado et al. (eds.), *Breaking Boundaries: Latina Writing and Critical Readings.* Amherst: University of Massachusetts Press, pp. 27–32.

1992 "My North, Your South." *New Mexico Magazine* 70/7 (July 1992): 86–91. Special collector's issue for the seventieth anniversary of the magazine.

1996 "Scenes of Home and a Dream in Green." *New Mexico Magazine* (Feb./Mar.).

Novels

1986 *The Last of the Menu Girls.* Houston, Texas: Arte Público.

1994 *Face of an Angel.* Hardcover. New York: Farrar, Straus and Giroux.

1995 *Face of an Angel.* Paperback. New York: Warner Bros.

2001 *Loving Pedro Infante.* New York: Farrar, Straus and Giroux.

Stories

1977 "Baby Krishna's All Night Special." In *An Anthology of Southwestern Literature.* Albuquerque: University of New Mexico Press.

1981 "Evening in Paris." *Nuestro Publications* (Nov.).
"Willow Game." *Nuestro Publications* (Jan.).
1983 "Evening in Paris." *Revista Chicano Riqueña* (University of Houston).
"Shooting Stars." *Writer's Forum* (University of Colorado at Colorado Springs).
1984 "Willow Game." In *Cuentos Chicanos.* Albuquerque: University of New Mexico Press.
1987 "Grand Slam." In *Voces: Anthology of Nuevo Mexicano Writers.* Albuquerque: El Norte Publications.
"Mamá Tona" and "Missss Rede." *Journal of Ethnic Studies* 15 (spring 1987): 48–67.
1988 "Love Poem" and "The King and Queen of Comezón." Novel excerpts in *Las Mujeres Hablan: An Anthology of Nuevo Mexicana Writers.* Albuquerque: El Norte Publications, pp. 114–118, 119–157.
1989 "The Last of the Menu Girls." In *The Norton Anthology of American Literature.* New York: W. W. Norton.
1991 "The McCoy Hotel." *Blue Mesa Review* no. 3 (spring).
1992 "Chata." In *Iguana Dreams: New Latino Fiction.* New York: HarperCollins, pp. 44–53.
"Saints." In *Mirrors Beneath the Earth: Short Fiction by Chicano Writers.* Willimantic, Conn.: Curbstone.
1993 "The Closet." In *Growing Up Latino: Memories and Stories.* Boston: Houghton Mifflin.
"Evening in Paris." In *Short Fiction by Hispanic Writers of the U.S.* Houston: Arte Público.
"The Private Journals of Denise Chávez." In *Writers' Choice: Composition and Grammar.* Glencoe, N.Y.: Macmillan, McGraw-Hill.
"Willow Game." In *Cuento Chicano del Siglo XX: Breve Antología.* Mexico City: Difusión Cultural UNAM.
1994 "The Last of the Menu Girls." In *Making Connections Through Reading and Writing.* New York: Wadsworth.
1995 "The Last of the Menu Girls." In *The Norton Introduction to Literature.* 6th ed. New York: W. W. Norton.
"The Wedding." In *Daughters of the Fifth Sun: A Collection of Latina Fiction and Poetry.* New York: Riverhead Books.
1996 "La Fonda del Recuerdo." *Border Beat—The Border Arts Journal.*
"Macha Grande." *Sí Magazine* 1/4 (summer).
"Missss Rede!" In *Walking the Twilight II: Women Writers of the Southwest.* Flagstaff, Ariz.: Northland.
"Space Is a Solid: Kari Lee." Story excerpt in *Modern Fiction about School Teaching: An Anthology.* Needham Heights, Mass.: Allyn and Bacon.

Poetry

1977 "On Meeting You in Dream and Remembering Our Dance." In *An Anthology: The Indian Río Grande.* San Marcos: San Marcos Press.

1987 "Birth of Me in My Room at Home," "For My Sister in Paris," "Legana of Lace," "Mercado Day," "Purgatory Is an Ocean of Flaming Hearts," and "Ya." *Américas Review* 15 (spring): 48–59.
"Legana of Lace," "Our Linkage," "Progression from Water to the Absence," "Sisters Sisters Sisters," "The Space Between," "This River's Praying Place," "The Train Whistles," and "Worm Child." *Journal of Ethnic Studies* (Western Washington University, Bellingham).

1993 "On Meeting You in Dream," "Tilt A Whirl," and "Worm Child." In *Infinite Divisions: An Anthology of Chicana Literature.* Tucson: University of Arizona Press.

1994 "Watching Mrs. Sedillo." In *Latino/ Latino Literature,* special issue of *Prairie Schooner.*
"Artery of Land," "Legana of Lace," and "Mercado Day." *New Mexico Poetry Renaissance.* Santa Fe: Red Crane Books.

1996 "La Pesadez," "I Am Your Mary Magdalene," "This River's Praying Place," "Tears," "Cloud," "Artery of Land," "Silver Ingots of Desire," "The Study," "Starflash," "Saying, Oh No," "Everything You Are Is Teeth," "Cuckoo Death Chime," "Door," "Chekhov Green Love," "The State of My Inquietude," "The Feeling of Going On," "This Thin Light," and "Two Butterflies." In *Chicana Creativity and Criticism: Charting New Frontiers in American Literature.* Albuquerque: University of New Mexico Press, pp. 77–97.

Plays

One-Woman Play

1989 "Women in the State of Grace" (an ongoing repertoire of characters). Unpublished.

Published Plays

1982 *The Step.* In Vera Norwood (ed.), *New America.* Albuquerque: University of New Mexico Press, pp. 49–51.

1988 *Novena Narrativas y Ofrendas Nuevo Mexicanas.* In *Chicana Creativity and Criticism: Charting New Frontiers in American Literature.* Special issue of *Americas Review* (Houston: Arte Público), pp. 85–100.

1989 *Plaza.* In David Richard Jones (ed.), *New Mexico Plays.* Albuquerque: University of New Mexico Press, pp. 79–106.

1990 *The Flying Tortilla Man.* In Charles Tatum (ed.), *Mexican American Litera-*

ture. Orlando, Fla.: Harcourt Brace Jovanovich. Reprint, *Prentice-Hall Literature Bronze,* 4th ed. Englewood Cliffs, N.J.: Prentice-Hall, 1996, pp. 642–687.

1996 *Novena Narrativa y Ofrendas Nuevo Mexicanas.* In María Herrera-Sobek (ed.), *Chicana Creativity and Criticism: Charting New Frontiers in American Literature.* Albuquerque: University of New Mexico Press, pp. 149–168. Also published in Ana Castillo (ed.), *Goddess of the Americas/La Diosa de las Américas: Writings on the Virgen de Guadalupe.* New York: Riverhead Books, pp. 153–169.

Unpublished Plays

1971 "Novitiates."
1972 "Elevators."
1977 "The Mask of November."
1979 "Nacimiento."
1980 "Santa Fe Charm Hay Posada" [Yes, There Is Shelter].
1981 "How Junior Got Throwed in the Joint."
     "El Santero de Córdova" [The Saintmaker of Córdova].
1982 "The Green Madonna."
     "Hecho en México" [Made in Mexico] (with Nita Luna).
1983 "Francis!"
     "Morenita."
1984 "Plaza."
1986 "Novena Narrativa."
1987 "Language of Vision."
     "The Step."
1990 "The Last of the Menu Girls."

Children's Plays Performed on Stage

1975 *The Flying Tortilla Man* (published extensively in anthologies for young people).
1979 *The Adobe Rabbit.*
1983 *El Más Pequeño de Mis Hijos.*

Children's Book

1992 *La Mujer Que Sabía el Idioma de los Animales/The Woman Who Knew the Language of Animals.* Bilingual children's play. Boston: Houghton Mifflin.

Edited Works

1979 *Jacques Linguini's Nuclear Eggs.* A novel by the students of the Park Avenue Elementary School creative writing class, Aztec, New Mexico.

1980 *Life Is a Two-Way Street: An Anthology of Prison Poems,* by the inmates of the Radium Springs Center for Women. Las Cruces, N.Mex.: Rosetta.

1998 *Writing Down the River: Into the Heart of the Grand Canyon.* N.p. (out of print).

Forthcoming

"Big Calzones." Story. New York: Knopf.

"Crossing Bitter Creek." Essay. In *A Place of Spirit: Journey Through the Grand Canyon.* Flagstaff, Ariz.: Northland.

"A Family of Feet." Story. In *Frank Magazine* (Germany), special issue on New Mexican writers.

Lucha Corpi

Poet, Novelist, and Educator

"Everything else is work, but poetry is my life, the air that I breathe."

L UCHA CORPI, an award-winning Chicana poet, novelist, and educator, is a writer of many voices. Born and raised in Mexico, Corpi did not become a U.S. resident until she was nineteen. This firsthand experience of everyday life in Mexico distinguishes Corpi from many other contemporary Chicana writers who were born in the United States. Her Mexican background provides Corpi with a deeper awareness of the basic conflicts encountered by Mexican and Mexican American women who are caught between the Mexican and Anglo-American cultures.

Lucha Corpi was born on April 13, 1945, to Miguel Ángel Corpi and Victoria C. de Corpi in Jáltipan, a small town in the state of Veracruz. In 1964 she married Guillermo E. Hernández. One year later the newlyweds immigrated to the United States so that Lucha's husband could study at the University of California at Berkeley. Their child, Arturo, was born in 1967. After a painful divorce in 1970, Corpi enrolled at UC Berkeley, where she also became active in the Chicano civil rights and education movement. In 1975 she received her B.A. in comparative and world literature, and four years later she earned an M.A. in the same field from San Francisco State University.

Corpi's increasing involvement in the Chicano Movement in the 1970s coincided with the beginning of her career as a writer. In 1970 she wrote her first short story, "Tres Mujeres," published under the title "De Colores" in *La Cosecha* ten years later. She has since published stories and poems in numerous magazines, journals, and anthologies, including *The Other Voice: Twentieth-Century Women's Poetry in Translation* (New York: Norton, 1976), *Fireflight: Three Latin American Poets* (Berkeley: Oyez,

1976), *Chicanos: Antología Historia y Literatura* (ed. Tino Villanueva, Mexico City: Fondo de Cultura Económica, 1980), and *A Decade of Hispanic Literature: An Anniversary Anthology* (ed. Nicolás Kanellos, Houston: Arte Público, 1982). El Fuego de Aztlán published her first book, *Palabras de Mediodía/Noon Words*, in 1980. The bilingual edition includes Corpi's lyrical and highly expressive Spanish poems as well as English translations by Catherine Rodríguez-Nieto. Ten years later, in 1990, Corpi's second poetry collection, *Variaciones Sobre una Tempestad/Variations on a Storm*, also a bilingual edition, was published by Third Woman Press.

In 1989 Corpi's first novel, *Delia's Song*, was published. Using stream-of-consciousness and other narrative techniques, Corpi tells the story of a young woman who leaves her family to study at UC Berkeley, where she gets involved in the Third-World Student Strike in the late 1960s. Corpi's second novel, *Eulogy for a Brown Angel*—the first of the Gloria Damasco detective series—deals with Chicano political activism as well. It opens in Los Angeles at the height of the Chicano Movement, and its protagonist, Gloria Damasco, is a speech therapist by profession but a Chicana activist, feminist, and detective by inclination. After Gloria discovers the body of a four-year-old boy killed during a 1970 Chicano civil rights march in Los Angeles, she becomes determined to solve the mystery of this murder. Allusions to Puccini's *Madame Butterfly* and to La Llorona in *Eulogy*, and to Native American rituals and artifacts in her next Gloria Damasco novel, *Cactus Blood*, are part of the combination of history, vision, and fantasy that Corpi presents in both of her feminist detective stories.

In addition to establishing herself as a writer, Corpi has worked as a teacher. She has been teaching English as a second language, primarily to adults, through the Oakland Public School System since 1973, and she has been an instructor at Vista Junior College for several years. She is also a founding member and past president of Aztlán Cultural/Centro Chicano de Escritores and a member of Sisters in Crime, an international circle of feminist mystery writers.

The numerous awards Corpi has received for her work include a National Endowment for the Arts Creative Writing Fellowship in 1979, first place in the Palabra Nueva literary competition for her short story "Los Cristos del Alma/Martyrs of the Soul" in 1983, and first place in UC Irvine's Chicano Literary Contest in 1984. In addition, Corpi was one of five writers awarded a Creative Artists Fellowship in Fiction by the Cultural Arts Program established in 1990 by the City of Oakland, California. That same year Corpi was Poet Laureate of the Indiana University Northwest. In 1993 she received the PEN Oakland Josephine Miles Literary Prize in Fiction, and the Book Award of Excellence in Adult Fiction of the Multicultural Publishers Exchange.

VOICES

My father taught me to sing
my mother to spin verses
and from my grandmother I learned
that truth can be found
through silence as well

There are so many voices in me
so many voices going down
to drink at dreams' edge
on winter nights

—reprinted with permission of Lucha Corpi
  from *Variaciones Sobre una Tempestad/Variations on a Storm*

KARIN IKAS   I would like to begin the interview with your poem "Voices," which was published in *Variations on a Storm* in 1990. In this poem you refer to "so many voices in me." Could you tell us a bit more about these many voices—for example, about the voices that influence you as a writer and as a person in general?

LUCHA CORPI   I suppose I was born with a certain gift for writing, although my gift is very small. I don't think I am a great writer or poet, but I try to make the best of it. I work hard at my craft, and I am as good as I can be. That is enough for me because it is the writing that is important to me. Publishing and the recognition that comes with it are desirable, but not the main reason I write.

Writing is a solitary occupation. It's hard work, harder for me because I write fiction in English, my second language. I didn't begin to learn English until I came to California at the age of nineteen. But when I write fiction, I am in the company of my characters. I hear their voices, and they speak to me in English. I am bound by their need to express in that language, within their bicultural context. They are with me during the long hours of intense labor writing a long work takes.

I write poetry in Spanish, however. When I write poetry, the voices in me are those of real people, people who in some way or another have formed me, taught me, or shared with me episodes of my life. Further-more, I also have in me the voices of those other poets I have read, in particular those I have liked and whose work has influenced my own poetry production. Like García Lorca, Neruda, Storni, de Ibarbourou, Agustini, Paz, and others, as a poet I partake of a poetry tradition in the Spanish language. On the other hand, I have also broken away from that tradition as the reality of my life in the U.S. demands.

I didn't start writing poetry until I was twenty-four. Looking back, however, I remember my mother's reaction when I finally dared to show her my first poems. She told me that she knew all along that I was a poet; I had just started later than other poets. I suppose my mother saw in me what I couldn't see in myself until then. But I believe my introduction to poetry was through music, in particular through my father's love of music and his singing. He had an eclectic taste in music. So since very young, I learned about music from different cultures, countries, not just Mexican music. In addition, I played the piano for many years, so I became familiar with the music of classical and Romantic composers, and later on, blues and jazz.

When I began to write poetry, I knew I had found something so akin to music. Music and poetry are the oldest of human expressions—prob-ably first music, then poetry. They complement each other and blend with each other to form a song. A song is powerful. It has the range of emotion music provides, and the power of ideas, images, memory asso-ciations, and speech governed by human intellect. Richard Wagner said something I found extraordinary. He said that the "reason for being of music is poetry." I wholeheartedly subscribe to that notion. At times, somewhere in my mind I hear the music of a poem long before the words come together.

K.I.   I understand that most of your formal education in Mexico was in the sciences. What made you get so interested and involved in the humanities and arts?

L.C.   That's right. In elementary school I had been exposed to poetry and short fiction for children. I loved reading mythology books and mystery stories. One of the first books I read and was influenced by was The Arabian Nights. I also loved reading books on astronomy, biology, and zoology. I loved adventure books. But most of the books I read were part of my schoolwork. My academic orientation throughout high school in Mexico was in sciences. I was basically interested in becoming a medical doctor or an astronomer—two careers not considered in Mexico suitable for girls who hoped to marry and have a family.

At age sixteen, I met Guillermo Enrique Hernández, whom I would marry and with whom I would come to Berkeley, California, three years later. He introduced me to literature and philosophy, from the classics to German and other European literary and philosophical works as well as Mexican and Latin American modern works. During the eight years I was with him, I got most of my literary education. Later on I became a student in comparative literature at UC Berkeley and honed my literary and critical skills.

During all these years, however, I had no idea—neither did my husband—that I was a poet or writer. People often told me that I had a very personal, even peculiar way of expressing myself when I wrote a letter, a composition, or any other school assignment. But I was never told my style of writing was particularly "creative."

K.I.   When was this sort of breakthrough for you as poet then?

L.C.   Well, when I was twenty-four years old, I had a strong need to express what was going on in me. At that time I had been in California, in Berkeley, for five years. I was going to get a divorce. I had a young child and very few friends. I spoke English well enough to get into Berkeley. I was working as a bilingual secretary, so I was able to support my child and myself. But there was a need to articulate all the ambivalence, all the contradictions, all the sorrow and pain carried within me. I did not have anyone to talk to. So I started writing, just to make sense of my situation and to express my feelings.

Writing at that time was a kind of healing ritual for me. For the first two years I never showed anybody what I wrote. Actually, the first thing I wrote was a long poetic prose piece called "Tres Mujeres/Three Women." That is the only work that I would really call autobiographical, besides a couple of personal essays. "Tres Mujeres" is an allegory. A young woman must choose between two worlds: to stay where she is or go back to Mexico. The third alternative is the one that provides something of both. The story depicted exactly the situation I was in when I started writing the story. I wanted to explore what would happen if I went back to Mexico or if I stayed in California. It seemed that I belonged nowhere anymore. In the end I decided to stay.

K.I.   What made you stay instead of returning to your family in Mexico?

L.C.   My parents were living in a smaller city in Mexico. It was a provincial city in attitude, away from the larger Mexico City. Everyone there was extremely Catholic, so any divorced woman would have a hard time. Imagine: I was twenty-four, not so bad-looking, with a three-year-old child. Although I could be self-supporting, I would have to live with my parents again if I went back to Mexico. Otherwise, as a divorcée, I would have to face the risk of social isolation and alienation. The only other alternative was to move to Mexico City, but I did not want my child to grow up in such an extremely large city. So I decided to stay in the United States.

K.I.   What were your feelings about Mexico and your Mexican roots at that time, and what are they now?

L.C.   At that time I was very angry at Mexico because of the way Mexican society viewed marriage and divorce. Not in political but in cultural terms, I felt like an exile. And I was very angry at my own Mexican culture for not allowing me as a woman to have the possibility of a wholesome life, a life of my own choosing. I think I still have some of that anger sometimes, though I have been able to reconcile to it a lot more, or at least to accept that I will always feel ambivalent as a Mexican woman, as well as Chicana, towards my culture.

K.I.   It would have been different if you were a man going back to Mexico?

L.C.   Absolutely. I mean, they would not have made a big deal of a man being divorced. He wouldn't have been tagged morally and socially as a deviant. Even now, in the late nineties, it is still very difficult for divorced women to live a life according to their own convictions and principles without pressure from society to get married. A woman alone, a single mother, is still an eyesore in Mexican culture.

K.I.   You have already mentioned the strong influence of the Catholic Church in Mexico. Would you say that this is one of the reasons, if not the major factor, for the still prevalent discrimination, stereotypes, and old-fashioned role models Mexican women have to face and deal with?

L.C.   The Catholic Church definitely contributes a lot to the way society perceives women and the place that is given to women in Mexican society. I think religion in general, when it does not particularly exclude women at all, is a way of keeping women in what men see as a woman's place. I certainly never fit in that mold when I was growing up. Since I was fourteen until the age of sixteen, I had a terrible spiritual conflict because I began to see all these contradictions and started to fight against them. Finally, when I was sixteen, I left the Catholic Church. I never told anybody. I just stopped being a Catholic. I still left home every Sunday and pretended to go to Mass. But I never went; I did something else instead. And my family did not find out until my son was already born and I told them. My father then was extremely afraid that my soul would be condemned. My mother felt sorry for me. My father asked me if I still believed in God, and I said, "I think so. God is something I have not dismissed."

K.I.   How would you describe your current religious belief?

L.C.   I belong to no institutionalized religion, but my ethics are still Christian. I believe in the Ten Commandments pretty much. They still rule me subconsciously sometimes, and at other times consciously. There are some common truths in all religions. I am still a Christian, but my intellect tempers my beliefs and [makes] them only a frame of reference when it makes sense.

K.I.   Many Chicana writers have a somewhat spiritual understanding of nature. The four elements and the moon, for example, are for some Chicanas quite often of special importance in their life and writing. Do you share that spiritual concept of nature?

L.C.   I grew up in the tropical part of Mexico, in a place where you had to respect nature. We did not see nature as separate. Still, as children we were always told to be careful, not to use firecrackers near dry wood or molest snakes that crossed our path. So there were a lot of things that we had to watch out for as children growing up in a junglelike place. All our senses were in tune with nature. Obviously that attitude toward and perception of nature color my work, but I can't say that it's necessarily spiritual.

K.I.   Were you also told to watch out for spirits like La Llorona, the Weeping Woman, who is said to haunt water places in search of children?

L.C.   Oh, yes, that was part of the lore. All children were told to be careful around certain places like creeks and swamps. In the region where I am from there was one particular type of figure called La Chaneca. La Chaneca was this nymphlike young woman who lured people, especially men, at night and took them into the swamp where they died. My grandmother used to call La Llorona, La Chaneca, the Devil, and the different personifications of death the "immortal ones."

K.I.   How would you describe the relationship with your mother?

L.C.   My mother has always been very conservative. As a matter of fact, she had a very hard time dealing with me because I was never one to just take things and conform. She always, *always* tried to make me conform, but I never could. I always questioned everything, since I was very young. She had only the answers that she had learned from all the other women around her—and from the men, of course.

Actually, my mother is the poet in the family. She used to write poetry. You know, she used to write poems on butcher papers. My father collected all her poems. When my father died, he left an envelope for me with all of my mother's poems in there. Her poems are sonnets with consonant rhyme.

K.I.   One poem in *Palabras de Mediodía* comes to my mind in that context. It is called "Protocolo de Verduras/The Protocol of Vegetables."[1] Did you think of your mother when you wrote that poem?

L.C.   Actually, I did not think especially of my mother when I wrote that particular poem, even though the poem imagined a woman, possibly my mother, who had eight kids and a great need to write. There are so many women who go through that and to whom this experience can be applied, not just to my mother.

I thought of my mother in particular in some of my other domestic poems. They are called "domestic poems" because they talk about being a poet and being constrained by housework or raising a family. Women nurture others, and many times we're not able to pull all of our energy into the writing. There is a long poem called "Labor de Retazos/Patchwork."[2] As I wrote that one, I did think of my mother many times.

K.I.   Who were the most influential people in your life?

L.C.   My grandmother and my father were definitely the most influential persons in my life.

K.I.   Your father because of his music?

L.C.   It is not only because of the music, but because he truly believed in educating the girls in the family, my sister and me. I have six brothers. My father gave my sister and me an opportunity to get a formal education. He insisted on it. He used to tell my sister and me since we were very young, "You have to do your homework, you have to study, you have to get good grades, you have to go to college, to the university, you have to have a career. It is more important to educate you, the women, than your brothers because when you educate a man, you educate an individual, but when you educate a woman, you educate a whole family. Consequently, your children's education begins with yours."

And that was my father's philosophy. In addition, my mother encouraged us to read and do well in school, too. She also took care that my sister and I got as good an education as my brothers. Within their means, both my parents helped us to get a good education.

K.I.   This kind of liberal and progressive attitude toward the education and role of women was not the rule at that time and still is not the rule among Mexican and Mexican American men today. Your father seemed to be a quite liberal, unconventional-thinking Mexican man in that sense, would you agree?

L.C.   Yes, my father was not a typical Mexican father, not at all. I am not exactly sure why. Maybe it is due to my grandmother. Her outlook on everything was so different. He was brought up in a different kind of environment, in a household different from others.

My female cousins did not go beyond the sixth grade, which is grammar school in Mexico, because they were going to get married. The idea was to have them marry men that were financially successful so that they would be well taken care of.

In a way my father had such an impeccable logic, but it was not necessarily what I wanted. When he gave me the choice for a career, he said, "Look, go into dentistry. You'll be independent, as you can work for yourself. You do not have to work for a man who can take advantage of you; you can choose your own hours; you can take care of your family, and you make a lot of money. So if your husband decides to leave you, you can always survive and support yourself and your children."

Wasn't that impeccable logic? The only problem was that he expected me to like a career in dentistry, but I could not see myself as a dentist ever. I enjoyed the first two years because it was very much like studying medicine in general. I liked doing the dental labs, but not the clinics. When I had to do my first molar extraction and the first ten fillings, I knew I was going to go crazy if I ever became a dentist.

That is when I decided to get married [laughs] and come to Berkeley. I met my husband first in San Luis Potosí when I was going to dentistry school, although he was not in dentistry. He was into philosophy, humanities in general, and literature. Later he told me that the reason why I caught his attention in particular was that he saw something in my eyes that was very different. I was different from all the girls, all the young women that he had met before. He wanted to find out what made me different. So he started talking to me and seeking my friendship. What he found in me was a kind of kindred spirit. Later on it turned out to be that I wasn't so kindred after all. We did look at things in a very,

very different way. During the time I was together with him—from age sixteen until we got divorced eight years later—I grew up a lot intellectually. I always say that he was the one who planted the seeds. Most definitely he was my teacher, just like my father was my teacher as well.

K.I.   So men have been very influential on your personal development and your writing?

L.C.   Yes. As I was growing up, I think I got most of my encouragement and support from men, not from women. Women seemed to always be saying that it was better to conform, or risk being unhappy.

K.I.   Your life sounds like the life of a feminist. Would you consider yourself a Chicana feminist and/or a feminist writer?

L.C.   You could say that I lived a kind of feminist life. But I never really thought of myself as being a feminist until I began to look into what feminism is all about. Then I realized that throughout my whole life I had been a practicing feminist, [but] I had not put a label to it.

With regard to the writing, I most definitely am attracted to the women characters that are strong, able to take responsibility for their actions and deal with the freedom they have. That is what counts for me.

The women characters in my writing are most important. It always surprises me what I have learned and still learn from them. Through all of them I have been able to gain a much wider perspective and to review some things I used to believe. So it is somehow like losing your innocence—I mean, not just sexually but culturally—when you begin to grow.

For example, if I think especially about the novel I am finishing right now, entitled *Black Widow's Wardrobe*—which is going to be the last one in my Gloria Damasco detective novel series—there are two women characters in there that have taught me a lot. They made me aware of many things I had never thought about before.

When you think of yourself as having become a superwoman, you also run the risk of becoming somewhat intolerant of other women in difficult situations. When I was younger, I had to fight for everything on my own. I had to juggle teaching and going back to get my M.A. In addition, I had a young child. I was a single mother. So there was so much to handle. In such situations, however, you learn to be so self-sufficient, self-contained, and self-possessed. Consequently, you begin to develop a kind of intolerance for other women who are not handling their lives well. You become harsh and judgmental because you think, "If I could get myself out of all my messes, why can't other women do that as well?" Your view narrows in that sense. I don't consider that being a feminist. It is more an inability to see beyond your own life. That is why you begin to lose some perspective. So through the writing of all these different female characters in my novels, I have been able to gain a much wider perspective and to review some things I used to not understand. These characters also helped me to regain some of the feelings that were lost in my struggle to survive as a woman.

K.I.   Could you tell us a bit more about your forthcoming novel, *Black Widow's Wardrobe?*

L.C.   The story has a lot to do with the renewal of the spirit and the soul. It is more about reincarnation. The two important women in the story are protagonist and detective Gloria Damasco and the woman she has to protect, "Black Widow." This woman believes she is the reincarnation of La Malinche. Gloria has to look into Malinche's life with Cortés and the conquest of Mexico to solve the mystery.

"Black Widow" killed her husband when she was twenty-four, when she was pregnant with his child. That is why the press names her "Black Widow." Her baby dies when she is in prison. Now, eighteen years later, she is out of prison and somebody is trying to kill her. Gloria witnesses the attempt; that is how she gets involved. The novel explores many themes, such as domestic violence, the history of Malinche, soul and spirit, the nature of love, et cetera: themes that are within the context of Chicano culture and against the background of Mexican history. Furthermore, the book explores the intertwined history of Mexico and the U.S.

K.I.   What kind of image do you present of Malinche in that story, and how do you feel about this female archetype in general, as she is still often used and abused to stigmatize Mexican and Mexican American women and so on?

L.C.   Chicanas have taken off La Malinche. Octavio Paz said that we are all "hijos de la chingada," "chingada" meaning the Indian woman raped by the Spaniards. But in the case of Malinche people have said that she was a whore because she gave herself freely to the Spaniards. Actually it was not freely at all. She was a slave, and so she was given to the Spaniards without having any choice. But she consented a lot more and used the arrival of Cortés for her own purpose. So when Octavio Paz talks about us as the "hijos de la chingada," he refers to us as the children of this raped Indian women, meaning that we are a bastard race. But that wasn't entirely the case of La Malinche.

But I think—and one of the characters in my forthcoming novel talks about that as well—that we are not *hijas de la chingada*—*hijas*, you know, meaning the daughters—so we are not the daughters of the raped woman. Instead we are daughters of La Malinche, the woman who had the intelligence and the ability to be Cortés's guide. Without her, he would not have been able to understand Mexican and indigenous culture, traditions, et cetera. She was his translator and mediator, so, actually, in a way she was his voice. And she was also the one who protected him from getting killed. The character in my novel says that we are not *hijos de la chingada*, meaning the woman who was raped, but *hijas de La Malinche*, meaning the woman who was very able, intelligent, and capable. That is very different.

I think Chicanas nowadays view La Malinche from the latter perspective. However, Mexicans still see her as the woman who sold out, if they talk about her at all. While being in Mexico this summer to finish my research about La Malinche, I came across two new biographies. They are very slim volumes because there is so very little known about her. Even Hernán Cortés mentioned her just twice in his letters to the king of Spain during the Conquest. He never even refers to her by her name but describes her only as a native girl who helped him, who interpreted for him. Although these two books are very slim, they show that there are at least more people interested now in finding out who she was. One of the volumes was edited by a woman, the other one by a man, both Mexicans, which is unusual. Their approach to Malinche is a lot more objective and a lot fairer with regard to the treatment of the historical figure of La Malinche than many of the other ones that had been published before.

But mostly Malinche has been a very popular character in literature, theater, and so on. For example, Carlos Fuentes and many others have written about her. She never did put in writing anything about herself. There are no letters or diaries. We do not even know where she is buried or how she died. Some people say that she died of smallpox. Others say that she was actually stabbed, that her husband—Juan de Jaramillo—killed her. She had just given birth to her second child, her daughter María, a year before Cortés was going to be brought to trial for a whole bunch of accusations more to do with morality and his sexual excesses than with his military ones. So they were accusing him, among other things—which might actually be true—that he had murdered his first wife, Catalina. He choked her to death when she came from Cuba to see him in Coyoacán. Malinche was already there and had a child by him. It is being said that Cortés was afraid that Malinche was plotting against him, and therefore he had her killed—stabbed thirteen times in front of her house in Mexico City. But there is no evidence one way or the other. The people who claim that she died in a smallpox epidemic have no more proof than those who say that she was stabbed.

K.I.   We have already talked about two important archetypes of Mexican women, La Llorona and La Malinche. The third one is the Mexican version of the Virgin Mary, La Virgen de Guadalupe. How do you feel about her and the mixture of Catholic and indigenous elements she embodies?

L.C.   Well, to me it is very interesting that she appeared just about three years after Malinche is supposed to have died. She appeared on the mountain Tepeyác, on which there was a temple to the native Indian goddess Tonantzin at that time anyway.

Today the cult to the Virgin of Guadalupe in Mexico is very strong. We women always had to live in between these two extremes, Malinche the whore and the Virgin of Guadalupe as the immaculate saint. If we moved just a little bit more to the left, we were a Malinche type, a kind of whore, and so we were bad women. If we moved a little bit more towards the Virgin of Guadalupe kind of role, we were good mothers, but we did not make good wives anyway. Men would always be looking at "loose" women for pleasure, but their wives had to be pure. There was not much to choose from as there was no in-between.

I do not have a religious or spiritual relation to the Virgin of Guadalupe or to any of the other icons of Catholicism either. I do not have an altar at home or things like that; however, I do have a little *retablo* with the name of Teresa de Ávila in my kitchen. I look at it quite often. I really enjoyed Teresa de Ávila's poetry, and I admire the kind of woman she was. Since I was very young, she has been a hero to me.

K.I.   If I think about your poetry and your whole emancipated life story in general, it seems that you have some affinities to Sor Juana Inés de la Cruz, the outstanding Mexican philosopher, poet, and nun of the seventeenth century. Would you agree with that?

L.C.   Yes, I enjoyed reading Sor Juana Inés de la Cruz immensely when I was growing up. I liked a lot of the other Latin American women poets as well. For example, I had read Juana de Ibarbourou, Sor Juana, Santa Teresa, and Delmira Augustín [of Uruguay], and the Chilean poet who was one of the first women to get the Nobel Prize in literature, Gabriela Mistral.

K.I.   You started writing and also publishing your work at a time when other Chicana writers—such as Sandra Cisneros and Ana Castillo, in particular—got started as well. Was there a kind of connection between all the Chicana writers at that time?

L.C.   Ana and Sandra are actually already a generation after mine. I would say they belong to a generation of younger writers. My contemporaries are more Chicanas like Bernice Zamora, Alma Luz Villanueva, and Estela Portillo-Trambley because of their age and the actual time we first started writing or publishing.

We find each other by accident and meet each other every now and again at conferences, readings, et cetera, but that is all. I have always moved in and out of the literary world at will. I spend a lot of time by myself also. Maybe that has to do with the fact that I write my poetry in Spanish and that I am considered as a more traditional writer, at least with regard to my poetry. And that is what I wrote for ten years before I attempted fiction. During that time I was part of the Chicano civil rights movement, and I was always accepted there with my poetry. Juan Felipe Herrera once told me that there is no one who cannot accept my poetry, as it addresses all those personal feelings a lot of us are afraid to express, so it seems that I speak to the soul of the Chicano people and the Chicano writers. I do that in a language that is considered the mother tongue. But I did not write about Chicano life in my poetry. Although my poetry has been political at times, I never intended to be a political writer. I wrote about what I wanted to write, and I never set myself limits of any kind in terms of expression or thematically. Therefore, my poetry has never been considered Chicana poetry. So I was always a kind of marginal Chicana writer. Even now, sometimes, there are people like a professor from southern California who once asked her students why I had chosen to write *Eulogy for a Brown Angel.* Someone replied that I wanted to exploit Chicano history. I did not grow up in the barrio; I came to the United States when I was nineteen, although it makes no difference to me what people think about my work in that sense. But ever since the sixties and the early seventies, when I started writing, I have felt marginalized.

I once talked with Marjorie Agosín, a writer from Chile, about one of her essays in which she deals with being a marginalized writer and a writer in exile. I felt very close to what she said because it was partly my experience as well. For example, I did not learn to express all these feelings—like my anger, my sadness, my happiness, and whatever emotions

I have—in English. Instead I always have felt and still feel them in Spanish. That simply is the language of my poetry, the language of my feelings. And I learned that in Mexico with my mother, my father, and my grandmother. For that reason I always write my poetry in Spanish. My whole experience just has not been that of someone growing up in the United States. Although I have lived most of my life in the United States now, I spent my first nineteen years in Mexico. Those were my formative years, especially in poetry.

K.I. What about your feelings about the United States?

L.C. When I came from Mexico, I came to Berkeley. So I did not come to the United States; I came to Berkeley, and there is a difference in experience there. The transmutation, the learning of the new way, in Berkeley was far from the average American way of life. Berkeley at that time, in 1964, was the center of the universe. Think of the free speech movement, Mario Savio, and all that. So my experience in the U.S. from the beginning has been quite different from that of other immigrants. Also, I did not come for most of the reasons other immigrants come. I came because I was married and accompanied my husband who was going to Berkeley. So I came as a student's wife.

With regard to society in the U.S. in general, I do not think I would call it a melting pot. At this point in the United States we have a number of different cultures trying very hard, but not successfully, to understand each other. We have so many different languages spoken and so many different cultures represented in the United States, but we do not pay enough attention to that at all. In Oakland, for example, which is 48 percent African American, we have languages like Black English, Ebonics, Navajo, Apache, Spanish, and English, of course, among many others. In particular, the Native American languages are often completely ignored. We have a uniquely difficult situation in cities like Oakland. I find living here very challenging but also very exciting. Cities like Oakland I see as the lab where the American Dream is tested every day, for we have to figure out a way to handle that diversity of ethnicity every day. So it is a challenge. I am not sure what is going to happen really.

K.I. Is this also a challenge for the writer Lucha Corpi? Is one of your intentions as a writer to enhance intercultural understanding?

L.C. Yes, of course, and it is a very important one. I have a story for children, for example, that actually deals with all that in particular. The story tells about the friendship between a Cambodian boy and a Chicano boy in the barrio of Jingletown, where both families live right next to each other. The Cambodian parents can't speak English, but somehow the Mexican parents try to communicate with the Cambodian parents. The primary element here and in many of my novels is that there is always a diversity of worlds in our society today. The Oakland I write about is very different from the city white middle-class authors write about. They don't see the Oakland I see. Instead, East Oakland, for example, is some sort of exotic place. That is the Oakland area where I live. I don't live in the Oakland hills, where all the middle-class people live, although I have friends there, and I certainly go there every now and then. But my Oakland is East Oakland.

In *Cactus Blood,* for example, I describe a park that is close to the school where I teach in East Oakland. Here you can see the interaction of many different ethnic groups. That is just an example of what you can see happening in any other park or street in Oakland as well. As a teacher in the Oakland public schools, I am a mediator between cultures. In my classroom I have to deal with all this cultural diversity every day. Being a writer is then just an extension of that view of the teacher as well.

It is interesting that I actually found out I was a poet and a teacher at the same time. More ironic still is that I never wanted to be a teacher, nor did I ever think that I was going to be a poet. But after I graduated from Berkeley, I needed a job. There was this job as a teacher that paid ten dollars an hour. I couldn't believe that I could earn much more money for teaching. In my former job as a bilingual secretary, I was making just three or four U.S. dollars an hour. I was so tired of being poor, of not ever having anything. So I took the job, mostly as transition. Then I started teaching. At first I felt exhausted, and I thought that there was no way that I could ever teach anyone anything. But then it became a challenge. Two months after I started teaching, I walked into my classroom and actually finished my lesson. As I walked out of my classroom, I realized that for all those three hours I had been there with the students, I hadn't thought once of anything outside my classroom. I began to really look forward to my teaching every day. At that moment, I realized I was a teacher by vocation, something I had never wanted to be. I wanted to be an astronomer, a medical doctor, almost became a dentist, but I never, never wanted to be teacher.

K.I.   When did you start writing?

L.C.   I was being formed as a writer at a very early age actually, but I didn't know it. I started school by accident when I was four years old. My brother had to go to school, as he was already six. We both were inseparable, and so I wanted to go as well, and my brother did not want to go to school without me either. My father talked to the principal, who finally agreed that I could accompany my brother to school. So I was given a little desk in the back of the classroom, but I wasn't officially registered. I learned to read and write already at the age of four. I moved on to second grade. A year later I officially started school myself. I was always the youngest in every grade. When I was seven, my father had a cornea transplant. He couldn't read for a long time. He had to wear a patch over his eye. So every afternoon after he got home, he asked me to read the newspaper to him. But my father always took out the crime page, the *página roja*, before I got the newspaper. I could read from anywhere in the paper to him, any section, but not from the crime page at all. Every time he took it out, folded it, and threw it away. But I always found the crime page, the *prohibido*, and the forbidden fruit kind of thing. I always read it. Then, after a while, I got tired of all the very gory descriptions, bloody things, the knifings outside dances, *macheteros* in the sugarcane fields killing each other, and whatever. Instead, I got more and more interested in the cases that showed there was some sort of intelligence behind the crime, some thinking going on. So I started following those cases, reading the newspapers every day. I started following the cases reported in the *página roja*, and I somehow became hooked on what is called "true crime." Next I began to read mystery novels. So when I started writing, my dream was to write a mystery novel and to write a play. Those were the two things I wanted to do. Of course, now I have three mystery novels written but no play yet. I feel writing a play will take a little more apprenticeship. If lucky, I might write a play before I die, as it is quite a challenge. The poet García Lorca, for example, has met this challenge brilliantly.

To me, the two ends of the literary spectrum are poetry on the one hand and plays and theater on the other. We go from the very extremely personalized and internalized process of the poetry to being spectators in the theater. The playwright is more removed and remains more distant from the material than the poet. Between those two extremes you have all the different genres and every kind of literary expression. So actually it takes quite a talent for a playwright to internalize and remain distant at the same time. I think that is why all the great playwrights like Shakespeare, García Lorca, and several others have been poets as well.

K.I. What is the difference for you between writing a novel and writing poetry?

L.C.   You know I always do things because they are a challenge. I think my natural voice is poetry, and there are still challenges in that as well. But I feel more at home writing poetry than anything else. Everything else is work, but poetry is my life, the air that I breathe, and I need it. I write one poem, and it is like having a love affair. Writing a novel is a long-term commitment. My forthcoming novel, *Black Widow's Wardrobe,* is probably going to be the last novel I write for a long time, as novels have a way of taking over your life. So writing a novel is like being married. It is a long commitment that is there every day, twenty-four hours a day. You cannot forget about it and just put it aside. Maybe you can, but it will cost you; you will pay a price for it.

I incorporate Chicana history into my novels. That is also why I write my novels in English, as most of the Chicanos and Chicanas today speak English and have to make their way in the English-speaking society. However, some of my characters still speak Spanish. In the barrio in Oakland there are quite a few families that speak Spanish at home. In that case, I then have to translate their Spanish to English. But for the most part my characters express themselves in English. My protagonist Gloria's dominant language is English although she knows Spanish as well, but Spanish is more considered as street language here.

Anyway, I attempted to write my very first novel, "Delia's Song," in Spanish, but I never could get past a few pages. I got lost and felt there was something fake about it. I was faced with the challenge of writing all my novels in English. It was and still is a challenge for me to write in English, as I will always feel inadequate in that language. I have to work much harder at writing anything in English. But for my novels it was necessary: English was the only language that worked, so there was no choice. I did not do it for any other reason—not to have it published or to qualify as a Chicana writer.

K.I.   If you think about the play you want to write in the future, what language will you use, English or Spanish?

L.C.   I have no idea. I have been reading and studying plays, both in English and Spanish, for a long time. In fact, I belong to a play-reading group where we get together every month to read plays and talk about them. But so far I have no concrete notion of what I would write about or the language I would use.

K.I.   Is Luis Valdez, the pioneer of Chicano theater of the 1970s, an important figure for you and your playwriting project? Will his style and technique influence the way you write your play?

L.C.   Luis Valdez is a unique case. His plays come from a very own and unique experience, his own. It was a time when everyone came together—the artist, the intellectual, the laborer, the farmworker—so there was no difference. Today the Chicano and Chicana experience is different. The activism, group solidarity, and so on of the sixties and seventies does not exist in quite the same way now. Nevertheless, the protagonist of my mystery novels, Gloria, went through that time of the sixties and seventies as a young woman. Therefore, her perspective is very much dictated by her activism and the friends she made during those years. So I deal with that world in my novels. But with a play it is different. I don't see myself trying to write a play like Luis Valdez. My experience is different from his. His particular style would not be my voice, my style. Anyway, before I attempt to write a play, I have to do a lot more apprenticing.

K.I.   With the novel *Delia's Song* you were one of the first Chicanas to write and publish a novel centered on politics, sexual awakening, and feminism from the perspective of a Chicana activist during the height of the Chicano/a student movement. And there are a couple of other things in which you have been a pioneer in Chicana literature as well, right?

L.C.   Well, I was the first Chicana to publish a whole collection of poetry, *Palabras de Mediodía: Noon Words.* Then I was the first one to write a mystery, too, *Eulogy for a Brown Angel,* which was published in 1992.

K.I.   What future projects do you have in mind?

L.C.   At this point I am finishing "Black Widow's Wardrobe." And once I have finished the first draft of that, everything else is only a dreary kind of work. It is just rewriting, speaking to the editor, and preparing the book for publication. Additionally, I am working on my first book for children, which is going to be published next year in August by Children's Book Press. It is a bilingual, illustrated edition, a picture book, entitled "Where Fireflies Dance/Ahí, Donde Bailan las Luciérnagas." I am very excited about it.

K.I.   A great number of Chicana writers— including Pat Mora, Sandra Cisneros, and even Gloria Anzaldúa—have published children's books recently. Do you feel that this is a current trend in Chicana literature?

L.C.   You are right. There are a lot of Chicana writers who write books for children right now, like Gloria Anzaldúa, Sandra Cisneros, and Carmen Lomas Garza. But I think that is more because publishers want especially Chicanas and Latinas to write bilingual children's books as they sell extremely well at the moment.

In my case, I got into children's literature through my son because I used to read to him a lot. And I always had such a hard time finding good picture books with good stories and told in an interesting way. Most of the books then were not worth even looking at, not to mention that there was hardly any reading material that was bicultural—forget multicultural. I first started to write longer stories for elementary readers in Spanish.

Then, actually, I started "Where Fireflies Dance" because Harriet Rohmer, the publisher of Children's Book Press, came to me and asked me to write a story for the press. We got together, and she gave me several ideas and suggestions for possible subjects. Writing a children's book, in particular a picture book, is very different from everything else I had done before. At first I really had a hard time getting used to that, in particular to its condensed form. I had written stories for children before. My shortest story was six pages long, far too long for a picture book. But Harriet was wonderful. She guided me through the whole process. I also had to collaborate with Mira Reisberg, the illustrator, a Chicana visual artist from San Francisco.

K.I.   What is the situation of Chicana literature right now if you think, for example, about the canon discussion or the growing popularity of Chicana writers—at least of some writers, like Ana Castillo and Sandra Cisneros, who have already been blamed several times for integrating too much into mainstream literature?

L.C.   You know, that is very interesting because in the sixties and seventies it was the male poet who dominated the movement, so the movement's voice was masculine. There were just a few women in the movement, like Estela Portillo-Trambley or Bernice Zamora and myself—poets mostly. The Chicanos, the men, invited us as tokens. They were already tokens, so we were the tokens of the tokens. The only reason why we were invited was because we were their friends and comrades in the political movement. As a favor they had let us come in and be part of the group. I am talking of the time from 1968 to 1975.

Sandra Cisneros, Ana Castillo, and other Chicana writers came later, towards the late 1970s and early 1980s. By the time Chicano writers gave Chicana writers credit, we were already a force to be reckoned with. Of course, we Chicanas knew of one another's existence and work—who was writing and what was being written. Chicana writers like Ana Castillo, Cherríe Moraga, Gloria Anzaldúa, Sandra Cisneros, among others, including Latina writers and poets, became the trendsetters and more popular writers. Still, very few of the many Chicana and Latina writers have been published by major presses.

K.I.   What about the future?

L.C.   When you consider that the largest minority in the U.S. will be Chicanos/as and Latinos/as by the year 2004, you have to ask yourself why it is that the literature hasn't been given its rightful place in U.S. literature. Why are there so very few films for TV or the screen that depict Chicano/a and Latino/a reality in an honest way? Why is it that only art and music have been brought to the forefront? At a certain level, the answer can be summed up in one word: racism. But there are other aspects to consider.

Chicano/a and Latino/a literature in the U.S. is formed by two very strong, conflictive cultural-linguistic traditions, a reality that presents a problem not only for those who live in its midst, but certainly quite a job for anyone trying to catalog it. Many publishers don't know what to do with such rich linguistic modes, from the writers who express themselves only in Spanish or English, to those who mix both languages to various degrees. Chicano/Latino literature is not homogeneous. It doesn't develop within clearly defined sociopolitical, geographic borders. Writers express various degrees from both major languages. It is perhaps best described by the metaphor of the mouth of a river, the place where violently, sometimes peacefully, where the water is at times sweet or salty, or both, runs deep or collects in peaceful pools, where marine, aerial, and terrestrial zoologies cohabit. It takes someone with a great vision to see the great potential in a place like this one. Someone will, I'm sure of that.

As for the Chicano writers who, like me, see their art as their life, they have no choice but to be faithful to the voices of their characters, be it that these characters express themselves in Spanish, English, and various bilingual modes. Otherwise, they run the risk of roaming the world with no more protection than a straitjacket.

NOTES

1. Lucha Corpi, *Palabras de Mediodía/Noon Words* (Berkeley, Calif.: El Fuego de Aztlán), p. 48.

2. Ibid., pp. 40–45.

BIBLIOGRAPHY

Poetry Collections

1976 *Fireflight: Three Latin American Poets.* Berkeley: Oyez.

1980 *Palabras de Mediodía/Noon Words.* Berkeley: El Fuego de Aztlán. Reprint 2001. Houston: Arte Público Press.

1990 *Variaciones Sobre una Tempestad/Variations on a Storm.* Berkeley: Third Woman Press.

Prose

1989 *Delia's Song.* Houston: Arte Público.

1992 *Eulogy for a Brown Angel: A Mystery Novel.* Houston: Arte Público.

1995 *Cactus Blood.* Houston: Arte Público.

1999 *Black Widow's Wardrobe.* Houston: Arte Público.

Children's Book

1997 *Where Fireflies Dance/Ahí, Donde Bailan las Luciérnagas.* San Francisco: Children's Book Press.

Other Publications

Poems in Anthologies

1976 *The Other Voice: Twentieth-Century Women's Poetry in Translation.* New York: Norton.

1977 *Contemporary Women Poets.* San Jose, Calif.: Merlin.

1980 *Chicanos: Antología Historica y Literaria.* Mexico City: Fondo de Cultura Económica.

1982 *A Decade of Hispanic Literature: An Anniversary Anthology.* Houston: Arte Público.

1983 *Women Poets of the World.* New York: Macmillan.

1985 *En Ruta.* High school reader. New York: Harcourt Brace.

1986 *Campeones.* Elementary reader. Boston: Houghton Mifflin.
Contemporary Chicano Poetry, ed. W. Binder. Erlangen, Germany: Verlag Palm & Enke.

1987 *The Americas Review: Chicana Creativity and Criticism* 15/3.
Dal Mito al Mito, ed. Lia Tessarolo Bondolfi. Milano, Italy: Editoriale Jaca Book.

1988 *Quarry West.* Santa Cruz: University of California.
Third Woman: The Sexuality of Latinas. Berkeley, Calif.: Third Woman.

1990 *Sotto Il Quinto Sole: Antología de Poeti Chicani.* Florence, Italy: Passigli Editori.

1992   *After Aztlán: Latino Poets of the Nineties.* Boston: David R. Godine.
1993   *Infinite Divisions,* ed. Tey Diana Rebolledo and Eliana Rivero. Tucson: University of Arizona Press.
       Vous Avez Dit: Chicano. Bordeaux, France: Centre de Recherches sur L'Amerique Anglophonet.
1994   *Light from a Nearby Window,* ed. J. Acosta. San Francisco: City Lights.

Works Published in Journals and Magazines

1977   *El Fuego de Aztlán* [Berkeley, Calif.] 1/4.
1978   *San Jose Studies* [San Jose, Calif.] 4/1.
1979   *Prisma* [Oakland, Calif., Mills College] 1/1.
       La Palabra [Tempe, Ariz.] 1/2.
1980   *Semana de Bellas Artes* [Mexico City, INBA] no. 133.
1984   *Imagine* [Boston] 1/2.
1985   *Poetry San Francisco* no. 3.
1987   *Beatitude 34* [San Francisco].
1988   *Poetry Flash* [Berkeley, Calif.] no. 191.
1992   *The Americas Review* [Houston] 20/3–4.

Other Publications in Which Works Have Appeared

1977   "De Colores." *La Cosecha* [Albuquerque, N.Mex.] 3/3.
       El Fuego de Aztlán [Berkeley, Calif.] 1/4.
1983   *Plural* [Mexico City] 13/1, no. 145.
1984   "Los Cristos del Alma/Martyrs of the Soul." *Palabra Nueva: Cuentos Chicanos* [University of Texas, El Paso].
1985   *Boston Review* 10/2.
       Revista Literaria: El Tecolote [San Francisco] 6/1.
1987   *Banderas.* [Elementary reader.] Boston: Houghton Mifflin.
1988   *Memorias.* Third Annual Congress of U.S.-Mexico Writers, Frontera Norte, Universidad Autónoma de Ciudad Juárez.
1993   *Cuento Chicano del Siglo XX,* ed. Ricardo Aguilar. Mexico City: Difusión Cultural UNAM.
       Hispanic Writers of the United States, ed. Nicolás Kanellos. Houston: Arte Público.
1995   *Las Formas de Nuestras Voces: Chicana and Mexicana Writers in Mexico,* ed. Claire Joysmith. Mexico City: UNAM and Third Woman.
       Latina: Women's Voices from the Borderlands, ed. Lillian Castillo-Speed. New York: Simon & Schuster.
1997   *The Hispanic Literary Companion,* ed. Nicolás Kanellos. Detroit, Mich.: Gale Research.

LOIS TEMA

Jamie Lujan

Cofounder of the Latina Theatre Lab and Actress

"Dare to be who you are and celebrate who you are."

JAMIE LUJAN is a Bay Area actress and the youngest cofounder (*co-madre*) of the Latina Theatre Lab.[1] (She is also a board member and volunteer coordinator for Brava! For Women in the Arts,[2] for which she has also taught beginning acting classes for women of color. Her students range from up-and-coming professionals to women just exploring new territory.

Jamie Lujan was born on July 28, 1966, in Albuquerque, New Mexico, to Dorothy and James Lujan and grew up in Denver, Colorado. From 1984 to 1988 she attended Emerson College in Boston, where she earned a B.F.A. in acting. In 1988 Lujan moved to San Francisco and participated in the summer training program at the American Conservatory Theatre. Two years later she was accepted to ACT's two-year advanced training program. At ACT Lujan was seen in the main-stage production of *Hamlet* (ensemble) and in studio productions of *Major Barbara* (title role), *A Midsummer Night's Dream* (Helena), *The Philistines* (Yuluna), and *Hayfever* (Jackie).

Lujan completed her M.F.A. in acting at ACT in 1995 with a thesis project on Cherríe Moraga's play *Heroes and Saints.* In the world premiere of this award-winning play, Lujan originated the starring role of Cerezita Valle (a disembodied head).

Having recently received a Writers Corps grant, Lujan is now teaching an autobiographical writing/theatrical workshop for Las Mission Girls at Brava. Also she participated in LTL's premiere production of *¿¡Qué Nuevas!?—What's New!?* at Brava. In addition, she was seen as Uuc (*el niño*) in Opera Piccola's world premiere of *Chac.* With WORD FOR WORD THEATRE CO. Lujan has toured schools and libraries in their production of *The Elephant's Child.* She is now touring with the Latina Theatre Lab in the cabaret *The Immaculate Conception.* With song, commentary, and salsa, LTL explores and challenges the virgin-mother-whore mythology and various other stereotypes.

KARIN IKAS Jamie, you are the youngest founder of the Latina Theatre Lab and currently on tour with LTL's newest production, *The Immaculate Conception,* a musical comedy about La Virgen de Guadalupe. But before we talk more about that theater project and the Latino/a theater scene in general, I would like to ask you to tell us a bit more about yourself, your family background, and how you were raised

JAMIE LUJAN I am an only child. I was born in Albuquerque, New Mexico, but grew up in Denver, Colorado, with my parents, who were very supportive in terms of what I wanted to do. Since I was little, I sang, first to the *río* [river] and then at school I joined the choir. When I was in high school, I started acting. I was very fortunate in that respect because at that time high schools had full arts programs. So I was in the theater department there. We had an international high school theater club as well and I received a U.S. $500 scholarship for college from them.

In terms of my family, I am very close to my grandparents. I do have a rich relationship with them. My dad's parents live in Albuquerque, and my mom's parents are in Colorado in a small town called Trinidad, which is almost on the border of Colorado and New Mexico. I consider myself a fourth-generation Mexican American. On my dad's side they were all Mexican. On my mom's maternal side, her people are indigenous from Colorado, as they've just always been there since it was Mexico. On my mom's paternal side, my great-grandfather was from Jalisco, Mexico. He had blond hair and blue eyes. His wife, my great-grandmother, was Spaniard. Her family immigrated to Chicago. There are pictures of her in gorgeous dresses and huge cars. Thus, when she married a Mexican—even though he was a landowner in Mexico—this was not acceptable to her Spanish family at all.

K.I. How would you describe yourself and your family background if you think about all these terms around like "Hispanic," "Chicana," "Mexican American," and "Latina"?

J.L. All these terms are somehow weird. But anyway, I would say I am a Chicana. I was born and grew up as a Chicana. Culturally I feel like a Chicana as well. My parents grew up at a time when they needed to get ahead in a white world. They had to work very hard for a better education. That also implied getting rid of cultural characteristics that hindered them, such as Chicano slang, which was just spoken in the barrio and not in the Anglo world. So I was never allowed to go and hang out with my cousins who lived in the barrio. My parents were trying to get out of the alcoholism, the gang riots, and everything else that was there in the barrio. But the Mexican American culture still stays with my parents. My father listens to *ranchera* music while he is cleaning the garage. Every Christmas we have *luminarias* at home. *Luminarias* are a New Mexican Christmas decoration around the house.

However, I don't speak Spanish at all. The only person in our family who actually spoke Spanish to all of us was my great-grandmother. My grandparents speak English fluently, without an accent, but to each other they speak only Spanish. My parents, however, just speak English to each other, even though my father didn't speak English till he was seven. But now that's changed, as it is really hard for him to speak Spanish at all. Both of my parents went to business school and got a two-year associate's degree in business. My mom has done everything under the sun— from bookkeeping to selling art to selling advertising to bookkeeping again—and my dad used to work for a bank.

K.I. Why did you choose an education in arts, acting, and theater instead of pursuing a career in business as both your parents did?

J.L. I just always was that way. When I was little, I knew every song on the radio, and I sang the whole day. Since I was the only child, I also had a very active play life by myself. To entertain myself, I always had a little scene going on with my toys and dolls. After high school I went to Emerson College in Boston as I didn't feel like going to New York yet. If you come from the West, New York is much different. After I got my bachelor of fine arts in acting at Emerson in 1988, I decided to apply for graduate school. I had several auditions at all the big board schools and ACT, and I got accepted to ACT's summer training program in San Francisco. And I really liked San Francisco, as it is similar to Boston. Later I auditioned for ACT again, and I got an ultimate position at the American Conservatory Theatre. The ACT belongs to the old school of theater companies where you have ensemble actors and theater companies that you use all year round. So there is a certain amount of minorities they have. I was an ultimate, and I guess the woman who decided she couldn't go, as a black, for whatever reason, was finally the cause why I got the spot. It was very interesting to see that kind of interchangeability in their minds; you know, there wasn't a Latina spot and a black woman's spot but instead just an ethnic woman spot. After two years of training at ACT I had three years to do my master's thesis. My thesis could either be on a one-person show that I researched or helped to produce, or a libretto, or so on.

K.I. You chose a very interesting project, creating and performing the role of Cerezita Valle, a disembodied head that is a leading character in Cherríe Moraga's *Heroes and Saints*.³ Cerezita was born without arms and legs as a result of her mother's exposure to pesticides while working in the fields. Can you tell us more about this project?

J.L. Yes, of course. As you've already mentioned, my project was to create and perform the role of Cerezita Valle and then talk about that process. Before I started, I didn't even know who Cherríe Moraga was. Therefore, I didn't have any clue about what the whole project was going to do for my career. You know, when you are finishing at ACT, you have to do these big auditions for agents who were looking for material. And I wasn't finding anything that I liked. As a Chicana, there is not a lot of stuff out there. One day someone told me, "Jamie, you should check out that Cherríe Moraga's work. She lives here. Why don't you give her a call and see if she's got an interesting play for you?" So I did contact her. Cherríe gave me *Shadow of a Man*⁴ and a first draft of *Heroes and Saints*. I had read *Heroes*. There is a scene where Cerezita and the priest have tried to make love, and it didn't quite work out. So the priest comes back and tries to apologize. And she says to him, "You know, it wasn't really about you. It was about me and what I wanted to be." And I said, "Wow!" that was really deep. Any woman should say that to any man any time. Therefore, I really wanted to do that play someday. However, I first put *Heroes and Saints* away, and I actually ended up doing a monologue from *Shadow of a Man*. A couple of months later, Ellen Gavin, the artistic director at Brava! For Women in the Arts, called me. She asked if I would like to audition for *Heroes and Saints*. Since I loved the play and I was keen on working with the well-known director Albert Takazauckas, who was going to produce *Heroes and Saints*, of course I went for an audition. Then at the callback Takazauckas gave me the final speech of Cerezita. I am a very physical actress, and this is a part where she has no limbs. Thus I began doing the monologue, but then all of a sudden I started doing something with my arms. As soon as I noticed that, I made an "uh-oh" face and put my arms under my legs. Cherríe and Albert both started laughing. Albert said, "You see, you have to do everything through your voice." In that way it was a real big challenge. Another challenge to me was that I had to do a lot in Spanish, as I knew just a little bit of Spanish. Thus, for me it was just a bit like working on a Shakespeare piece: You say, "OK, where are the operative words? Which words are the nouns and the verbs?" Then, "What does this sentence mean? What is the correct pronunciation?" The pronunciation was the first thing I learned because I got one of the women in the cast to speak my part in Spanish on tape. The next day I came back with the hundred-percent part, and everyone was quite impressed. I wanted this language issue to be my last worried thought. Therefore, I went through that Spanish every night when I was driving across the Bay. In the end, people were coming up to me talking Spanish. I had to apologize and say, "Sorry, I don't speak Spanish." They were like, "Whaaaaat! You are Mexican! I am looking at a Mexican girl, so you have to speak Spanish!"

K.I. How important was this project for your whole career? Did your acting style change after playing Cerezita?

J.L. First of all, it was great working with professional actors and actresses, and, of course, with Cherríe and Albert. It was my first professional show, and I learned a lot from all of them. Then, when all this preshow press came out, I soon started to realize what a famous women-of-color and lesbian playwright Cherríe Moraga is. We were featured in the *American Theatre* magazine and many others. We got a lot of great reviews, and often my photo was included in the article. So in terms of showcasing me, it was excellent, it was great. At that time I thought I was getting known all around and that it would last for a while, so I wouldn't have any problems finding further roles. However, I learned that here, in the Bay Area, that was not going to be the case; my popularity didn't last. When I called in to audition later on, for whatever reason I was just never getting passed. For example, I auditioned for a role of a secretary in a classical play by Strindberg. I was told that I was so good, but that I was just not plain enough. Whatever that is supposed to mean, I don't know. I think it is mainly a physical aspect, as a lot of times Latinas are told things like: you are too exotic, too fiery, too dark, or even you are too light. I've also gotten comments like, you are not Chicana enough, as I don't speak enough Spanish, or I am not down or from the street enough. Well, I am not.

You know, Jamie Lujan may not be that or that, or whatever your perception of me is. But I am an actor! And if that is what you require, whether it be dialect or a vocalic item, I can provide it for you. So I've gotten it from both sides. Either I am not Chicana enough, or I am too dark and too much Chicana. I think Latinas get that a lot in different ways, whether it is their speaking voice or anything else. Some women are first generation here, and they do have a Spanish dialect of a kind. Therefore, they are often told, "Oh, you can't play Shakespeare because no one is going to understand you!" That happened to Wilma Bonnet,[5] who was told that by several reviewers. They all mentioned her dialect. You know, to me that is totally incomprehensible because in conservatory theater you are taught the American speech, so that everybody in America sounds the same. That's at least what they try to do.

K.I. Were these discriminating and/or universalizing tendencies in the established American theater scene part of the reason why Wilma Bonnet, Dena Martinez, Tessa Koning-Martinez, and you finally decided to found the Latina Theatre Lab?

J.L. Yes, they definitely were. We were frustrated about what was going on. We got an excellent training in the classical and the Latina theater scene, and we just couldn't understand why we weren't cast. We figured out that it was because there is a certain bulk of actors that they start using and which they know. It is incredible, because if you are not in that circle, it is very hard for you to get in at all. Dena Martinez[6] had just come back from Los Angeles where she had to deal with the whole gross L.A. scene. She was very burnt out back then in 1994. We knew each other through mutual friends. We met and talked about starting our own theater company. But first, everything was just an idea. At that time, I was a volunteer coordinator at Brava! For Women in the Arts. I was coordinating a fund-raising event to get money for purchasing a house that provided enough office space. The board offered a lot of raffles. One of the board members at Brava was the arts consultant. She had given an hour with the art consultant as one of the raffle prizes, and Dena won that prize. So we both looked at each other and thought, "Wow, here is our open door, do we take it? Do we want to walk or just going to talk?" We decided to go for it. Thus we met the artistic consultant Ellen Gavin at Brava.

K.I. Do you think *Heroes and Saints* also attracted support from Brava and other sponsors for the Latina Theatre Lab?

J.L. Well, my work at Brava was first of all due to my financial situation. I started volunteering at Brava to do low things first just to earn money. Of course, I was very interested in their work and their productions as well, and I could keep the connections with Brava alive. And that helped a bit to get started with the Latina Theatre Lab.

Everything started with Dena and me having the first meeting in a café. There we decided to put our energy no longer in just complaining about our situation and in lamenting that we never get casted, but instead take that energy and do something. As there are hardly any Latina writers or directors out there, we had to cultivate within ourselves. It is like, "Hey, I know someone who is a playwright, I know somebody who likes to direct, et cetera." For the second meeting we then invited Wilma Bonnet and Tessa Koning-Martinez.[7] Wilma Bonnet is a twenty-year theater veteran. Tessa Koning-Martinez is a Puerto Rican street-theater-based actress and producer of radio dramas from New York. She has also worked with many of the established Latino theater companies like Teatro de la Esperanza and El Teatro Campesino. So we four—Dena, Wilma, Tessa, and me—we were the artistic core.

The next question for us was, "What are we going to do? What should be our first project?" We thought about having a cabaret showcase, a showcase of Latina talent. The response we got for that was really amazing. You know, the Bay Area theater community is very small; the Latino theater community is even smaller. Consequently, you pretty much know everybody who is out there. We put an advertisement, an audition notice for "Latina theatre artists for a cabaret showcase—bring your own act" in the *Callboard*—that is, the auditioning theater magazine here in the Bay Area. After the ad was published, we were stunned about how many women we have never seen or heard of before came to audition. It was quite obvious that there was really a need for a project like the one we were about to start. All these women, who were all aspiring actresses, did their different acts. They were all really good. We had a hard time to choose just the eight to twelve women we needed. What we did was to take the acts they brought in and then look at them to figure out if there is a kind of through line in all of them. The issues we wanted to deal with were stereotypes—in particular, stereotypes that were within the entertainment industry, meaning that we are always playing the maids, the nurse, the drug addict, or the drug addict mom. I mean it is OK to play those. I would play a maid, as my great-grandmother, for example, was a maid. But it is the way these roles are written; they are very one-dimensional and very straight. Therefore, we decided to focus on this issue in the cabaret. We videotaped the women who we were casting. Then we had an interview with them, and we talked about the first time they encountered racism in the entertainment industry. Many women first started saying, "Well, I really can't remember that it actually happened to me at all." But then when they kept telling their story, they pretty soon realized that it did happen. So the major problem was to get aware of it in the first place.

K.I. Did you have to go through that as well? Or have you been aware of that kind of subtle discrimination right from very early on?

J.L. No, it happened to me as well, however, in a somewhat different way. I wasn't aware of others perceiving me as a Chicana until I was seventeen and participated in a beauty contest for Miss Sorrora. Miss Sorrora is next to Miss Colorado, which then is next to Miss America. And the only reason why I participated was to get the prize, a scholarship for college. We were only five competitors, and everyone had to go in for an individual interview with the panel. When it was my turn, there was one white male, very cocky, asking me with a very condescending voice, "Well, Miss Lujan, why don't you tell us the history of Cinco del Mayo?" It was sort of like to see if the little Mexican woman knows her history. I have never felt such overt prejudice before, or at least I have never registered it. So I told him in a very cold voice, "Oh, you want to know? OK, I break it down for you." Afterwards I was incredibly mad, as I had never experienced such a humiliation and such racism before. Finally the woman who was tall and Anglo won the contest. Then this guy came up to me to tell me, "You are definitely going to do it next year as you are so young." And I just said, "No, I will be in Boston next year. Besides, I will never let such plain racism happen to me again."

K.I. There was already a common bond between you and all the actresses auditioning for the Latina Theatre Lab project because of the fact that all of you had to face similar discrimination and racism in one way or the other, right?

J.L. Exactly. So we interviewed the women for our first project that was called *¿¡Qué Nuevas!?— What's New!?* By the way, the title of the comedy *¿¡Qué Nuevas!?— What's New!?* came from "What's new! Wow, let's look at these women." The question mark means "What's new?" thinking about all these stereotypes we have to deal with, and to emphasize the importance of dealing with all that, it is written with exclamation marks as well.

We also asked the women about what they would like to do on stage but had never been allowed to do so far—whether it would be playing Shakespeare, *ranchera* music, or whatever. In one of the interviews, for example, a woman was playing a scene of Shakespeare's *Hamlet,* and in another one an actress was performing as a *ranchera* singer, and she had a very beautiful voice.

Anyway, we took all that material to check out how to incorporate everything in our project. We started with the Jamie scenes, as they had to be performed by a young girl. So the cabaret starts out with a girl standing in front of the mirror singing one of the Carmen Miranda songs.[8] Songs that go like that, "Mamá, yo quiero. Mamá, yo quiero. Mamá, yo quiero, mamá."[9] Then the light changes, and she is in an audition where she speaks with the same whispering voice. Afterwards there are some other, different scenes. One of them is a mass audition for Carmen Miranda, and we do a Carmen Miranda show tune. Three of the characters are men, three are women, and all are dressed in the Carmen Miranda style. When each woman shows up and does a pose, the audition process goes like that: "She is too dark, she is too short, she is too old, too this, too that . . ." Afterwards, in the top of the second act, the Jamie character, now a couple of years older, comes back again. This time she speaks a bit louder. However, still being very nervous, she forgets her text. Then the third time Jamie comes back to audition, which is at the end of the show. This time she is the grown-up Jamie who, besides all her self-doubts, starts getting at the beginning of this audition again. She is finally able to make a stand and get through the audition as a self-confident, strong Latina woman and actress.

K.I. Is there a scene in *¿¡Qué Nuevas!?—What's New!?* that can be directly traced to an actual event in the life of one of the actresses?

J.L. Yes, there is one scene dealing with stereotypes. It actually happened in a casting office. By the way, first of all you have to know that in the commercial industry the manifestation of stereotypes is even worse, and the "general Latina" is just called for the maid, the nurse, or for the one-line role. One day we were all called in for a film entitled *Village of the Damned*, which is a scary thriller screen show. And, of course, all of the Latinas had been called in for the role of the nurse, which had about three lines. However, the funny thing about it was that all of us Latinas were very different. So they really didn't know what they wanted. In addition, we noticed a general manifestation of stereotypes. It took place during the casting, as all the Latinas were reading for the nurse, all the Asians were reading for the doctor, all the black men were reading for the garbageman, et cetera. Eventually, all of us started laughing. Then someone suggested going up to them and telling them to change the title to "Barrio of the Damned." And we actually did it; we went up and acted out the whole thing. It was great. This scene is now part of our show as well.

K.I. Can we go more into detail about the stereotyping going on and how you work with that in your shows? I noticed, for example, that it has become a major subject in your current show, *The Immaculate Conception*.

J.L. You know, in the advertisements you never see Latinos using products. To me that means people in the commercial industry are not concerned about their Latino consumers. I have never seen Latinas promoting dish soap, toilet paper, or toothpaste; they imply we just don't use these products. They never presume the "real" Latino consumer in the barrio. If they use Latino and Latina characters at all, again, it just happens in a stereotypical way. For example, Latinas in particular are often shown in ads for beauty products and perfume, as they are considered to put a seductive, passionate, and sexual touch to it. To criticize that, we picked up some of these images and other misleading commercial messages in *The Immaculate Conception* and made fun of them.

K.I. In *The Immaculate Conception* you deal a lot with female archetypes such as La Malinche, La Llorona, and La Virgen de Guadalupe. The opening scene, for example, starts with a demystified Virgen de Guadalupe giving birth to all the other—mostly stereotypical—Latina characters. Is this LTL's present strategy: to combine distorted historical Latina images with pop-cultural twentieth-century stereotypes in order to show new perspectives?

J.L. Yes, after we finished *¿¡Qué Nuevas!?—What's New!?* we did want to deal more with these female archetypes, in particular with their actual meaning. Thus, we looked at the stereotypes, preconceptions, and realities associated with them today. As all of these characteristics are based on Latina women who are *mort*, we also checked questions like: What's their reality? Why are they dead? You know, the fact that they are dead doesn't mean that they are less valid. When we started with the new production titled *The Immaculate Conception*, we took the virgin-whore mythology and all these stereotypes in order to comment on them in a very critical, but also quite funny way.

The original version we did in February 1996 started with Malinche. But the three different monologues we finally had for her seemed too heavy, too Shakespearean in the end, compared to all the other funny stuff we had. It would have been too hard for the audience to give up all that laughter, we thought. Additionally, I personally didn't like the show to start already with such a complex monologue. The idea then was to let the Virgin of Guadalupe give birth to all the stereotypes and other archetypes. As you might know, the Virgin is pregnant in the original picture anyway. So the question is: What is she about to give birth to? Jesus? The baby? No, we thought, let's have her give birth to women because she ultimately is the Goddess who gives birth to us all, to all of us women. So that's where that whole concept comes from. Then we also continue criticizing the industry and its racist behavior. To do so we dramatize the birth of Marisa Tomei by the film industry. Marisa is an actress. She was cast in a Puerto Rican film or a film about a Puerto Rican family although she is not Puerto Rican at all. There are plenty of talented Puerto Rican actresses out there who could have played the role, but they used Marisa Tomei. And there was talking about how she used brown body makeup and gained all this weight to look like a Latina. All that is just really offensive to us. That's why we comment on that in particular through a little musical comedy we incorporate in the first scene. That is the part where the Virgin is giving birth to all the characters. When Marisa Tomei is born and claims right away: "I can do Cuban accents and Puerto Rican . . . and Mexican . . . arriba, arriba, an-da-lay!!!," all the Latina women show their protest by pushing Marisa back into the Virgin's womb.

K.I. You have a maid, a *soldadera,* La Malinche, and La Llorona as characters in the play as well.

J.L. Right, we have the Adelita, who is a *soldadera* character. Then there is the *campesina* who has just crossed the border. Also, we have La Llorona. Originally La Malinche and La Llorona were born together, like twins. In addition, there is the *salsera,* which I play this time.

K.I. In the play you also make fun of some of the images Chicanas and women in general often have to face in the mass media. I think in particular of the "Cross-over Make-over" scene in the cosmetic *palacio* of Estee Leedia facial products, and then the scene where you play the character of Francisca, desperately fighting with her weight problems. Could you comment on these scenes?

J.L. In that scene we were looking at body image and at what society says is beautiful—you know, like those tall, beautiful, gorgeous models or the thin weight keeper. However, women's bodies in real life are not like that, whether you like it or not! I think that is one of the reasons why the play is really a kind of crossover to all women, as they can all relate to these issues.

In the first version we didn't have the "Diet-Slim" scene. We just had the "Barbie Twins." The latter is based on an actual interview we found in a magazine with these women who were called the Barbie twins. They are really alive, have tons of breast implants, and big blond hair. They posed for *Playboy* and other magazines. When you see the Barbie twins interview in our show, that's pretty much how the real interview was like, too. They really talked about all the stuff they took without thinking about the side effects. It all sounded like this: "You know, we took all these laxatives and lost weight, and everything was just great." So first we thought about presenting this scene in a very cartoonlike way. But then we decided to incorporate the interview more or less in its original version and deal with the issues of weight and dieting in an additional scene instead. So that's what became then "The Miracle Diet" scene. Here we show how the scene's main character, Francis, tries everything—from yoga to meditation—in order to distract her from food and eating. Eventually, however, nothing works out and she has a complete breakdown.

K.I. How did the audience react to these two scenes in particular?

J.L. It is really wild to perform that, as "The Miracle Diet" scene in particular is also very funny. But we didn't want to make it only funny—you know, like in the way that Francisca is just weak and goes crazy with food. We also wanted to show the reason for that behavior, the desperateness. So there is a switch in the scene, and I think that is what makes the audience feel uncomfortable. First, when Francisca is trying to use spirituality and meditation to forget about food, people in the audience laugh a lot. Then when Francisca has the breakdown and is desperate, all of a sudden the laughter in the audience stops. I believe that this is a very deep thing for the people in the audience, because they recognize themselves and realize how they have been in similar situations as well. However, as the scene continues, the laughter comes back. That is part of our technique. Overall, we want to keep a certain strain of fun in the play.

But what is so sad and sick about those two scenes is the fact that situations like these really happen quite often in everyday life. They are the result of all these wrong images we are perpetuating in magazines, such as the notion that everybody has to look like the Barbie twins, et cetera. Therefore, we put the "Barbie Twins" scene after "The Miracle Diet" one. We wanted to show: "Look, Virgen, this [the Barbie twins] is what my ultimate goal is." The Barbie Twins are also a way for us to comment on this "Miracle Diet" scene. Nowadays, we have gone so much into this notion that looks are most important and that the way you look has to be a certain way. So we want these two scenes to be our criticism of all that. We should no longer accept and try to follow or adopt all society says is right or beautiful, as this is not what matches with women's life. It is just not how real life is.

K.I. The issue of crossing over into the American world is a central theme of the show as well, would you agree?

J.L. Of course, I do. The two scenes just mentioned as well as the one about the "Crossover-Makeover on the Campesina" demonstrate that. The "Crossover-Makeover" scene is a big scoff on the cosmetic industry. The actor Lydia, who plays the Estee Leedia character in that scene, actually works for Estée Lauder. So we are showing Estee Leedia, the owner of a cosmetic *palacio*, and her two employees, the Lip Liner Locas, trying to crossover the working-class Latina Fejita Cruz into what is supposedly beautiful. Fejita is a campesina who has just arrived from Michoacán.

Actually, I think this "Crossover-Makeover" or "Estee Leedia" scene could be its own play as there is so much in it. I would love to see that happen. In that case I would go on with the part like that: I would have Estee Leedia to come back in the second act, and for the Lip Liner Locas to be bold, wipe off their wigs, and say: "No way! We go back to our roots!" and then do a wild salsa number and convince Estee Leedia to take off her wig as well. Maybe in the future Estee Leedia gets its own play.

K.I. Another element you deal with in the play is machismo, a prevalent issue not just in everyday life of Chicanas but also in the theater scene. The Chicano and Latino theater scene—for example, Luis Valdez and the Teatro Campesino—has a reputation for being, or at least for having been, pretty much male-dominated. How was your project received there? And what's your personal impression of the present situation of Chicanas in theater in general?

J.L. Well, some blame us for putting too much focus just on women and, therefore, being exclusive. But I don't mind because our theater project is exclusive. The reason why it is, and actually even has to be, exclusive is due to the fact that there aren't many opportunities out there for us. So we have to make nucleuses on our own.

With regard to all the major Chicano theater groups, I personally never worked with Luis Valdez or any of these other male-dominated Chicano theater companies like Teatro Campesino or Teatro de la

Esperanza. One of the reasons why I never got calls from them is, for example, that I don't speak Spanish. In particular, Teatro Campesino puts much emphasis on Spanish, yet many of their plays are bilingual. Another reason is that all these organizations are entirely run by men. Some of the women have worked for them but never got promoted or even recognized. They are not supportive at all to women. Just think of Luis Valdez, who has become one of the first and most famous Chicano playwrights and producers of the 1970s, eighties, and nineties. He could do a lot to help other young and promising playwrights and actors—in particular, us still so strongly underrepresented women—to get started in the theater business. But he doesn't care much about us. Ask Cherríe Moraga, for example, who has worked together with Luis Valdez at the beginning of her career. Cherríe will tell you that Luis wasn't supportive at all. He didn't do anything to open the door for young Chicanas. Maybe men are scared, jealous, or afraid of losing their power. Additionally, they run their companies in a different way. Our philosophy at LTL is more based on the concept of working together with the whole ensemble. Everybody needs to share the whole workload, and we always try to nurture a supportive atmosphere. Otherwise it would be really easy for jealousies to happen. I mean, of course, it is okay that men and women as well as the older and younger generation have their different approaches. However, what is not OK is that we don't talk about it. Instead we keep pretending that there is no difference, but that we all have the same approaches, ideas, and opportunities. We have to deal with such intergenerational issues within the Latina Theatre Lab as well. Wilma, one of our four cofounders, is from the old school. Therefore, she is strongly influenced by traditional ways of how theater works. Let me give you an example: For the second round of *The Immaculate Conception* I wanted to invite some new actresses to participate in the new performances. As we already knew their potential for the roles, we just wanted to hire them and skip the traditional procedure with auditions and stuff like that. But first, Wilma was completely against that. It took her quite a while till she finally accepted our decision and agreed with us that just because oneself had to make one's way through all those rigid and discriminatory regulations and procedures doesn't justify to perpetuate all that now as well. How could the situation for women and younger actresses become better if we are not about to implement changes ourselves and start to support and nurture each other? There should be this kind of female bonding that helps us to learn from each other and to cooperate with each other. Thus we might be able to improve the situation for all of us. My philosophy is that everybody has his or her place in the universe. That also defines the things that are happening to us. So if Christina gets a particular part instead of me, it is because she was supposed to get that part, and there is going to be something else which I am supposed to be doing in that time frame, whether it is personal or professional stuff.

K.I.   How would you describe the situation of the Chicano/a and Latino/a theater scene at the moment?

J.L.   Part of the reason why the Latino community hasn't succeeded in terms of the arts—theater, television, et cetera—so far is that we simply don't work together. We don't support each other and the ones from our own community. At Latina Theatre Lab we therefore try to create a home and to foster the philosophy of cooperation and nurturing each other. It is this notion of: "Your success is my success. If you are out there succeeding and promoting Latina Theatre Lab, as you came from that Lab, that helps all of us."

I got a writer school grant. Last year I taught young Latina women, ages fourteen to seventeen, a writing and performance workshop that Cherríe had actually started at Brava. It is called Mission Girls and is a project with the YMCA. Cherríe worked on that for two weeks. Then Ellen and I were trying to find a way for me to work at Brava and get paid. Thus I finally got the chance to continue with this workshop and work together with these young people. One of the young women in that program actually works with Latina Theatre Lab now. She is a stage manager in training and is doing a very good job. It is really great to see that happen and to see her and other young women foster.

K.I.   You are here to give several performances at La Peña Cultural Center. However, Berkeley isn't the first stop on your *Immaculate Conception* tour, right?

J.L.   Correct. We actually started with a slightly different *Immaculate Conception* version, which was performed in San Francisco at Brava for four weeks in February 1996. We used these performances also as an opportunity to check the play out, see what works and what has to be changed and so on. In October 1996 we then started our tour with the revised version. Our first performance was at Stanford University on Día de los Muertos. Afterwards, we performed with Culture Clash in the Culture Clash Comedy Slam at Brava. But for that we just did the Estee

Leedia number. Now, after La Peña, we will be in San Jose at City Lights Theatre in January 1997 and at the Working Women's Festival in San Francisco in March 1997.

K.I. What are the future projects of Latina Theatre Lab?

J.L. We are thinking about working together with another theater company called WORD FOR WORD. They take novels and short stories and put them into a theatrical scope. They do that word for word, with "he said, she said," so they are going to work with us for a while. For us that is somehow like doing some research. Maybe later on we are trying to find some pieces of Latina writers, some short stories would be good, to produce them with that new technique. Most probably that is going to be our next project.

K.I. How do your personal plans for the future look? Do you want to concentrate on the Latina Theatre Lab in particular, or do you have other projects in mind as well?

J.L. The Latina Theatre Lab will probably be part of my life for a long time. It is getting more and more exciting to see its further development and influence on improving the situation for women artists and theater. However, I am also very open towards whatever other acting comes along. A thing that I might start again is singing. I sang some time in school; I even trained. Right after school I did some cabarets. Although I have to admit that this cabaret thing first seemed to be a little bit beyond my scope, as I never had done an open mike, much less my own kind of cabaret or singing show before, but I just went ahead and did it. I took twenty songs to have two sets, and I had a couple of monologues in between. First everything went well. But then I got some problems with the guy who played the piano, and the whole thing turned out to be a disaster. It took me quite a while to get over that. That's why I eventually quit singing at all. But I think now I am ready to try anew. I take up singing again. So maybe one of my new projects will include my singing.

K.I. Do you want to stay in the Bay Area?

J.L. I think so. If I move anywhere, it would be to New York, but not to Los Angeles.

K.I. What about New Mexico, the state you were born in?

J.L. I couldn't live there. The theater scene is not so rich and diverse in New Mexico. Here in the Bay Area it is different, as there is a great mixture of Chicanos, Chicanas, and Latin Americans. That is one of the things I like so much about the Latina Theatre Lab as well, as it reflects all that. LTL is extremely diverse within, culturally, as we have people of

Chicano, Argentinean, Puerto Rican, or Nicaraguan background. That's why it is called *Latina* Theatre Lab. It is not specifically Chicana. What is also very interesting is that there is a range of ages from twenty-two to forty-five, and a range of depths of experiences. It is called "Lab" because there is an experimental ethic there, too. For us "Lab" means an organized activity involving experimentation or observation in a field of study or practice in a skill. Group spirit is very important for us in that context. Everyone is part of this one group, the Latina Theatre Lab. It is a give-and-take relationship for both sides. The Latina Theatre Lab as a whole gets forward in the same way. Each individual member contributes to its success and vice versa. In the group we have to figure out what everybody's strength is so that we can use it effectively in the performances. In addition, we have to create a very open and honest atmosphere so that we can try to handle problems by talking about them. It's a bit like being a large *familia*.

K.I. What does your audience look like? Are there also white and/or Anglo women in the audience?

J.L. There are several white women in the audience. I think they are very interested in our work. Maybe they are interested because LTL productions are not just particularly Latina, but also very women in general. Latina issues are women issues. However, you have to keep in mind that our stories are told from a Latina sensibility, of course. This means we show our point of view and our experience as Latinas. I think that is true for any actor, as every actor brings his or her own sensibility with him/her—whether it is an African American point of view, or a Russian, et cetera. They all have their different sensibility, their way of being. As an actor you just can't separate your physical person and feelings from the character, as a merging happens.

K.I. So does being an actress mean, "Dare to be who you are"?

J.L. Yes, exactly. Dare to be who you are, and celebrate who you are!

NOTES

1. The Latina Theatre Lab (LTL) is a theater company as well as a support group for women artists and is fiscally sponsored by Brava! For Women in the Arts, San Francisco. Its main purpose is "to provide particularly Latina theatre artists with a professional environment in which they can write, act, direct, and produce their own work, while also providing an opportunity for development

and advancement of younger upcoming theatre artists." Dena Martinez, Jamie Lujan, Tessa Koning-Martinez, and Wilma Bonnet, four Latina actresses who were exasperated with limited roles for them on stage and screen, founded the Latina Theatre Lab. They felt that the existing theater environment did not address the need for portrayals of positive and empowered Latina women in their community. In order to fill this void and to work on eradicating limiting stereotypes, they founded the LTL. Being quite aware that "what we have to offer culturally has not been fully explored on stage," the members of LTL nevertheless are convinced that "the Latina sensibility, that we bring to every role we create, has the potential to give a new voice, not only to the classics, but to the modern contemporary American Theatre" (Latina Theatre Lab information sheet, 1996). The lab's productions include ¿¡Qué Nuevas!?— What's New!? (1995), Good Grief Lolita! (1996), and The Immaculate Conception (1996).

2. Brava! For Women in the Arts is a ten-year-old organization located in the San Francisco Mission District that promotes and produces women playwrights on a broad base—not just Chicana playwrights, but also other women of color and sometimes even white women. It focuses on women's issues and on bringing out new playwrights. People working with Brava also occasionally perform classical plays, but in a slightly altered interpretation, from a woman's perspective. Ellen Gavin, a community activist and renowned theater producer, initiated the creation of Brava in 1986 and is now its executive director. She describes Brava's mission as "to agitate, if not outright incite. Entertainment is incidental. Theater—in the flesh, in the real moment—has to be about making a change. . . . It's about disturbing people into action." In that context, and with regard to the under-representation of women and minority playwrights in the theater, Gavin emphasizes Brava's efforts to "raise the awareness of women's theater in general, and black and Latino artists in particular" (Michel Fox, "Producer Gets Cheers for Brava," San Francisco Chronicle, April 1, 1992).

3. Cherríe Moraga's Heroes and Saints (in Three Plays [Albuquerque: West End Press, 1993]) deals with the effects of environmental pesticides on a Chicano farmworker family in the San Joaquin Valley in California. The play had its world premiere in April 1992 at the Mission Cultural Center in San Francisco, produced by Brava! For Women in the Arts. Jamie Lujan played the leading character, Cerezita Valle. Heroes and Saints is divided into two acts: the first consists of sixteen scenes and the second of thirteen. In a cinematic style the action moves rapidly from place to place as it develops the situation between the family members, the surrounding community, and the power structure that refuses to acknowledge the problem. Although Heroes and Saints is fiction, Moraga based the story on real events that happened in the 1980s, such as protests against pesticide poisoning. Doing so, she goes beyond the struggle and the experience of the farmworkers and addresses issues of sexual and cultural identity as well as problems of assimilation and the strong influence of the Catholic Church. For

further analyses and reviews of *Heroes and Saints,* see Michel Fox, "Exposing the Effects of Pesticides: 'Heroes' Entertains While Elaborating on the Issues Affecting the Chicano Community," *San Francisco Independent,* April 12, 1992; Dean Goodman, *"Heroes and Saints*—Mission Cultural Center," *Drama League Weekly,* June 4–10, 1992; Judith Grenn, "Two Up-and-Coming Writers Explore Minority Community," *San Francisco Weekly,* Apr. 8, 1992 ; Monica Hernandez, "Woman in Hiding: Cherríe Moraga's New Play Draws Some Provocative Analogies," *Bay Area Reporter,* Apr. 9, 1992; Karen Hershenson, "Hero Has Head—That's All—for Farm Fight," *Contra Costa Times,* Apr. 3, 1992; Heather Mackey, "Down on the Farm," *San Francisco Bay Guardian,* April 21, 1992; Scott Rosenberg, "Injustice Stays All in the Family," *San Francisco Examiner,* Apr. 20, 1992; Randy Turoff, "Heroes and Saints: Playwright Cherrie Moraga presented by Brava," *San Francisco Bay Times,* Apr. 23, 1992; Jorge Huerta, "Moraga's *Heroes and Saints*: Chicano Theatre for the '90s," *Theatre Forum International Theatre Journals,* no. 1 (spring 1992): 49–52.

4. Cherríe Moraga's play *Shadow of a Man* was initially published in an earlier version in Linda Feyder (ed.), *Shattering the Myth: Plays by Hispanic Women* (Houston: Arte Público, 1992), pp. 9–49. It was republished in Cherríe Moraga, *Heroes and Saints & Other Plays* (Albuquerque: West End Press, 1994), pp. 37–84.

5. Wilma Bonnet, a Latina, is an accomplished award-winning actress whose many hats include playwriting, directing, and teaching. She is known in San Francisco and the Bay Area for her work with local major theater companies, including ACT, Berkeley Repertory Theatre, and El Teatro Campesino. She was also a member of the popular Tony Award–winning Chicano theater group the San Francisco Mime Troup (SFMT), with which she toured the United States, Canada, Europe, and parts of Latin America. Since SFMT, she has performed at L.A. Theater Center and the Bilingual Foundation of the Arts in Los Angeles, the Old Globe Theatre in San Diego, Eureka Theatre, Magic Theatre, El Teatro de la Esperanza, Marin Theatre Company, and the Dallas Theater Center in Texas. In 1995 she was a company member of California Shakespeare, and in 1996 she could be seen at ACT in Tennessee Williams's *Rose Tattoo* and Charles Dickens's *Christmas Carol.* She has also appeared in numerous films, commercials, and the PBS children's series *You Can Choose!* For three years she was a board member of Latin American Theater Artists, and she is one of the four cofounders of the Latina Theatre Lab. She directed LTL's premiere production of *¿¡Qué Nuevas!?— What's New!?* and she is currently participating in LTL's *Immaculate Conception* Tour.

6. Dena Martinez is an actress and director from the Bay Area. She has been on national tours with El Teatro Campesino and the San Francisco Mime Troup. She also served as road manager for the comedy group Culture Clash, and she has worked with many Bay Area theaters, including the Berkeley Shakespeare Festival, Eureka Theatre, Magic Theatre, San Jose Repertory Theatre, Teatro Nuestro, and others. She played the leading character Maria in El Teatro Cam-

pesino's production of Josefina López's play *Simply María or the American Dream* and worked with them on the PBS *Great Performances* production of Luis Valdez's *La Pastorela* as well. She is now host for a new PBS children's show, *Short Stories and Tall Tales,* and she has her first starring film role as Maggie in the Big Production's *93 Miles from the Sun.* For her directorial debut, *Praying Mantis* at City Lights Theatre in San Jose in spring 1996, she won a *Drama League* award for best production. Martinez has also taught the Vibrant Being Workshop created by Luis Valdez.

7. Tessa Koning-Martinez was born in New York City and is of Puerto Rican ethnicity. In 1972 she enrolled in theater arts at Antioch College and studied with members of the Polish Laboratory Theater and the Otrabanda Company. The following year she began a professional residency with El Teatro de la Esperanza in Santa Barbara, California. Later she produced radio dramas and public affairs programming for WYSO in Yellow Springs, Ohio. With the Theater Group of Seattle, she cowrote an original musical about the fall of the Allende government in Chile. Between 1979 and 1982 she lived in Mexico City, where she performed with Mexico's Grupo Mascarones, studied with Teatro Galpon of Uruguay, and led acting workshops at the University of Puebla. Back in the United States she has performed with Teatro Latina, Teatro Adelante, El Teatro Campesino, Tale Spinners, and Brava, and for several plays she has created new roles. Recently Koning-Martinez completed her fifth year as artist-in-residence for the California Arts Council multiresidency program. She also works in film and video.

8. Carmen Miranda was a Latina icon. If someone wanted some Latin flavor in a movie, there was Carmen Miranda in it. She was used as a Cuban, a Mexican, a Puerto Rican, whatever, although she was Brazilian.

9. Translation: "Mama, I love you. . . ."

BIBLIOGRAPHY

1992 Michel Fox, "Producer Gets Cheers for Brava." *San Francisco Chronicle,* Apr. 5, Datebook.

1993 Cherríe Moraga. *Three Plays: Giving Up the Ghost, Shadow of a Man, Heroes and Saints.* Albuquerque: West End Press.

1994 Jamie Lujan. "Heroes and Saints: Cerezita Valle—A Masters Thesis." San Francisco. Unpublished script; courtesy of the author.

1996 *The Immaculate Conception.* Conceived and written by Latina Theatre Lab Ensemble (Cat Callejas, Cristina Frias, Tessa Koning-Martinez, Jamie Lujan, Dena Martinez, Andrea Cristina Thome, Leedia Urteaga). Directed by Dena Martinez with Wilma Bonnet and Francine Torres. San Francisco. Unpublished script; courtesy of LTL.

Information sheet of the Latina Theatre Lab, Oakland, Calif.

Programs of LTL Productions

1992 Program of the world premiere of *Heroes and Saints* at Brava! For Women in the Arts. San Francisco, Apr. 4–May 3, 1992.

1995 Program of *¿¡Qué Nuevas!?— What's New!?*
Program of *Good Grief Lolita!* (written and performed by Wilma Bonnet).

1996 Program of *The Immaculate Conception*.

JEFF SMITH

Demetria Martínez

Author and Journalist

"The message of my work is to always question authority."

TUCSON, ARIZONA, APRIL 29, 1997

A JOURNALIST, POET, and fiction writer of strong political conscience, New Mexico native Demetria Martínez was a focus of nationwide attention in 1988 as the first reporter to be prosecuted in connection with the Sanctuary Movement. She is also the first Chicana writer to have one of her poems used in court against her.

In 1960 Demetria Martínez was born in Albuquerque, New Mexico, where she also grew up. After attending public schools in Albuquerque, she went to Princeton University.

As an undergraduate in the Woodrow Wilson School of Public and International Affairs at Princeton, Martínez took her first poetry workshops with Maxine Kumin, Stanley Kunitz, and Ted Weiss. She also attended courses in religious social ethics with Gibson Winter at the Theological Seminary of Princeton University and worked as an intern with the *Albuquerque News* and *Time* magazine. In 1982 Martínez graduated with a B.A. from Princeton and returned to Albuquerque, where she devoted most of her time to poetry. Her poetic drama *Only Say the Word* was performed at the Albuquerque Museum in 1984. It was later adapted for the stage, and its Spanish version was presented at a United Farm Workers meeting in Arizona. In 1985 Martínez began her work as a correspondent for the *National Catholic Reporter* and in 1986, as a religion writer for the *Albuquerque Journal*.

As a reporter and human rights activist, Demetria Martínez became involved with the Sanctuary Movement. Although she was indicted on charges related to smuggling Central American refugees into the United States, the court was not able to prove that she and Lutheran minister

113

Glen Remer-Thamert conspired to violate immigration laws by helping two pregnant Salvadoran women enter the United States in the fall of 1986. In 1989 she was acquitted on First Amendment grounds.[1] The poem used against Martínez is part of her first collection, *Turning*, which was published in 1989 as part of a collection of works of three Chicana poets entitled *Three Times a Woman: Chicana Poetry*.

After her experiences in court, Martínez decided to stay away from poetry writing for a while. In 1992 she started to write her first novel, titled *Mother Tongue*. Quite experimental in form and style, *Mother Tongue* is compiled of journals, recipes, poetry, and even grocery lists. Influenced by her own experiences, Martínez set the novel in the times of the Sanctuary Movement of the early eighties. The story is about Mary, a dreamy young Chicana, and her decision to provide sanctuary for the pseudonymous José Luis Romero, a refugee from El Salvador. *Mother Tongue* was published in 1994 and won the Western States Arts Federation's annual award. One World: Ballantine Books reissued it in 1996. It is available in England, Australia, and in translation in Spain, Holland, Brazil (Portuguese), and Germany (German title: *Der Himmel ist ewig* by Europaverlag). In 1998 it was published in Israel and Greece.

Demetria Martínez lives in Tucson, Arizona, where she continues her writing—both poetry and prose—as well as her work as a journalist. She works as a columnist for the *National Catholic Reporter*.

KARIN IKAS Can you tell us a bit more about yourself, your roots, and your background?

DEMETRIA MARTÍNEZ I'm New Mexican. My family has been there since the 1500s. My family, for example, helped to found Old Town Plaza Albuquerque in 1706. Then, on the other side of the family, which is the indigenous side, the origin stories have us here in the New World since the beginning of time. Many of my people there are also Jewish descendants of those who fled Spain during the Inquisition and ended up in New Mexico. I refer to all that explicitly because in New Mexico we usually have a very strong sense of roots. We don't feel like recent arrivals. The immigrant experience isn't always ours. Many of us had a world based on Spanish grants. My closest ties in time to Mexico would be my grandmother Martínez. She is my father's mother, who came up to New Mexico with her dad after the Mexican Revolution.

K.I. How do you feel about Mexico? Do you have close ties with Mexico—any family bonds or Mexican roots?

D.M. Again, the New Mexican experience is very unique because we were Spain, we were Mexico, and then we were part of the United States. We were very, very isolated from Mexico City. And those of us who have been here in New Mexico for a long time often still feel this isolation from Mexico, even though there are growing numbers of immigrants from Mexico who were coming through the States.

As I already said, my connection to Mexico is my grandmother, who came to New Mexico after the revolution. In addition, there is my *tía* [aunt] Elvira of Albuquerque, who talks about Mexico like this: "Oh, yes, we went over there to buy some groceries." You know, as if Mexico were just like another Albuquerque barrio. Thus I am planning to do a tape with an interview with her. She was in the circus with her father as a performer. Both her mother and her father performed throughout Mexico. She did everything from high wire to pantomime to clowning. And her father wrote up performances for the circus, like little skits, which I've got at home and I want to copy. So that's another strong connection to Mexico that I feel through her. And then there is, of course, my living here at the border.

K.I. In *Mother Tongue* the protagonist, Mary, is concerned about her son José Luis's learning his father's language, Spanish. How about you? Do you speak Spanish?

D.M. I listen to it. My father always spoke Spanish to all of his relatives and his friends. My cousin tells me that I did understand it very clearly when I was between the ages of one and five. When I went to school, it just faded away. The irony is that my father, before he became a Democrat, served on President Nixon's first bilingual education commission. He was a great advocate of bilingual education. Since that time I have always taken classes in Spanish, and I listen to Spanish on the radio all the time. Also, I read a lot in Spanish. Then, for political and cultural purposes, all the political work I do involving human rights abuses along the border, Spanish is very important.

Additionally, it feels very familiar and very soothing to have spent the first years of my life living with my grandmother and my mother when my father was off in Okinawa. It is becoming very clear to me now how much that Spanish language is part of my life in an emotional sense, even though I don't really have all the words yet. That is a key concern in my novel *Mother Tongue* as well.

K.I. Can you tell us a bit more about your early beginnings as a writer? How did you get started?

D.M. I started writing when I was little. When I was about fourteen years old I kept a journal. I tended to be overweight, and no one asked me out for a date. At that time I had a very bad body image. I think this is something Chicanas often don't talk about in their works, you know, that sense of rejection. The blessing was that I started keeping a blank notebook and began to write. Just literally, I learned to write my way out of that depression. My experience of writing was very much a transcendental experience, before I ever knew that people took it up as a career. Writing to me was very spiritual. That is where I am coming from. As a writer I see writing as a spiritual space.

K.I. Are you writing particularly for yourself or are you a community writer first?

D.M. I don't distinguish between writing for myself and writing for my community. I don't see those two things as separate. When you are writing genuinely from your heart and from your experience, you are automatically writing out of the energy of the community. Like I have always said, "It takes more than one person to tell a story." So every time we are involved in the act of writing, it is like the whole community, and in particular the ancestors and the ancestral voices, is there in that room.

K.I. You already talked about how you started writing while you were a child. When did you actually choose writing as a profession?

D.M. Oh, not until later. I graduated from Princeton in public and international affairs. I had sworn that I would never take a job that requires heels and hose from nine to five. I would never survive that. I would either become a paid activist and live on the edge all my life or be a writer, even if I had to live on the edge all of my life, too. It was just a decision to follow my bliss, as Joseph Campbell says. And that bliss involved becoming a poet. It was returning to that bliss I had experienced in high school, getting up early in the morning or sometimes after school, lighting a candle, getting a cup of coffee, and just doing writing. In addition, I was listening to all the psalms, which my grandmother Martínez, who was in the Assemblies of God church and always read biblical texts, had been saying. These were poetry to me. It was a sense of a calling, I guess. I always have kept a saying with me. I am not sure who said it, but I'd like to find out, as it has followed me around since I wrote it down in 1979: "It is important to make a living, but it is more important to make a life." And that has been my guiding light. I realize what a privilege that is. For my father it was a much different experience, an emphasis on financial security. He was the first in his family to go to college. On the other hand, my father has always done so much out of his heart for the community; for example, his twelve years on the school board where he never saw a cent.

I've had the luxury to make a choice to "just write," and I used to feel guilty about that. But when you look at what our community needs, it is not a luxury. Because we have to have our soul and our politics nurtured. That's the role of the writer, not to be off in an ivory tower.

K.I. What made you write poetry first, then a novel, and now you seem to continue doing both? What influences or motivates you to choose a particular genre?

D.M. I just started to write the novel *Mother Tongue,* and it took me only nine months. That, of course, was a miracle. I had never, ever intended to write a novel. In addition, I had a full-time job. It all began with the hearing of a voice, and I just wrote down that first sentence. Then in nine months, it was done. It was so easy that I wondered if I would ever write poetry again.

Before *Mother Tongue* I had published an early poetry collection entitled *Turning,* which is part of *Three Times a Woman,* a collection of Chicana poetry. For ten years I saw myself primarily as a poet, and I didn't want to write a novel. But then in the summer of 1996, I was teaching at the Center for Study of War and Social Consequences at UMASS Boston. I was surrounded with faculty that included primarily Vietnam veterans (established writers) as well as other people whose lives had been affected by war. The other woman who they had recruited that year, and who was new there as well, was Daisy Zamora, the Nicaraguan poet. She has been a major influence on my work. Then there was the "former enemy" who came in a delegation from Vietnam, all artists. The majority of them were poets, and I just relate to that kind of intensity, love of the word, love of a few words. It was a very intense experience, and we all became very close friends. I experienced a kind of healing by talking to these Vietnam veterans. They have been through "the dark night of the soul" and came out on the other side.

It took me a long time to really get over what had happened to me in the trial once, you know, that sense of shame, of guilt, of being violated, that sense that I asked for it. I mean, I must have been a bad girl to do something like this. To be in this position, even though they found me not guilty, is a very powerful mind game. Talking with these Vietnam veterans who spoke of their own drama, I really saw the healing power of words. There was something profound about being around that energy. Then one day I was just sitting there at my bed-and-breakfast place, and it was like a miraculous gusty wind, which just came down into the room where I was sitting there with my coffee and my journal. I started writing. About three or four poems just came out, full-born then, and I knew that was it. I barely needed to eat or drink that summer. I concluded the summer at Rudy and Pat Anaya's summer home in Jemez Springs, New Mexico. That was where the work, the new poetry collection, entitled *Breathing Between the Lines,* was finished. It includes my first bilingual poem, where I had started writing a letter to a friend in Spanish. That was like bicycling with training wheels. Somewhere I looked back and I realized that the training wheels were just kind of dangling there, and I was actually going on my own. It was a really different emotional space to be writing in Spanish. Thus, I continued the poem and then switched over to English. That was a breakthrough for me. It is something that I want to do more often now.

K.I. Do you write for a particular audience?

D.M. No, I just write. It has to be something that I enjoy and that makes me laugh. And if it does, then I suspect it will have a pretty broad audience as well. It is more organic if you write a story. Then the story finds its community, and the community finds the story.

K.I. How important is autobiography in your work and for your writing?

D.M. It is hard to say; everything is autobiographical. I see a lot of myself in all of my characters except for Soledad, who is my wanna-be when I grow up. In a way she is like my grandmothers and my mentors all collapsed into one character.

K.I. Are other women—your mother, grandmother, aunts—very influential for you and your writing?

D.M. I was very fortunate in that I grew up with a mother who really encouraged my education. Very strong female mentors have always supported me. Consequently, there has always been that sense of being surrounded by these strong female teachers, many of them poor mothers who have struggled to get their educations while already being mothers. I think to see how women, how mothers have created their lives had a profound impact on me, as this is a very creative act to me. But the biggest influences on me are mentors over the age of fifty who raised their kids while hiding and smuggling refugees on the side or protesting the war, and yet can throw together a bowl of beans and chili at the very last minute. Also, they have a profound sense of humor.

The mother figure that I want to write about, but I don't want to romanticize it, combines motherhood and political activism. The symbol of that would be a woman marching against war with a baby in the knapsack. I have always been exposed to that, to a generation of mothers where private life is not separate from political or public life.

K.I. In *Mother Tongue* you deal with the refugee problem, and by doing so you offer a sharp criticism of the U.S. policy toward El Salvador. By calling attention to war, brutality, torture, and abuse of people, the novel also reflects a general antiwar attitude. Furthermore, it mirrors your general criticism of any form of violence toward human beings, no matter when and where it happens, be it in developing, fascist, or even democratic countries. I think in particular about such issues like sexual abuse of children, as in the novel [*Mother Tongue*] the protagonist, Mary, was abused as a child by a neighbor. How did you become such a devoted political activist and consequently a political writer as well?

D.M. My parents have always been activists. My father was the first Chicano ever elected to the school board in Albuquerque. We were taught to be out there to do something for your community one way or the other and to speak out against injustice.

The other reason has to do with living on the border and coming of age during the Central America wars: the U.S. government-funded disasters in El Salvador, Guatemala, and Nicaragua. That was my political and spiritual coming-of-age. I was too young for Vietnam. When I understood that our government, which had no money for scholarships, managed to spend $1.4 million a day in military aid in El Salvador, I began to wonder what the hell was going on. Especially when I saw the victims of our policies coming here, being denied political asylum, and having to go underground, wearing handkerchiefs on their faces in order to tell their stories safely at the Quaker meeting house or whatever. Boy, if that didn't give me pause! Then there was, particularly, the example of people of faith who helped politicize people. They said, "That is completely unacceptable. I will not let my money, my tax dollars, pay for war, for deportation of its victims." It was a very powerful experience for me.

K.I. What do you associate with the terms "border" and "bridges"?

D.M. I live on the border and so we are bridge people in so many ways, both linguistically and culturally.

It also has to do with my own experiences with the INS [Immigration and Naturalization Service]. In 1986 I took a trip to the border with a Lutheran minister who was helping two Salvadoran women cross over into this country as part of the Sanctuary Movement. He invited me to come along with him, and he hoped I could write a story about that. Of course, I said yes, and I ended up writing a poem about it. A year later I was indicted for conspiracy against the United States government: twenty-five years in prison and $1.25 million in fines. It was a seven-month indictment, and it included a more-than-two-week trial. Finally, I was found not guilty on First Amendment grounds. The jury concluded that a reporter has a right to get up as close to the story as possible and is under no obligation to turn in the sources to the government. In a way it is funny because I still haven't integrated that experience of the trial; I still don't see it as central to my experience. But I know it has left a scar on my psyche, which on the good side has opened me up to the larger world. It globalized my vision.

K.I. What do you associate with the term "intercultural understanding"?

D.M. Just the words "empathy" and "solidarity." I think the latter is the political action arm of empathy.

K.I. Do you consider yourself a cosmopolitan person who is at home in more than one culture?

D.M. Yes, very much. My roots are Spanish, indigenous, Jewish, Moorish, rural, and urban. The Chicana and the mestiza have so much wealth to draw from.

K.I. Is border crossing therefore a quite natural and also unproblematic thing?

D.M. Yeah, I would say so. I don't know where that comes from: maybe from being an introvert for so many years and therefore being able to watch people. Nevertheless, I belong to many communities. In my early years my mentors were primarily white and Jewish feminists. Then in the past five years, my mentors have become the women I do political work with. There are all these very powerful Chicanas who have been involved in the *movimiento*, the anti-Vietnam work, and everything else since the beginning of time. They really know the history of Mexico and the Southwest as well.

Now I am meeting a lot of women, many of them Chicanas, who are ten or fifteen years younger than me. And that's just opening up a whole new world for me, too, across a generation. I sometimes attend services at a Jewish congregation, too, because I have a great-grandmother going nine greats back. She married into a Jewish family and was accused of *brujería* [witchcraft] by the Inquisition. I am trying to figure out how to do her right, now more than three hundred years later. Her name is Isabel Holguín.

In general, I believe that our energy must be drawn from many world communities because our identities are made up of many elements. Nationalism is dangerous; it denies human complexity. The writer's task is to explore ambiguity and to make us more at home with our contradictions.

K.I. Who are your favorite writers? Whose work do you read at the moment?

D.M. I read anything I get my hands on in the way of poetry. I am reading Cornelius Eden, the African American poet, and Joy Harjo, the Native American poet, who is my favorite poet. Then, Sandra Cisneros's stories are pure poetry. I also listen to a lot of musical lyrics. Milan Kundera and Marguerite Duras have influenced me. The greatest living writer to me is Toni Morrison. Her book *Jazz* is a work of genius.

K.I. What are some of the current developments you are worried about?

D.M. I'm particularly worried about this development of the rich getting richer and the poor getting poorer. You are seeing that here in the United States as well as globally. I fear this process is just in its early stages. We can't even begin to comprehend what the movement of capital—and NAFTA—means. People cross lines, seeking work. Yet politically borders are opening up even as we are trying to shut them down. In addition, the environment concerns me. That is one of the other things I'm really interested in, in particular with regard to how Chicanos and Chicanas respond to these environmental issues. Environmental groups traditionally have ignored our issues—such as toxic waste in poor communities—completely. We had to concern ourselves with the pesticide issue because of our migrant farmers. Interestingly, third world activists are really ahead of the U.S. in terms of environmental issues. They don't separate these from issues of poverty and land rights.

K.I. In *Mother Tongue* religion seems to be very important as a source of strength for individuals to get through pretty tough situations. You mention, for example, the little community-oriented, politically active parishes in Central America, as well as their priest and cardinals, who have to face particular violence and terror but don't give up their social activities. Also, the Virgin Mary plays an important role, in particular with regard to the protagonist, Mary, who believes very much in the support of La Madre de los Desaparecidos [the Mother of the Disappeared]. Can you tell us a bit more about that? How do you feel about all these female archetypes—the Virgin of Guadalupe, La Llorona—who are quite important among Mexican Americans and within the Mexican American community? How about the Madre de los Desaparecidos?

D.M. I think it is important to talk about spiritual diversity within the Mexican American community, because La Virgen de Guadalupe isn't that major of a figure in New Mexico. She is more of a recent immigrant, brought by recent immigrants from Mexico. Historically, we were very isolated from Mexico. Thus it was that the French priests and other clergy—not necessarily from Mexico—were forming people spiritually. Many Chicanas see the Virgin de Guadalupe as a feminist symbol, which is wonderful. My spirituality was formed by icons painted by Robert Lentz, such as Oscar Romero and the Mother of the Disappeared. The latter is a woman wearing a white handkerchief and holding a crown of thorns. The handkerchief is used by the mothers at the plaza in Argentina or other places of the world. It became a very powerful symbol for me. The Mother of the Disappeared would always be there, waiting and watching over that part of our psyche that had been disappeared through sexual abuse or any form of trauma. She would even be there when we couldn't.

Another important feminist spiritual concept is shown in the opening image in *Mother Tongue*—the goddess Ishtar. She says, "A prostitute compassionate am I" (p. 5) as she takes the war out of men when they come to the temple after having been to war. Later in the novel, Ishtar reappears as the Mother of the Disappeared.

K.I. What about your current religious belief? How about Catholicism, spirituality?

D.M. I hope that people begin to take a closer look at the themes of spirituality in my work. That is so much a part of our heritage. Not only through Catholicism, but also in those places where Catholicism never quite took. In New Mexico we draw from indigenous spirituality. I also draw from my Jewish spirituality. Currently, we are living in a world where we have access to such a wide variety of practices. I always had a very strong interest in theology, especially feminist theology, liberation theology, the new eco-theology. Therefore, I am hoping that people take a look at my book at many levels because sometimes people have studied my book and downplayed the part of the book that is concerned with spirituality.

K.I. For your first novel you chose the title *Mother Tongue*. Why? What do you associate with terms and metaphors like "tongue" and "mother tongue"?

D.M. "Mother tongue" has to do with two things. The first issue is Mary's recovery of her voice after reclaiming her memories of her affair with José Luis. It is really critical that she recovers her voice after all these years, and after finding out—through that process—how she had been silenced through abuse as a child.

The second key element was her son's decision, which is typical of my generation, to learn Spanish. He goes to El Salvador to learn Spanish, but also takes Spanish classes in the U.S. It's the recovery of his mother tongue.

Finally, in Salvador, if the military wanted to send a message to the people who were trying to work for a change and who were speaking out against the fourteen families who own most of the land and thus protect their privileges with death squads, oftentimes the military would cut out your tongue as a sort of a warning to the village. Therefore, this process of how a community find its voice under state terrorism is alluded to in the title of my book *Mother Tongue*.

Then, Teresa Márquez, a mentor of mine who also works at the Zimmerman Library at the University of New Mexico, pointed out another meaning of "tongue," which had never occurred to me: La Malinche (who was the translator for the Spaniard Hernán Cortés) who became the mother of the Mexican people.

Another important point with regard to the meaning of "tongue" is that it refers to the voice of the indigenous people. They do have their own mother tongues.

Sometimes older people think that they are more Latino because they speak Spanish. Meanwhile the younger generation is struggling to learn Spanish. My answer to all of them is: "You know, if you are really concerned about identity, Spanish was the language that was imposed upon us, so why don't you go learn one of the indigenous languages like Tiwa or Tewa or a Mayan dialect. Chicanas, by definition, are heirs to countless mother tongues, many of which the Spaniards tried to wipe out.

K.I. What is your current writing project?

D.M. I am working on another love story that I've called "Mexican Rubies." It is set in Santa Fe.

The protagonist, Emma Sánchez, falls in love with this guy. Currently,

I'm not sure yet if he is going to be white, or half and half and hiding the Mexican part. Then it includes another protagonist, Mrs. Raquel, who runs a seed store that saves endangered seeds and species.

K.I. How do you see the future of Chicanas and Chicanos? How about Chicana and Chicano literature?

D.M. I see more globalization of the literature as we encounter more of our brothers and sisters from Central and South America. Not just there, but here in the United States as well. I see an increased concern with the issue of losing the Spanish language and the struggles to regain it.

I would like to see greater concerns with Native American issues. Joy Harjo and I are talking about working on an anthology. It has to do with water because we are running out of water in this country, and the U.S. would gladly steal it from the Indians. The whole area of water rights is very fascinating. It is a great time for Chicanos to build alliances with Native Americans about that issue because they are brothers and sisters. There is a tendency sometimes to go back in history and romanticize the Aztecs. In New Mexico we don't have to; our relatives are all around us. We have about twenty Indian pueblos in New Mexico, for example.

K.I. What is the ultimate message you want to communicate to the reader through your work? How about the impact of your work on Chicana literature?

D.M. I am hoping that political movements like those of the Sanctuary Movement can add to our experience of spirituality. Also, I think we need to reclaim our mystical roots through Sor Juana, through our indigenous spirituality, and through our Jewish spirituality. These are rich areas for writers and readers to explore! Then I certainly hope there will be education, too, because when I go to a class at some of the universities to talk and I ask students, "Do you guys know what the Sanctuary Movement is?" these young twenty-something kids often ask, "The Sanctuary Movement, what is that?" And I go on, "Did you know that your government spent $1.4 million a day in military aid?" "Did our government really do something like that?" So it is a kind of educational process about questioning authority. That is what my writing is all about as well. The message of my work is to always question authority.

NOTE

1. The First Amendment covers the right of a reporter to gather news and information.

BIBLIOGRAPHY

Poetry

1989 *Turning.* In *Three Times a Woman: Chicana Poetry,* ed. A. Gaspar de Alba, M. Herrera-Sobek, and D. Martínez. Tempe, Ariz.: Bilingual Press.

1997 *Breathing Between the Lines.* A poetry collection. Tucson: University of Arizona Press.

Prose

1994 *Mother Tongue—A Novel.* New York: One World/Ballantine Books.

1999 *Der Himmel ist ewig.* German edition of *Mother Tongue.* Translated from American English to German by Sabine Hübner. München: Knaur Verlag.

Forthcoming

"Mexican Rubies: A Love Story."

Pat Mora

Poet, Writer, and Educator

"The issue is not so much ethnicity or gender. It is about the way we reach a point of communion as human beings sharing this difficult journey called life."

SANTA FE, NEW MEXICO, OCTOBER 1, 1996

C HICANA AUTHOR Pat Mora is a native of Texas and has earned distinction as a poet, an author of multicultural children's literature, and an educator. Her published work includes five collections of poetry, ten children's books, and two non-fiction books (*Nepantla: Essays from the Land in the Middle* and *House of Houses,* a family memoir. She has also had several essays and poems published in various anthologies and journals. Her work has been translated into Spanish, Italian, and Bengali.

Pat Mora was born on January 19, 1942, in El Paso, Texas, where she grew up. In 1963 she married William H. Burnside, and they had three children. After a divorce in 1981, Pat married the anthropologist Vernon Lee Scarborough in 1984. Five years later they gave up their life in El Paso and moved to Cincinnati, Ohio, for the first time. Mora and her husband now split their time between Santa Fe, New Mexico, and Cincinnati.

In 1963 Mora was awarded a B.A. in English from Texas Western College. She then worked as a teacher in El Paso, where she also attended the University of Texas, earning an M.A. in English. From 1971 to 1978, she was a part-time teacher of English and communication at El Paso Community College. In 1981 she became assistant to the vice president of academic affairs at UT El Paso. During this time she also served as a poetry judge for the Texas Institute of Letters and was director of the University Museum at UT El Paso. From 1983 to 1984 Pat Mora hosted the radio show *Voices: The Mexican-American in Perspective,* on KTEP, a

127

National Public Radio affiliate. A Kellogg National Leadership Fellowship allowed her to study international and national issues of cultural conservation in 1986–1989.

Among the several awards she has received are a Harvey L. Johnson Book Award from the Southwest Council of Latin American Studies (1984), a Leader in Education Award from El Paso Women's Employment and Education (1987), and a Chicano/Hispanic Faculty and Professional Staff Association Award (for her outstanding contribution to the advancement of Hispanics at UT El Paso). In 1988 she was named to the *El Paso Herald-Post* Writers Hall of Fame. She was awarded a National Endowment for the Arts Fellowship in 1994, and she is the recipient of four Southwestern Book Awards.

According to her belief that people's sense of identity is firmly rooted in their culture, Mora has dedicated much of her life as a writer and teacher to the preservation of her culture. A central theme in her writing is the concern for the Mexican and Mexican American cultures and their conservation; another one is the recognition of the interrelatedness of natural and cultural diversity. She explores various kinds of borders—political, cultural, social, emotional, and sexual—and tries to develop new ways to overcome them.

Growing up in the Southwest, Mora developed a keen sense of and appreciation for the desert. In many of her poems and children's stories, the desert is portrayed as a place that offers solace and inner peace. The desert also plays an important role for female identity as Mora believes the latter to be shaped tremendously by woman's close connection with the earth. Particularly in her earlier works, Mora focuses on the desert and the southwestern landscape she grew up in, for which some critics have labeled her a regionalist. Her recent publications, however—*Nepantla* and the poetry collection *Agua Santa/Holy Water*—demonstrate once more that Mora is interested not just in the Southwest, but also in global issues concerning women and the overcoming of borders in general. Mora's present writing merges centuries-old values, languages, and cultures with contemporary perspectives of Mexican Americans and global issues such as equality of women, the harmony of cultures, and cross-cultural understanding.

KARIN IKAS In *Horn Books* you mentioned in 1990 that you "take pride in being a Hispanic writer. I will continue to write and to struggle to say what no other writer can say in quite the same way."[1] What does this particular and somehow unique way of writing and articulating special things look like? What is it that makes your writing special in comparison with other, also non-Chicano/a, writers?

PAT MORA Well, I think what I was referring to was the uniqueness of each human voice on paper. For example, I have a new book coming out in spring 1997 that is a family memoir entitled *House of Houses,* and I spent a lot of time on this book. Once my nephew said to me, "Oh, Aunt Pat, I wanted to write some of the stories in the book." And I said, "But I could never write the book that you would write." What I was trying to suggest is that even if two people have exactly the same experience, as soon as they write about that experience, it would be two distinct literary occasions. That is due to the uniqueness of each perspective and of each voice. Now, in a general way, I think the fact that I am a Chicana writer means that there are certain values that are embedded so deeply in me that I am not aware of them. That is one of the things that fascinate me about culture, the way in which culture is so much a part of us that we cannot tease it apart from ourselves.

K.I. What are the most important elements of this culture for you?

P.M. First of all there is the importance of family and then the presence of religion as a force. And because I am a Chicana from the desert, another strong force is the presence of this desert. In my own family I think the presence of women is another strong element. I have a very strong mother who is also very articulate, bilingually articulate. She was always a reader. In many ways she defies a lot of the stereotypes that we have about a Mexican American parent. My mother was the kind of person who was always involved in school, who was present at the PTA (Parent Teacher Association). . . .

Therefore, I always had as an example a woman who was a very strong, articulate woman, a book lover, et cetera. So that was completely natural to me, and it was nothing I had to reach for or work for. It was part of my everyday experience.

K.I. Thinking of your work and also of what you just told us about your mother, I get the impression that your mother seems to have been a vital force in your childhood and still is for your life and writing career. Could you tell us a bit more about that and about your childhood, your education, and career? What about your Mexican roots?

P.M. Well, I can answer the question better this year than I could have answered it two years ago because of my work on the family memoir. What it did is that it really caused me to go back. And that is one

thing that I am really trying to say to new writers and to students, teachers, or librarians: There is an incredible wealth that is there for us when
we go back and do this sort of excavating work and find out about our
own particular family. What I found out was that all four of my parents
came to El Paso, Texas, at the time of the Mexican Revolution, and all
four came with very limited economic means. On my mother's side, my
grandfather had been a judge, a circuit judge in northern Mexico, and
the party that he supported was the one that was being ousted. Therefore, he had to leave and bring his daughters with him. Those daughters
became my mother's half sisters, because my grandfather's first wife
died. One of his daughters, his eldest, was Ignacia Delgado, who we also
called Lobo. You know I write a lot about her in my works. She is in
every book, also in the book of essays, and she is a very strong voice in
the memoir, *House of Houses,* too.

Back to your question, I grew up in a bilingual home, and my parents
always moved back and forth between English and Spanish very easily. I
probably have a better sense of my father's place in my life because he
has been dead three years now, and I think that is when you really assess
a person's impact. With regard to my mother's role in my life, I can't be
in any way objective yet because I don't have this distance so far. But I
always describe my mother as my first good editor. From the time I
started to write as a child, I would always take everything to her because
she had a very fine sense of language and was always making good suggestions. She also loved public speaking, as I do. When I was in grade
school, I started doing public speaking, and I would always give her my
talks. Therefore, I think her voice is a very strong force for me, but like I
said, I haven't got the distance to fully assess it yet.

K.I. Do you recall the time everything started? Was there a book or a
personal encounter that motivated you to devote yourself to writing?

P.M. In grade school both writing and public speaking were already
present in my life. I loved school. I was a good student, and I was not
necessarily shy. So when they needed someone to volunteer to give a talk
or something, I was always happy to do that. In some of the interviews I
have said that I remember that when I graduated from eighth grade—I
went to Catholic school from kindergarten to senior high—my parents
gave me a grey typewriter. I remember that one day there was a party in
our house. My parents had given me some stationery, thus I sat down,
and I wrote very religious poetry. And I know that in high school writing
always came easy to me but I really did not think about being a writer.

Instead I wanted to be a nun. Actually, for the first seventeen years of my life I did not consider anything other than being a nun. The nuns were my heroines. And I refer in this context primarily to the nuns at my school who had taught me. I didn't know much about the Mexican icon, philosopher, and writer, the nun Sor Juana Inés de la Cruz, back then. The reality was that at the time I grew up in this country, and this is probably still true today, most Chicanas or Mexican Americans in high school today have never heard of Sor Juana. They have never been asked to read her. The process of incorporating the Chicana or Latina voice in the literature of this country and in educational institutions is very slow. Although I have a master's in English, I never was asked to read writers who wrote in Spanish or bilingual writers, not even if they were writing in English or in translation. Throughout my whole education experience, it never happened.

K.I. How did you find out about Chicana and Chicano writers then?

P.M. I was teaching at a community college in the early 1970s, and I decided to use a book entitled *Bless Me Última*, a novel written by the New Mexican and Chicano writer Rudolfo Anaya. Of course, I had read the book before already, but now it was the first time that I consciously remember choosing a book like that for my class and using it as a teacher. Many of the students attending my night classes were adults, and among them were a lot of Vietnam veterans. At some level I was probably impressed by the impact this book had on my students. Most of the students, particularly the male ones, were very open and told me their impressions and how they were moved. Some told me: "I never read a book by somebody like me before."

K.I. What were the major influences on you and particularly on your writing? Not primarily Chicana and Chicano literature?

P.M. Correct. Looking back I believe that some of the early influences for me were really very traditional Euro-American writers like Edna St. Vincent Millay, Amy Lowell, and Emily Dickinson. In my adult years the Canadian writer Margaret Atwood had an impact on me as well. Particularly Margaret Atwood was a very strong force for me early on.

As I got nearer and nearer to turning forty, I had kept notes in a journal when my children were little telling why I should write a poem about that, an essay about that or a children's book about another thing. But I didn't do very much about it. Every now and then I wrote a few things, and then they would be rejected, and I would just stop. But then, when I was about to turn forty, I thought: it is now or never. At that time, reading poets like Atwood, I remember very clearly that there was something about the hard edge of her voice that fascinated me. So as an early writer, she was a strong factor for me.

As I became more and more interested in writing, then I went back and said, "Well, what about this Mexican heritage, and how does it braid into my life?" One of the things I say to teachers a lot today is that it is a real challenge in a country with all the many stereotypes that we have here to find a way in which we teachers lure all that a student is to the page. What I had done, and what often students do very effectively, is that they leave part of themselves at home. They figure out what might not fit in at school. So they make arbitrary decisions, and many times this is about their cultural background.

K.I.   And your students are mainly Mexican Americans?

P.M.   No, I am not referring to the students in a class. I am just talking about the situation I discuss when I speak at conferences. OK, now I do the writing and speaking full-time, so that when I talk to students, it is while I am visiting a campus. Also it is something that I talk to teachers about a lot.

K.I.   What is your favorite: to write or to teach?

P.M.   As I said, I really don't teach anymore. I concentrate on writing and speaking, and I like that very much. However, it is a very hard way to make a living because there is no security. So it is possible that I would go back to teaching, but just if it would be necessary, because that really does diminish my writing time. On the other hand, the kind of writing I do is not the one that leads to best-sellers. That's why it makes it so difficult to be able to support myself by that. Therefore, I have thought about writing fiction, but the problem is that then I come up with these other nonfiction projects that I like very much, and so I don't get around to thinking about the fiction. But I haven't ruled writing fiction out. And with regard to the children's books I am writing, in a way I am already doing fiction although it is just, or primarily, for children so far.

K.I.   Do you write for a particular audience?

P.M.   In *Nepantla* I said that I write for people of conscience, which may be true of my essays. The ideal reader is the person who really hears what I'm saying, who is so open and attentive that the words have a chance of entering the reader.

K.I.   You already mentioned the issue of stereotypes. What would you say about your—let's call it "definition" or "concept" of "American"? Has it changed since your childhood days?

P.M. I think it definitely did change. When I was growing up I was very interested, as most children are, in belonging. And I think psychologists would tell us that when we are young, we are really struggling with identity formation and want to have a positive identity. Even today it is difficult for Chicano students, Mexican American and Latino students—and this also applies to Native American students, Asian American students, and African American students—to figure out where to get positive images, images that would let one see one's own background as a source of strength and, what particularly interests me, as a source of creativity. So I discovered that this was exactly what I had not focused on, and I had not seen as a creative resource, until I began to write.

K.I. In that context some of your poems, "Immigrants" [*Borders*, p. 15] and "Now and Then, America" [p. 33], come to mind. In "Now and Then, America," for example, one line goes, "Risk my difference, my surprises. / Grant me a little life, America."

P.M. Well, I appreciate your focusing on the line. I think it is a sort of a sassy plea to the forces that tend to shape society, be they educational or political forces, to create more space for this overused word of "diversity." I am very interested in biological diversity; you know, the diversity of the desert or the diversity of the forest, for example. And I think it just enriches us all, and therefore it is such a tragedy that people find it frightening. But if you analyze what the media in this country offers—or if you look into the prestigious magazines, it is the same thing—it suggests that if you are white and economically comfortable, you somehow might be more intelligent. That is one of America's myths, and many of us write in particular to counter this myth.

I would like to resist stereotypes on all sides. And that is why in *Nepantla* I say that at the broadest level the audience that interests me is people of conscience. In a particular way I am interested in a Chicano and Latino audience because of the void, of course. However, I am also interested in people with a good conscience, and this has nothing to do with skin color. Obviously, there are Mexican Americans or Hispanics who have little use for low-income Chicanos. So it would be too facile to think that it is merely about ethnicity or merely about skin color. And yet I do not want to ignore those issues, as they are real. And I think one of the reasons why there is so much fear of difference is that the power is controlled by a few. I believe that there is a need to keep raising this issue of why we do find difference and diversity threatening. In *Nepantla* I ask, "Why is it that we are more fascinated by birds of color than people of color?" and I don't ask this question just to be flip. To me it is a very serious issue, and I want people to really ponder it in their hearts.

K.I. You just mentioned the term "people of color." Do you feel comfortable with the term, or maybe even the label "woman-of-color writer"? How do you get along with other writers of color: Native American, Asian American, or African American writers, for example? Would you say that there is a general bond between all these writers?

P.M. There is a bond that springs from lack of access, the bond that springs from histories of oppression and discrimination. But again, the bond I hope for is the bond that has to do with conscience, and I mean conscience across cultures. However, there is something comforting when we are with someone who has shared a similar kind of experience. For example, if you have lost a close relative—and I have lost a close relative—then we would come together in a particular way when we talk about that loss, that grief and sadness. I think that is the point at which Native American, Asian American, Afro-American, Chicano, and Latino writers come together. And there is also that desire to rectify those sorts of literary inequities.

K.I. Do you think that all these writers of color are seriously interested in coming together at all? Sometimes I get the impression that, let's say, for example, African American writers and Chicano writers both concentrate more on their own ethnic and cultural specifics, and they don't seem to be interested very much in working together. What is your impression?

P.M. Well, I think that has to do with just time constraint more than anything else. You know, the job of a writer is to write. There is a daily struggle, how you keep protecting that, and it is very difficult. The sister whose birthday is today likes to call me in the morning from Los Angeles, but when I start on a new book, I say to her, "You can't call me in the morning anymore because I won't be answering the phone." As you have experienced yourself, I usually don't answer any calls in the mornings, as I reserve that time for my writing. So there is that struggle to carve out enough time because there is so much noise in your life that you experience while you are writing that you have to carve out enough quietness to do your work. Therefore, in terms of just priorities, I feel a special responsibility to my fellow Chicana writers first, then to Chicano writers, and then to Latino writers, and so on.

K.I. Which Chicana and Chicano writers were most important to you?

P.M.   In terms of Chicana and Chicano writers, we have to talk about some of the wonderful writers in New Mexico now, of course. I think in particular of Rudolfo Anaya, Denise Chávez, and there is Demetria Martínez, who is from this area although she lives now in Tucson, Arizona. Then I think about Sandra Cisneros in Texas and Helena María Viramontes, who is now teaching at Cornell. Somehow I almost hate to mention names because the list just goes on and on and on. Going back, of course, to a very important Chicano writer, Tomás Rivera, and how to keep strength and support is part of my life.

However, I was very influenced by African American writers as well, like Toni Morrison and Alice Walker, for example. And then there are two contemporary poets whose works are very important to me, Lucille Clifton and Mary Oliver. What amazes me most about Lucille Clifton and her work is that she has a very powerful and distinct voice. Then I am very moved by Mary Oliver, who some people describe as a nature poet in a way to categorize her. To me she is a very important voice, as she is a very attentive writer. Oliver has written very eloquently about working not only between words, but also between sounds. She exercises that kind of care.

Other writers that I hope have an influence on me are Pablo Neruda and García Lorca because of the music that I find in their work. That is why I really want to be influenced by them, and why I wish I had more time to read them.

So again, one of the major problems I have to struggle with is time constraint, a problem all of us have to live with to some extent. Although I tell myself that I am going to take a break after each book, that never happens. Therefore, I already started thinking about the new book while I was still working on the memoir. Right now I am discussing this new book with a publisher, and I think it will be a poetry collection on the saints. What happens then is that I immediately shift my reading towards reading the lives of the saints I am interested in for the new book. My sadness is that I do not have the time anymore to read fiction as I used to in the past. There might be about ten books out by Chicanas, for example, that I would like to read, but I just never have the time to do so. Instead, at the moment, what I am writing really guides my reading. By the time I have done the reading and then try to do the writing, the day is gone. And, you know, I have family responsibilities, too.

K.I.   How is the situation among Chicana writers themselves in terms of cooperation, alliances, support? Would you say that most of the writers prefer to emphasize their geographical and cultural and/or sexual differences, or is there a tendency to establish a kind of united Chicana writers' alliance?

P.M. Chicana writers are very supportive of one another, I believe. Certainly I have benefited from the support of writers like Sandra Cisneros, Denise Chávez, and Lorna Dee Cervantes. State boundaries are political constructs. I can't speak for any writers other than myself, of course. I'm committed to women, for example, and feel a strong bond whether they are lesbian or heterosexual.

K.I. Let's now talk a bit about genre issues. You started as a poet, but you have also published a collection of essays and several children's books as well. How do you decide which genre to choose for a piece of writing?

P.M. My favorite certainly is poetry because I consider it the greatest challenge. I have always loved the essay form as well. In that sense, writing *Nepantla* and now just recently writing the memoir gave me a lot of pleasure. By the way, I already have an idea for a third book of nonfiction. But it is a very different process. Sometimes when I am working in prose, I feel like somebody feels in a basement that is full of spiderwebs. It is like I am caught in all this language. Therefore, I love it when I somehow can escape back into poetry.

I love the leanness of poetry, its insistence that we carve away. To me this is much more like sculpture already. But I think that my motivation for nonfiction and children's books includes an element of practicality. Poetry might be an impractical choice in the sense that it is impractical financially, and it is impractical in terms of a readership. Particularly in the United States, there is this sense of whether poetry sells at all.

I became interested in nonfiction both because I had always loved the essay form and because I had friends who would say, "Well, why don't you write something I can understand?" That is why I think of prose writing as being practical. It is a way of reaching an audience that my poetry may never reach.

This is true for children's books, too. I have said that there is a close connection between children's books and picture books. Both are very spare. It is not unusual for poets to write children's books. That is a natural combination somehow, and I love the form. But, again, I had a practical goal, which was that it was important to me that the Latina voice become part of the field of children's literature because I feel that early on children do or do not establish a relationship with books. Although it is possible for someone to become a reader later in life, I don't know how often that happens. Most of us who are book people are book people because books filled some sort of an emotional place in our life early. We developed an emotional loyalty to words, and so I want Latino young-sters to see themselves in these picture books when they are little and to feel at home in this world of English in which they will spend their lives. It has been a world that has excluded them traditionally. You know, we were just not there.

K.I. Most of your children's books are bilingual, in English and Spanish. The poetry collections and all your other books—including the essay col-lections—are written primarily in English although you have some code switching in between. How would you consider yourself with regard to language? Are you a bilingual writer?

P.M. I would say I am a bilingual writer, but I am English dominant. And I am English dominant because my entire educational experience has been in English. What that means is that you develop your profes-sional vocabulary in that language. For me, in a way, Spanish might be a more emotionally loaded language because it is a slightly more private language. But I can't say it definitely because in my home and even with Lobo, the woman I wrote about a lot, most was bilingual. I was always able to speak both languages, English and Spanish. But, like I already said, there is privateness to Spanish that gives it a special place. I try to suggest to writers, particularly beginning writers of whatever age, that if they are lucky enough to know another language, whatever that might be, it gives them another range, and it would be foolish not to seek to incorporate it in some creative way. That might be through the use of the language itself, or it might be—and this is something I am hoping to do this year myself—through exploring the poetic forms that come out of that language. As I haven't had technical training, for example, in poetry in Spanish, one of my hopes is to do a little more of that this year and see if the form might interest me.

During your stay here in New Mexico I am sure you have seen all those carved *santos* in the churches and altars. They were a strong force in giv-ing me the idea for my new book, the book of saints I am thinking about at the moment. The *santos* are carved many times using traditional style, and then some of the carvers incorporate new styles. I am always fasci-nated by that intersection of drawing on tradition, yet incorporating it and in some way contributing to it. So I have thought in this book of the saints that if I learn more about poetic forms in Spanish, I might decide to do some other poems about the saints in English using the forms in Spanish. It is just a thought at the moment. It can be a sort of another gift, then, that being bilingual could give me, in the same way that a Chinese American might look at Chinese poetic forms. He or she might then also find a certain source of excitement that might guide his or her writing in a new direction.

K.I. Here we come from the bilingual poem already to the international poem, right? Do you consider yourself a cosmopolitan writer?

P.M. No, probably not. I would prefer to call myself a southwestern writer, not in a negative or provincial sense, of course, but in a sense that this here, the Southwest, is the land that is my source of inspiration. You know, I was born and grew up in Texas, where I also got my education. Then later on I moved over here to New Mexico, where I feel very comfortable as well. In between I spent a couple of years in the Midwest, in Cincinnati, Ohio, but I didn't feel very happy over there as I missed the Southwest quite a lot. So I think you can definitely say that my roots are here, and that I do write from here.

However, as you can tell from my writing that also focuses on international and cross-cultural experiences and themes, that does not mean that I am not keenly interested in our various international voices. I am definitely interested in them, although I think this southwestern land shapes my vision.

K.I. How would you then define your identity? Do you feel comfortable with terms like "Hispanic," "Chicana," "Mexican American," "Latina"? Which term would you apply to yourself?

P.M. Well, talking about all these labels, I heard a wonderful response to this question not that long ago. It was by a young Chicana, actually the daughter of Tey Diana Rebolledo, a dear friend and colleague. Tey Marianna Nunn told us that she had been at a Smithsonian Institution symposium some time ago together with a group of other young Latinos. When they were asked that particular question there, she said she heard one of the best answers possible, and she just wished she had said it herself. The answer was: "situational or situational identity." What that means is that we all have multiple identities. In that context I would say, "Yes, I am a Chicana writer, I am a Mexican American writer, I am a woman writer, I am a southwestern writer, I am a U.S. writer, I am a bilingual writer." So I don't have any trouble with any of those terms, and I don't view them as limiting. I mean, there are women writers who feel that label is limiting—that is, to be in an anthology of women writers or something like that. They are all part of what I am. In this part of New Mexico where I am living now—that is, Santa Fe—people tend to define themselves as Hispanic, a word that since 1992 I tend to avoid. But I believe that people have the right to self-definition. And so if I am speaking to a group of women here, and they are bilingual, and in my own mind they are Mexican Americans or Chicanas, but they define themselves as Hispanas, which is fine with me. I mean, I am not here to tell them who they are; that is not my issue.

But with regard to my own identity, I would say it is situational. What is very important to me is that I am trying to increase and not decrease communication. And if labels are getting in my way, I would hope that I could convey to my reader or listener why I am choosing the labels I am choosing. However, I am very much interested in that communication. Today I was reading a book that had the very interesting idea that we should ultimately seek to move from communication to communion. And I think that is true. You know, if I give a poetry reading, for example, I can feel or see if the audience really listens, really listens with their hearts. So then the issue is not so much ethnicity or gender. It is about the way we reach a point of communion as human beings sharing this difficult journey called life.

K.I. Do you think literature can be an effective means to foster a deeper understanding of different cultures? For example, if I take your books with me to Germany and teach them there, do you think German students can get some idea about the Southwest and Chicana literature by reading and studying them?

P.M. I hope so. Of course, that would be an aspect of the work that would delight me because I am very interested in international issues. I think we can't ignore boundaries, and I am very impatient with that, as we need to be respectful of cultural differences, seek to understand them, and also realize our limitations. For example, even if you and I were to become best friends, I would never be able to understand what it means to be German, and on the other hand, you will never be able to totally understand what it means to be a Chicana. But if we approach one another and our words with a sort of deep interest and respect, we move much closer to that understanding, a kind of intercultural understanding, if you like.

K.I. Writing, reading, and also communicating about what one writes or reads could be an effective means to overcome old-fashioned stereo-types. Is this one of the most important tasks of writers today, particu-larly with regard to the multicultural societies we all live in?

P.M. Well, of course. However, it depends a lot on the writer, if she really takes the chance to use this possibility of contributing to intercul-tural understanding. I would say many of the people who are very suc-cessfully published in this country are very effective in reinforcing stereotypes and that is a very big problem. Quite often these are people who are very influential, as they get published by very large presses, and so they can have huge publicity campaigns. For example, there is a book entitled *In Defense of Elitism,* and it did very, very well. This book certain-ly was not promoting intercultural understanding. However, personally, I do hope that my work in some way causes people to rethink stereo-types that they might have about Chicanos and Latinos, of course.

K.I. Another element closely associated with particularly female stereotyping is the use of archetypes. Female icons, mythical or religious figures such as pre-Columbian goddesses, La Virgen de Guadalupe, La Llorona, La Malinche, but also the Mexican artist Frida Kahlo comes to mind here. In your most recent poetry collection, *Agua Santa: Holy Water,* you deal with these legendary figures in a very interesting and, let's say, pop-cultural way. In the central poem, "Cuarteto Mexicano," you imag-ine in a slightly sardonic way what four of these women—that is, the Aztec goddess Coatlicue, the Virgin de Guadalupe, Malinche, and La Llorona—might say on a television talk show. Can you tell us a bit more about that? How did you come across this idea?

P.M. You know, usually as a writer you are so glad when you come up with a good idea that then you forget when or why you came up with it. So I don't know exactly when and how this idea came into my mind. I know that I wanted to do something about them but I didn't have any particular concept at first. I am not a television watcher myself, but it could have been that something quite as simple as one of my daughters being home and watching an Oprah Winfrey talk show might have influ-enced me finally. Actually, I remember that I was quite stunned to realize what power people like Oprah Winfrey and other television hosts, et cetera, have.

Then all of a sudden I wondered what some of our female icons might sound like if they were on talk shows. So something as simple as this could be the starting point for "Cuarteto Mexicano." This talk show concept gave me a way of portraying these female icons in a way that I hope would add something fresh to the portrayal.

Actually, that is always a challenge: Not to redo what has been done and just put your name on it, but instead trying to push the boundaries of it. In letting them speak for themselves—although I am quite aware that I am, as the author, somehow the filter for them, of course—I thought, this might help us to see them as more human and not as such distant icons, which I think is what can happen.

It often seems to me that the more distant a thing is, the less attention is paid to it. For example, maybe one of the reasons that people are fascinated by talk shows is because those shows are so immediate. When something is very distant—like the *Mona Lisa* in the Louvre in Paris, for example—there is a gap. We don't have any sense of her voice, and we don't have to interact with her as intensely. So in making Coatlicue, La Virgen, La Malinche, and La Llorona—and in particular, their voices—more human, it is more likely that we might really listen to them.

K.I. What female icon is most important to you then? Is it one of the four mentioned in "Cuarteto Mexicano," or perhaps another one, such as Sor Juana Inés de la Cruz?[2]

P.M. Of the four mentioned in "Cuarteto Mexicano," which is Coatlicue, the Virgin de Guadalupe, Malinche, and La Llorona, I would say that probably Our Lady of Guadalupe is most important for me. Her image was in my house every day of my growing-up years. The others were not, so she was—and still is—there on this sort of subliminal level. Another reason is that she is such a strong figure for Mexico. However, I don't think that Our Lady of Guadalupe is so important for me that I would define her as a force in my life. And that is true with Sor Juana as well. I mean, I admire Sor Juana very much, but I don't know if I would define her as a force. The presence of fate and religion is a force. I have always joked that the nuns made me who I am because of my thirteen years of Catholic education. But I would now define "catholic" with a small *c* and not with a capital *C*.

K.I. Let's talk a bit more about that issue. Your poems "Nun"[3] and "Maybe a Nun After All"[4] display quite a strong commitment to religion and, in particular, to the Catholic Church. "To Big Mary from an Ex-Catholic"[5] is completely different, as this poem demonstrates a woman's emancipatory move away from the Catholic Church and all the repressions she associates with it. So how important is the Church for you?

Altar of *santos* in a New Mexican church

Adobe church
in New Mexico

Shrine in la Basilica de Nuestra
Señora de Guadalupe, Mexico
City

Portrait of Sor Juana Inés
de la Cruz

P.M. I am still a Catholic, however only in a cultural sense. As my brother once said very wisely, "Catholicism is our myth system." And I totally agree with him; it definitely is our myth system. Those are the symbols I know, and they will always reverberate in my life. So there are aspects of institutionalized Catholicism that are very distant from me. Not too long ago I was telling a friend that I feel about the Catholic Church with a capital *C* the way I feel about returning to the home in which I grew up. I have very affectionate feelings.

K.I. You seem to have very affectionate feelings about nature, too, particularly about the desert, which can be found in most of your writing. Is nature and, with it, mysticism and spiritual cultural elements like *curanderismo,* part of your spiritual or religious belief? How would you define your current religious belief in general?

P.M. Just last night I was thinking that I really try to avoid hierarchical labels. At conferences I talk about linguistic hierarchy and how it is so prevailing in this country. Cultural hierarchy is such a part of the Southwest, and quite often it is also so negative. In addition, there is a lot of religious hierarchy. Sometimes it can be very much a part of institutionalized religion. For example, if you are Catholic with a capital *C*, then Protestants are somehow inferior or vice versa, et cetera. I find that very repugnant, and I try to resist.

What I am very much interested in is the power of faith and spirit in our lives. And the natural world is part of that interest, how we can deepen our awareness of what our work should be in this world. But I do not tie it to a particular institutionalized religion. I will always be fascinated by Roman Catholicism because of its role in my life as well as its role in the history of Mexico and the Southwest. With regard to the oppression that can be associated with the Church in some parts—think about the underprivileged role of women, for example—I believe anger should not be the prime emotional response. At least, I don't feel it. However, there are still moments when I might think, "Well, it is preposterous to think of a totally male-centered religion like the Catholic Church as being the truth." At moments like this I often feel sad. Then I ask myself: "How could this have happened, and how could this keep happening?" It is somehow the same way you might feel about a very paternalistic home if you are feminist, right?

K.I. Do you consider yourself a feminist?

P.M. Yes, definitely. I am a very strong feminist.

K.I. With regard to all the different terms or, let's say, areas of feminism that one can find now, how would you define your feminism?

P.M. Well, again, I would try to resist the label though I understand the impetus for the labels. However, focusing so much on the subpieces keeps us from coming together. I am very interested in issues of power. A question like, "How can I be a Chicana and a Southwesterner?" is an issue of power as well. And in my whole life I have seen how divisions within one group can diminish the ultimate power of the group.

K.I. Speaking about power, feminism, limits, and also about efforts to avoid borders or overcome them, the Chicana writer and feminist Gloria Anzaldúa has written a very powerful book entitled *Borderlands/La Frontera* in which she deals with these issues as well. What do you think about this book, and did it influence you?

P.M. I think *Borderlands/La Frontera* is a very powerful and important book. And I like, in particular, Gloria Anzaldúa's emphasis on the space in the middle, the space in-between borders. However, I can't precisely answer the question about the book's influence on me as well as my writing. For writers, in general, I think it is very difficult to talk about the influences. There is a certain mystery that is an element of certain kinds of writing, and it is a mystery that I like to respect. If you are doing a critical paper and there were certain authors or certain journals that were very important for it, you have a clear sense of an influence by this. But I think with really deep interior writing, the roots are much more elusive than that. So it is impossible for me to say precisely what forces shape my writing. I don't know the influences exactly.

K.I. In the first chapter of *Nepantla* you mention that one of the aims of Latina/o writers nowadays is, or should be, "writing in order to resist internalized oppression" (p. 8). Can you explain this concept a bit more here?

P.M. This issue of internalized racism is very deep, and that's why I touch on it at least a little bit in *Nepantla*. When I started out in children's books, Mexican American teachers were as likely or even more likely to pass them up because of internalized racism and a sense like, "If she is Mexican American, can she really write?"

The same thing can happen on the other side of the border, like in terms of how Mexicans view Chicanos. Particularly upper-class Mexicans might often tend to look down on Chicanos as being uneducated, low-income, and so on. This has to do a lot with class and with image.

Just think about the image of our U.S.-American society that people in Mexico would get from television. They might see a riot and other negative things and thus they associate these negative images with Chicanos—that is, Mexican Americans living there now, in the United States. As we are such a visual society, those images seep into us. It is very difficult to confront them and erase them. This is as true in terms of the educational establishment. Just look at something prestigious as the Guggenheim Fellowships. One day last week I was looking at the list from last year. They gave out about seventy fellowships, and not one of the recipients was a Latina or a Latino. That would suggest, then, that there is not anyone who is doing good enough work. What it means is that the committee begins with a bias but they would never be ready to admit it.

They do not want to believe that, but I am convinced that once the compositions of selection committees change, so do the awards. But that is a very touchy issue because people in the establishment—for example, university professors, critics, et cetera—like to say that they are so intelligent that they can rise above these things. Most people in the establishment believe that very firmly. The argument they always use in that context is quality. As if you could be objective about quality at all; you just can't.

K.I.   Why did you move to Cincinnati, Ohio, in September 1989 and thus leave behind such inspiration and cultural southwestern influences and inspirations like the desert? In particular, the desert seems to be a very prevailing subject in most of your writing [e.g., see "Mi Tierra," *Borders*, p. 33; "Desert Woman," *Borders*, p. 79; "Desert Pilgrimage," *Communion*, p. 20] and I believe it is very important for your whole life, too, right? So how did this change of place influence your writing, life, and way of thinking? Do you have any plans to go back to the Midwest?

P.M.   Well, I don't know if I can go back to the Midwest as that would be very hard for me. My husband has to go back, so that is the hard decision. We were here in Santa Fe a year before last year, and we are going to be here this year. He is a professor of archaeology, and so his position is there in the Midwest, in Cincinnati, Ohio, although he would love to be in the Southwest. At the moment he is just on a sabbatical. So it is very hard for us to decide what we are going to do next. You know, the only reason why I went to the Midwest was because of my husband. But as you know quite well, it was not easy for me to move to the Midwest a few years ago. I am a person who loves the desert and the whole southwestern landscape and culture tremendously. So I missed that very much. However, looking back, I think it was good to stay for a few years over there, away from the Southwest. As I say at the beginning of *Nepantla* ["Bienvenidos," pp. 3–14], there were things I said about the border that I would have never said if I hadn't left it. And then I looked back and I thought, "Why is it I never read these authors? You know, all these questions that could be obvious to an outsider, but when you are in it, the culture can be so oppressive that you don't even have the questions in your own mind. So I think it was good for me to leave for some time, but also now, I think it would be good for me not to leave again. There is so much work to be done here now, and there are so few of us to do it. However, it will be a very hard decision because my husband definitely has to go back. My three children are grown. They are twenty-nine, twenty-six, and twenty-three years old, and nobody lives in the Southwest. Two of them live in Austin, Texas, but technically, to me, that is not the Southwest.

K.I. Why not? Is it because of the more internationally oriented university town of Austin itself, or is it more an issue of the geographic location?

P.M. The second point you mentioned is the reason for that, I would say, because we think of West Texas as the Southwest, and that does not include East Texas and Austin, at least not for me. El Paso in the south is part of this Southwest, as it is right there by New Mexico and by the border to Mexico as well. It is right there on that edge.

K.I. That's why you feel so comfortable in El Paso, your hometown, and now in New Mexico, right?

P.M. Right. I mean, I am a Texas writer. However, I also have to say that I love New Mexico very much.

K.I. You would never consider yourself a New Mexican writer then?

P.M. Well, I think the New Mexican writers would probably hit me over the head if I say I am a New Mexican writer, because they are New Mexican writers and their cultural background is a bit different from mine. Therefore, I prefer to say that I am a southwestern writer, and so I won't offend anybody.

K.I. What would you say is the major difference between Texan and New Mexican writers, then, with regard to Chicanas and Chicanos? Does it have to do with the different levels of Native American influences?

P.M. Maybe. However, it also has to do with the different kinds of experiences in general. Those boundaries are very arbitrary, and they are political. That's another reason why I prefer the term "southwestern writer." But if someone were going to tie me to a state, they would say: "You spend most of your time in Texas so you are a Texan writer." I don't have any troubles with that.

K.I. In *Communion* and *Nepantla* you write a lot from your experience as a tourist and traveler to several countries all over the globe—including Pakistan and Middle America. How important is traveling to you and to your writing?

P.M. Travel has been a great source of inspiration and learning. I feel so grateful to have traveled and to have heard other languages surrounding me, to have participated in different customs, to have been so enriched by the generosity of others.

K.I. Do you think tourism can enhance a global mutual understanding? Or does it just separate people into two categories or classes: the haves and the have-nots, as you show in your poems "Fences" (*Communion*, p. 50) and "Peruvian Child"? (p. 60).

P.M. Let's talk about travel rather than tourism. Travel has the potential to increase our knowledge and understanding, but our observations are often quick takes, quick conclusions. Travel per se doesn't separate people; however, insensitive tourism can, because of global economic dominance. It is easy to be seduced by service and to conclude that certain people deserve to be waited on.

K.I. You already mentioned some of your new projects. Can you tell us a bit more about other projects you're working on right now? How about your future plans?

P.M. I am just beginning to explore the possibilities of a book of short meditations. There is a book that was written in the United States called *Gift from the Sea* by Anne Morrow Lindbergh. And she went down to the beach for a week or two—at least that is the way it is in the book—and picked up shells, and she would describe a shell and relate it to something about life. So I thought that might be an interesting idea to pursue in the desert. And at this point in my life, I think about how we can simplify our lives and what keeps us from simplifying our lives. So the tentative title for this is "Desert Reflections." At the moment it is too early for me to know if I think it is going to work and lead any place or not.

NOTES

1. *Horn Books* (July–August 1990): 436.
2. Cf. "Sor Juana," in *Communion*, p. 77.
3. In *Communion*, p. 76.
4. In *Borders*, p. 76.
5. In *Borders*, p. 77.

BIBLIOGRAPHY

Books

1984 *Chants*. Houston: Arte Público.
1986 *Borders*. Houston: Arte Público.
1991 *Communion*. Houston: Arte Público.
1993 *Nepantla: Essays from the Land in the Middle*. Albuquerque: University of New Mexico Press.
1995 *Agua Santa: Holy Water*. Boston: Beacon Press.
1997 *Aunt Carmen's Book of Practical Saints*. Boston: Beacon Press.
       House of Houses. Family memoir. Boston: Beacon Press.

Children's Books

1992 *A Birthday Basket for Tía*. New York: Simon & Schuster.
1994 *Agua, Agua, Agua*. Glenview, Ill.: Good Year Books.
       The Desert Is My Mother: El Desierto Es Mi Madre. Houston: Piñata Books.
       Listen to the Desert: Oye al Desierto. New York: Clarion Books.
       Pablo's Tree. New York: Simon & Schuster.
1995 *The Gift of the Poinsettia: El Regalo de la Flor de Nochebuena*. Houston: Piñata Books.
       The Race of Toad and Deer. New York: Orchard Books.
1996 *Confetti: Poems for Children*. New York: Lee & Low Books.
       Uno, Dos, Tres: One, Two, Three. New York: Clarion Books.
1997 *Tomas and the Library Lady*. New York: Knopf.
1999 *Delicious Hullabaloo: Pachanga Deliciosa*. Houston: Piñata Books.
       This Big Sky. A poetry collection for children. New York: Scholastic Press.
2000 *My Own True Name: New and Selected Poems for Young Adults, 1984–1999*. Houston: Piñata Books.
2001 *The Bakery Lady/La señora de la Panadería*. Houston: Piñata Books.

Children's Literature Anthologies

1981   *Kikirikí: Stories and Poems in English and Spanish for Children.* Houston: Arte
      Público.
1986   *Tun-Ta-Ca-Tun: More Stories and Poems in English and Spanish for Children.*
      Houston: Arte Público.

Forthcoming Books

María Points the Hills. New York: Viking.
With Pat Mora et al. (eds.), *The Rainbow Tulip.* Children's book. New York:
   Viking.

© JEAN WEISINGER, 1993

Cherríe Moraga

Poet, Playwright, Essayist, and Educator

"My bottom line is always that I want to get better and better and better, which means keeping an open heart and an open mind."

SAN FRANCISCO, CALIFORNIA, JANUARY 2, 1997

C HERRÍE MORAGA is a Chicana poet, playwright, essayist, scholar, and activist. She became a central figure in feminist, lesbian, women-of-color, Chicana, and American literature when she started publishing her work in the 1980s. Her writing is highly politicized, intensely personal, and eloquently honest.

Born on September 25, 1952, in Whittier, California, Moraga is the offspring of a mixed-race marriage. Her paternal roots go back to Missouri and Canada, and her maternal roots to California, Arizona, and Sonora, Mexico. Like Southern California, where she grew up, Moraga is the product of Mexican and Anglo influence. She experienced Mexican customs at home and American traditions in school, and she was surrounded by the Spanish and English languages. Due to her relatively fair skin, she could "pass" for a white woman in society. Thus she did not experience the pain of prejudice that many Mexican Americans and Latinos face. However, as a lesbian, Moraga had to cope with another type of discrimination: homophobia. The anger and frustration about all these different types of discrimination, as well as her belief that change must be instigated by the oppressed themselves, contributed to Moraga's passion for writing. In 1974 she earned a B.A. degree from a private college in Hollywood, and after several years of teaching English, she decided to concentrate more on her writing. In addition to writing poetry and critical essays, she began her thesis for her master's degree in feminist writing at San Francisco State University.

Together with Gloria Anzaldúa, she collected essays, poems, letters, and conversations of women of color on issues like feminism and lesbian-

153

ism for a book. With this work, entitled *This Bridge Called My Back: Writings by Radical Women of Color,* Moraga completed requirements for her master's degree in 1980. Shortly after it was published in 1981, *This Bridge Called My Back* was recognized as a groundbreaking collection of third-world feminist writing and theory that also challenged Anglo-American feminism. It was republished in 1983 and received the 1986 Before Columbus Foundation American Book Award. In 1988 a revised, Spanish edition entitled *Esta Puente, Mi Espalda: Voces de Mujeres Tercermundistas en los Estados Unidos* was published. In 1981 Cherríe Moraga cofounded Kitchen Table: Women of Color Press in New York City to allow more feminists and women of color to express themselves textually. Two years later Moraga's first collection of works, *Loving in the War Years/Lo Que Nunca Pasó por Sus Labios,* was published there. In that work Moraga discusses the effects of Chicanas' cultural heritage on sexuality—homosexual and heterosexual. She asks all Chicanas to free themselves from the sexual and cultural oppression that has taught them to think of the needs of their men before their own. *Loving in the War Years* was the first published book of writing by an avowed Chicana lesbian. With Norma Alarcón and Ana Castillo, Moraga edited *The Sexuality of Latinas* (1989) and the already mentioned edition of *Bridge, Esta Puente, Mi Espalda.*

Moraga's experience at INTAR, the Hispanic-American Arts Center in New York City, provided her with the skills needed to write and produce plays and contributed to her success as a playwright. Her play *Giving Up the Ghost: Teatro in Two Acts* was published in 1986 and performed in 1987 in San Francisco and Seattle. In it Moraga deals with the brutality of heterosexual love as opposed to the homosexual love the play's female characters Amalia and Marisa share.

Moraga has received several awards, including the Fund for New American Plays and the National Endowment for the Arts Theatre Playwrights' Fellowship for *Shadow of a Man* (1988) and *Heroes and Saints* (1989). Some critics, such as Catherine Wiley, regard *Shadow of a Man,* for example, "in many ways as a radical revision of Arthur Miller's *Death of a Salesman* with the sexual tension of Miller's subtext placed in the foreground."[1] In her latest plays Moraga puts more and more emphasis on social problems and political activism, and adds these elements to her ever present criticism of various forms of oppression. In "Watsonville: Some Place Not Here" (1996) a cannery workers' strike, a miraculous vision, a single mother's sexual breakthrough, and an earthquake are brought together. In *Heroes and Saints* (1992) Moraga displays the human drama of a Chicana family suffering the effects of pesticide-related deaths, birth defects, and poisoning. In an unusual blend of political theater, realism, and surrealism, Moraga develops the action of *Heroes and Saints* around the female protagonist Cerezita, who—due to birth defects—is just a head poised on a wheeled cart. Moraga's book *The Last Generation* is a collection of highly politicized essays and poems. Moving freely between Spanish and English and also crossing literary genres, Moraga argues for a new conception of gender, sexuality, race, art, nationalism, and the politics of survival based on a radical transformation of consciousness and society.

Moraga is artist-in-residence and instructor of theater and creative writing at Brava Theatre Center of San Francisco. She is also president of the board of directors of Latin American Theatre Artists, teaches at Stanford University in Palo Alto, and lectures around the country.

KARIN IKAS We are now almost at the end of the twentieth century. Your first works were published in the 1980s. How have things changed since then? How would you describe yourself as a person and as a writer now in the late 1990s?

CHERRÍE MORAGA Well, my first book published was *This Bridge Called My Back* in 1981. Then *Loving in the War Years* came out in 1983. I think the major difference is that at the time that both of those books were published, there wasn't very much in print and no real dialogue where women of color were articulating perspectives about feminism. Within the context of the Chicano literary movement there was virtual silence concerning lesbianism and, to a certain degree, concerning feminism as well. Therefore, when those two books were published in the 1980s, they were unique in the sense that they somehow introduced the fact that one could be both lesbian and Chicana in the same human body. Also, these books showed that feminism wasn't a compromise of one's Chicanismo but that in fact one could define feminism from a Chicano cultural perspective.

I have taught at the university for many, many years now. I see in the way Chicano issues come up that much of these things are already understood now. So they are grounded; they are now established. Therefore, as we are moving into the twenty-first century, people can go on to ask more complex questions about how class, gender, race, and sexuality intersect. You no longer have to question whether you have the right to look at it at all—which was the case twenty years ago.

K.I. Would you say that there is a generational gap between the younger Chicana/o writers and the ones of your generation? Or do you support and help each other?

C.M. Obviously, with each generation there are new sets of questions and concerns. But there is not a generational gap because we were mostly in the role of teaching that younger generation, and they are reading our work. So I feel like there is continuity. In terms of my own generation of writers, we were very much starving at the beginning. To have a twenty-year body of literature on Chicana feminism, that's nothing. And that's just barely coming of age itself. The younger generation may look at us as *ancianos*. But I feel that we just really understand the ways we want to write; if you ask anyone of my generation, everyone just feels this way. Culturally we have a whole body of work in front of us. So I see all of us as still very young, and I feel like the younger people, the new generation coming up, can take a greater risk in theme and concern. Maybe other people see it differently but I think—because I work so much with young people—that there is incredible continuity.

K.I. Your first writing is very angry. Are you still angry about your situation?

C.M. I have never lost my anger.

K.I. Can you describe that anger to us? Are you angry about the society as a whole? For example, if I think of *The Last Generation*, in which you deal a lot with global issues, your anger seems to be put into an international context. Is this the way your anger goes now?

C.M. I think that the only people who have a right to write with anger are white people. I just feel that categorizing our work as "angry" is a way to totally trivialize it. So I always ensure that no matter what I am writing about, even a love poem, I remain angry. It has always been a tradition in the United States that the standard American literary perspective on that is that somehow art is antithetical to anger and anger is antithetical to art. But I don't see these distinctions at all. I believe there is only a difference when you're younger. For example, I myself as a younger writer didn't feel as though I had the right to write, and I see this with a lot of younger writers today as well. So the anger has more to do with what helps you to get the stimulation and the motivation and to feel that you can put your ideas in print. It's almost like you need the anger as the impetus to feel like you have the right to do it, because it's not a given that you should have ever written. And I think the difference is that now, as I understand I have a right to write and that no one is going to take that away from me, I feel less embattled about that aspect, but certainly not less embattled about my perspective. And yes, I agree that my work has become increasingly more international. But I feel like that just has to do with one's evolution and one's understanding of the causes of injustice, oppression, and even love.

K.I. I would like to talk a bit more about *The Last Generation*. What did you have in mind when you started this work?

C.M. Well, it was partly motivated by both personal and political concerns. The personal concerns are that most of the elders in my family are now into their eighties and nineties; they are passing as we speak. I feel that the generations coming up in my own family are much more assimilated and less conscious of their Mexicanism, their Chicanismo. I lament that. So there is a certain sense in which, as a writer, I feel like I am the last one in my family to remember and record that we're Mexicans. But I also see that in this country there is such a movement toward multiculturalism—which is just a sort of acronym for the melting pot—making "nationalism" a dirty word. This reaction to nationalism has happened all over, internationally as well. However, some of the roots of Chicano nationalism are still very valid. This has to do with remembering that this was initially our land, and that the land was stolen from us. This is similar to what Native American people do. And that kind of cultural nationalism in terms of one's consciousness—for example, having a right to land, like the Palestinians or anybody else—is very, very important. Although I feel that there is a move in this country to Hispanicize us, to Europeanize us, and make us another immigrant group that we are not, and to ratify us. So the book was motivated by both the personal concerns and then by the much more political concerns. The latter is about the passing of a generation, of a movement, and the refusal to let this movement go underground. It is not the last generation. When you say something like "the last generation," it is to stop it from being the last generation; it is a conscious political movement. So those were the two primary motivations for this work.

K.I. In this book you deal with lesbianism as part of "the last generation" as well. It seems that, in that context, you see yourself as the last of your generation also because of your homosexuality and the consequent difficulties in having children. However, now you have a child yourself. You have a son who is about three and a half years old. Did this motherhood experience change your writing and you as a person?

C.M. At the time I wrote the book, I didn't have children. What I always try to do is to make a distinction between the life of a writer and the life of a book. In the life of that book, that writer has no children. So when she says no one is going to call me "mami, grandma, *abuelita*" or whatever, that writer meant that. But my concern about family and the re-creation of family, including queer *familia,* has always been the same. I think by virtue of being Mexican, family is so culturally important. And I came from such a huge extended family that, whether I'm queer or straight or whatever, I always tried to re-create that, even if it was just with lovers and their children. You know that kind of re-creation of a *familia* that countered the nuclear family model. So to me having a child is a kind of logical extension of those ideas. But I was never guaranteed a pregnancy or any of that. So the fact that I have a child now almost seemed to be in my role. It was my part to do that, and it just happened to me. However, it may not have worked. I mean, it could have been that I didn't get pregnant. So the fact that it did happen showed that it was in my path to do that.

What it has changed, however, is that it reinforced how necessary it is, even in the rearing of children, to draw from the positive elements of one's culture in terms of values and respect for elders and ancestors, for example, and to get a more collective understanding of how the formation of family happens. In addition, we should not copy the problems that the typical American nuclear family has put up for itself. We do need to create new models about how to raise our children. Queers are in the position to do that because we are outside of society. That's why we are never really interested in domestic marriages and all that kind of stuff. I have become even more committed to trying to draw from certain cultural traditions that I think work and to critique those traditions that don't work. This happens in particular with regard to raising my own child and sharing him with the other people who are helping to raise him.

κ.ι. If you think about white feminism, women-of-color feminism, and lesbianism—the three major issues in your work—is it more important for you to concentrate on women-of-color lesbians, and are you therefore not so interested in making alliances with white feminists?

c.m. Well, I make alliances with white feminist individuals, but not with the white feminist movement. I mean, there are numbers of white feminists who really are my allies because they are antiracist, and they practice what they preach. But as a movement, white feminism has nothing to offer me. Just calling it "white" feminism shows it excludes. In large part, the institutionalization in terms of organizations that are dominated by white feminists is one reason why white feminists still are not able to really integrate concerns of not just women of color, but working-class and poor women as well. But that has nothing to do, necessarily, with individuals. I mean, I will build coalitions with anybody whose work I feel a common cause with. So that can be a white woman, that can be men. And there are a lot of women of color I don't work with because we don't share a common cause either. But when you're talking theoretically, when you're talking in terms of your political analysis, white feminism has nothing to offer me. What it did was to provide a base twenty years ago from which I could then critique what was missing. Not just me but us as a collective body of people. Women of color could critique what it had to offer and what were the missing parts, and on that we built a broader-based movement, one that makes sense globally as well.

K.I. What was most influential for your writing at the beginning, and what is most influential now?

C.M. As a poet, Adrienne Rich had a great impact on me. I studied her work a great deal. In the mid-seventies I was reading all the work that came out, like Mary Daily and Juliet Mitchell. I read all the work of white women and the "bibles" of feminism, Marxist feminism, radical feminism, and social feminism. They were all providing a base of analysis for me to understand feminism and to figure out how Marxism coheres with that or how it doesn't. I wanted to get a handle on understanding my own oppression, the oppression of the women around me, and of my culture. So what happens is that you read all that stuff, and then you ask, What's missing in the picture? That's what then made me primarily reflect on black feminism. By and large, black feminists at that time were not writing theory, with some exceptions, of course. I was reading the poets and the novelists like Toni Morrison, Pat Parker, Audre Lorde, and Alice Walker. I read Walker's *Meridian* in the early days. At that time black feminists were the only ones who were articulating a kind of class, race, and gender analysis. So that's sort of your natural progression. You think about what is missing in that picture, and you bring it to your own kind. Those were my first influences.

In recent years I read much more Native American women's work than anything else; for example, Leslie Marmon Silko and Linda Hogan. I feel an affinity within to these women's work. Their writings run closer to the Chicano experience, given the fact that we both have native roots here in the United States.

к.ı. What about the Asian Americans?

с.м. I've read plenty of Asian American literature. I see similarities in terms of the kind of repression that women experience in relation to very patriarchal societies. We build coalitions against common threats. But I think it is the passionately political nature of black literature in this country that makes it most influential. Every people-of-color movement will tell you that they draw from models of the African American movement because racism is so pervasive in the United States. African Americans have always had to be at an extremely cutting edge in their radicalism to counter that racism. So that always inspired me politically. When I draw from the Native American tradition, it is more in a cultural and spiritual sense.

к.ı. Do you feel there is a common bond between African American and Chicana/o writers?

с.м. No, because I think we know a huge amount more about them than they know about us. By and large, as a general rule, I don't think that it is mutual. We Chicanos/as remain very invisible within the U.S. literary scene. Even very well read and very well published African American writers in the U.S. hardly know us. If you ask them about Chicana writers, the only person they know is Sandra Cisneros. So they usually only know people who have really crossed over to the mainstream. There isn't the motivation to do the same research we do. African Americans have more mainstream writers. So they and their literature are more accessible to us. I think that we have always taken the examples of leadership from the black movement. However, I don't think the relationship is reciprocal, which is a kind of a shame.

к.ı. If you think about the future of feminism as a whole, and women-of-color feminism, in particular, what will it look like in the twenty-first century?

с.м. The most hopeful start has been made in terms of the international connections among diaspora people; for example, the African diaspora and black American feminists creating international connections. Or Native American women during the quincentenary, when there were international conferences happening, connecting native people, indigenous people, from all over the globe. I think there is an incredible amount of potential, of women, of nations of women, coming together that doesn't recognize these national boundaries. It is a very patriarchal and also a very imperialist capitalist notion to allow these geopolitical borders to separate us. Although women are doing many other things, I feel somehow hopeful when women connect with each other, violating those boundaries. That's really exciting to me.

K.I. Can white women and white feminists be part of that, too?

C.M. That happens in terms of international conferences. The problem is never that it can't happen. It's just that, by and large, when you're dealing with the dominant class—which tends to be white people, Euro-American and European women—it is rarely a dialogue. It never is. That is my experience, from all the work I've done with white women. When you go to an international conference, you always know what to expect in terms of it being dominated by European methodology. So when you have an international conference where European women and Euro-American women are there, the dialogue is still dominated by that cultural perspective. I have never experienced it any other way except that it is happening within a different context and so it is different people who define the terms. It doesn't mean that it is impossible. It is also a question of who is running the show, who has the power, who determines the nature of the debate. By and large, if you have international conferences that include both women of color and white women, white women continue to be the ones who define the nature of the debate and the conversations. That always limits what can really happen.

K.I. If you think about intercultural and cross-cultural understanding that goes beyond current borders between women of color, people of color in general, and white people, are you pessimistic or optimistic that it is going to happen in the future?

C.M. It's not that I am pessimistic about it. I just think the real work in that context begins locally. It's like that saying: "Think globally, act locally."

Like in your case, you're from Germany. There are people of color there, like there are in every other city and country around the world. That's where the work begins, in your own country and community. It is not about going across the world to have conversations with people. It is about—and I don't want to sound too Christian here—how you treat your neighbor.

I remember going to Germany, to Berlin. I was staying in that area where there were mostly Turks living and other people of color. So to me it was almost like any other American city where you can find people of color everywhere. And it became very clear that the people who invited me to Germany to give a talk about us Chicanas and Chicanos in the United States were very liberal about us. They could say that we were interesting and exoticize Chicanos/as or natives or blacks in the United States. But in their hometown, very little has been done in terms of dealing with people of color there. And that's where the real work should be. It is not about being pessimistic. It is about believing that real change happens at the most intimate level first. All these are good gestures and stuff, but they don't impress me. What impresses me, and what I believe in, is that kind of contact work in your own community.

K.I. Let's talk a bit about your essay writing. Do you have a particular theory in mind when you write your essays?

C.M. No. I have a particular question in mind. Some essays are also driven by personal experience. Right now I am finishing a book called *Waiting in the Wings*. It has to do with the birth of my son and deals with personal and philosophical questions. But usually I write essays motivated by questions I have, contradictions, what I see politically in society that I can't find an answer to. I don't necessarily have a theory I want to work out. It is more like I have a question I want to ask in public. I may not have an answer. I just want to ask the question so that people will talk about it.

K.I. At a poetry reading you gave at San Francisco State University on November 21, 1996, you mentioned that "theater is hard but very revolutionary, it's three-dimensional and in the flesh." Can you tell us a bit more about that, especially because you are one of the few Chicana playwrights?

C.M. It has to do with the fact that things are different once you give them a voice. Reading is a very private act. The readers can shut the book, open it, or do whatever they want. They can interpret the writing any way they want to. Theater is more confrontational. You have to open your heart and take a play in or not. But it is also an opportunity to do that in a very visual way. With a book you don't have that possibility. You can keep your mind—at least to some degree—separate if you want to. I find it very exciting that theater is so much more confrontational.

K.I. What is most important for you when you write a play?

C.M. Characters are the most important element for me. Usually I am always motivated by a character first or an image.

K.I. What about the audience? Do you feel that it is sometimes difficult for the audience to deal with the sometimes very outspoken lesbian elements in some of your plays?

C.M. It depends on who is in the audience, homosexuals or people who are homophobic. But I don't worry about that. In that context, for me writing theater is somehow a bit like writing a novel. The characters are talking to you, and you have to listen to them. If you try to superimpose your ideology of that time, the work gets very flat. So I never am concerned about how the audience is going to respond. I never censor anything based on who the audience is. I write for my ideal audience that is probably made up of people who are not homophobic, not racist, people who are open-minded. So if you assume your audience is open-minded, and you write well and with enough depth, then whoever is in the audience—white person, person of color, whatever—will be able to see the other—maybe for the first time in their life—just as humans. That's where your hope is.

K.I. Your theater seems to be very political. I think about *Watsonville* or *Heroes and Saints*, for example. In those plays you deal with the situation of Chicana/o fruit pickers who are exposed to pesticides. In *Heroes and Saints* the protagonist is Cerezita, a disembodied head [due to her mother's exposure to pesticides during pregnancy]. How important is that political content in your plays?

C.M. Well, of course there is a political message in my plays. But again, my theater is in particular about trying to have the character's humanity express that message. Otherwise we are just polemical, and people think you are lecturing them. Then they don't open their hearts. Of course, I want to raise consciousness. I want to wake people up. The way I do that is by creating fully dimensional characters.

K.I. What does Cerezita, the protagonist of *Heroes and Saints*, stand for in particular? The issues you bring up with her are manifold. I already mentioned the bad situation of fruit pickers. Other topics include sexuality and love from the point of view of the handicapped woman, Cerezita, then religion—in particular, the Catholic Church—and there is also love for a priest. Then you have an overprotective mother, hypocrisy, and several other elements in there.

C.M. Most important about Cerezita is that she is a Mexican American woman who has great vision and who is imprisoned. She is a symbol for all of us, for any young Chicana who has great vision and is not allowed to be fully dimensional in a world dominated by sexism, racism, and all of that. So she is somebody who is so brilliant, who can see so much, almost everything. She sees truth, and you are not supposed to be able to do that. Her not having a body is the representation of that. She is completely physically disabled from being able to speak the truth. That's how I feel about so much of the potential of young Chicana and

Mexican American women. There is all that beauty and vision. So probably at the heart of it, that's what that play is about. You can say that the things that stop Cerezita are the environmental racism, the Catholic Church, homophobia, and the list can go on. But nonetheless, part of it is that she is just a human being who is not allowed to have her full humanity. And that is the biggest crime of racism, sexism, and homophobia: it keeps people from achieving their full humanity.

K.I. We are here at Brava! For Women in the Arts, a nonprofit organization that encourages and supports women to pursue professions in the arts. It also sponsors female theater projects like the experimental Latina Theatre Lab. If we think about the male-dominated history of the Chicano theater, in particular by Luis Valdez's Teatro Campesino and others, how do you feel about the situation right now?

C.M. Now there is no longer a real Chicano theater movement at all. Some of us are writing Chicano theater in a Chicano context; others are writing within a mainstream context. But very highly politically motivated work—that is really about social change—by and large is not being written by Chicanos anymore—at least not right now. It doesn't mean that our plays have to be about strikes and social protests. However, they should involve issues that are very necessary for Chicanos, for our own evolution as a people. But at the moment, plays often are either so highly personalized that they don't have enough of an impact on Chicanos/as, or they are too superficial or too pedantical. Therefore, I feel that right now Chicano/a theater in general—written by women or men—is kind of biased. Additionally, like you have already said, as the history of Chicano theater is very male-dominated, the plays written by women are just gradually about to get more recognized anyway.

K.I. Who are the most important contemporary Chicana playwrights to you? And what would you say are the major difficulties they have to cope with?

C.M. There are many talented Chicana playwrights, like Denise Chávez and Josefina López. But by and large, almost no Chicana has the opportunity to fully concentrate on writing drama. Most of us are doing other things as well, like acting, writing for TV, et cetera. In terms of looking at the time when theater was really part of a revolutionary movement, when there was a political movement to support it, that's no longer the case. We are writing as individuals now. And even on an individual basis I feel like the work is not progressive enough. It doesn't reach far enough and doesn't challenge the mainstream enough. It is too colloquial. I think that is the trouble with our literature, too. There is not enough Chicano/a literature that is really challenging the preconceptions about who we are as a people by the mainstream. Also, we don't critique ourselves as people so that we can become better people.

This applies to all of us today, that is, on January 2, 1997; we have to change that. We need to do the kind of intercultural critique that will make us a stronger people, and also the critique that challenges the status quo. It is hard to do that and still get the mainstream attention we need to survive as artists.

Coming back to what you asked about Chicano theater in relation to mainstream theater, we remain very ghettoized and tokenized. None of that has changed yet. There is very little progress in that area. None of the work—with the exception of Luis Valdez's works—has really crossed over into the mainstream. There are a few writers, Latino writers, not just Chicanos—like José Rivera, Caldo Solice—mostly men, however, who had made some crossover more to mainstream regional theaters, but by and large we remain a ghettoized theater.

K.I. Have [you] ever thought about adapting one of your plays for the TV screen?

C.M. Sure, but I have to be offered that. I would not waste my time coming up with a screenplay and pushing to get it on the screen since that is like winning the lottery. In the past there has been some interest in my work for that, but nothing has worked out so far. It is so expensive to do film or TV. As a writer you constantly get invitations to do these things, and some projects go further than others. But to actually see something realized into a film is very rare. Well, I respond to those invitations if they seem interesting. And, of course, I am interested in that to the degree that those two mediums have incredible access in a way to many people. They also reach people who don't read or don't go to see a play. But I would never put my time and energy into being a screenplay writer because as a screenplay writer you are no longer able to control the production of your work. The director does this. So if you do want to have control, you don't write screenplays.

K.I. What projects do you have in mind at the moment? What about your future plans?

C.M. I am finishing a book right now that is called *Waiting in the Wings: Portrait of a Queer Motherhood*. It basically deals with my son. He was born premature. It is actually about what it means to give birth to a child when the generation that raised me is leaving the earth. There are also some more philosophical questions involved. Then I have a play called "The Hungry Woman, the Mexican Medea" that I am finishing this spring.

K.I. Do you incorporate the La Llorona myth in that new play?

C.M. Yes, that's what it is. It is kind of a turn-of-the-century Llorona. It is now a feminist Llorona as opposed to the patriarchal interpretations of her. In my play the Medea myth runs parallel to the one of La Llorona.

K.I. Focusing a bit more on your theoretical work: you started doing theory in the 1980s with Gloria Anzaldúa when you edited *This Bridge Called My Back: Writings by Radical Women of Color.* At that time you were one of the few Chicana writers doing theory. How has the situation changed since then? Do you still work with Gloria Anzaldúa?

C.M. Gloria Anzaldúa and myself, we have our own different approaches. The only collaboration I did with Gloria was *This Bridge Called My Back.* That was about fifteen years ago. Now there are plenty of people writing theory, such as Norma Alarcón, Yvonne Yarbro-Bejarano and Ana Castillo.

K.I. With regard to Chicana theorists and Chicana writers, how does the situation look like right now? What seems to be most important at the moment?

C.M. The problem right now is that we are cultivating more critics than we are cultivating artists. So many young Chicanas are going into literary criticism. There are plenty of them if you think about all the dissertations done in that area by young Chicanas in recent years. So there is a lot of that happening, but not much in the cultivation of really good writers. And that's what I am really interested in. So these theorists are doing academic criticism, which I think is different than what Gloria Anzaldúa and me or even Ana Castillo are doing. We are writing as creative writers. We are running personal essays, essays that have theoretical components. But it is not that we are trying to sit down to write academic essays. It's about creating theory that also is very experimental. It is also based on research. The essays are literary to me, as opposed to academic essays. I don't consider myself an academic even though I teach at Stanford. I consider myself a professional writer and that to me is different. I am looking for young writers really coming into the work. I mean, I think of someone like James Barth, who wrote incredible essays. That's the kind of theory you can use. Otherwise, to me standard academic writing presents you with language that is less accessible and more exclusive and requires a more formally educated readership. I am looking for essays, philosophies, and ideas that can change people. It has to be written like the mind that filtered to the heart.

K.I. What kind of philosophy is important to you? Sometimes it seems that you create a kind of personal philosophy, in particular with regard to your theoretical writing.

C.M. Yes, to some extent I create my own philosophy. I agree with Gloria Anzaldúa, who mentioned already years ago that she always wanted to be a philosopher. That's a beautiful thing. It is not that she wants to make a career in the academy. It is that she wants to think. Like Jackie Alexander, who teaches in New York, said, "Our great philosophers were the eldest in our village who sat on the porch and had the ideas." This idea of a real solid base of ideas is what is important to me.

K.I. In that context another vital element in Mexican and Mexican American culture comes into my mind, *curandismo* [folk healing] and the *curanderas,* the women who practice it. They deal a lot with Chicano/a traditions and cultural elements and incorporate them to heal. Can a writer or writing itself function that way as well? Do you feel like a healer sometimes?

C.M. I don't like to use that language because it is too overused. But, of course, I've seen that writing can save lives. I've seen young writers who saved their own lives by writing. So I know the act of writing is very cleansing, and sometimes it also can save your life. But that's not what being a *curandera* means. A *curandera* is somebody who has practiced the art of healing, who uses herbs, and who has a special relationship to *indigenismo*, rituals, and prayers. *Curandismo* has its own folk tradition. I respect that, but I would never use that word to describe my thoughts.

K.I. Crossing borders and even dissolving borders are some of the keywords of your writing. Postcolonialists deal with dissolving borders as well. Are there any postcolonial theories that you feel can be applied to Chicana literature? Do you sometimes feel like a postcolonialist yourself?

C.M. No, I never use the postcolonial theory in my writing. Whatever theory I read, and I have read a lot of different philosophies—Buddhism, for example—I try to get some answers to my questions. In postcolonialist discourse there is language that is useful. But I try not to use that language in my writing. I find it alienating to my readers and myself. I like language to give tools that help people to get a hold of understanding their situation and their experience. If I understand it, I read it and translate it to other languages. So it has its validity in my own reading.

But for the most part I tend not to re-create or use that language in my own writing. Instead I try to use a language that I feel is original to my own perspective.

K.I. How do you then feel about critics who call you a postcolonial writer?

C.M. Lots of people do that, and that is fine with me. I have read a lot of things in which people refer to me as a postcolonial writer. The way people use my work has nothing to do with me. The book has its own life once it is published, so I don't have to agree with everything. However, that's not important to me anyway. It's just the conversation that has to happen. You have no control over how people react and interpret your work.

K.I. So as the book has its own life once it is written, I assume you also never go back and rewrite some of your essays or books?

C.M. Right, I wouldn't. However, I hope that each book reflects a development. I mean, sometimes people come to me and say: "How could you say that? That contradicts what you said ten years ago." And I tell them: " Thank God, thank God it contradicts it!" I mean, if I am not changing, I would be really worried. I would expect work, whatever new work, to be a kind of reflection of my own evolution. But certainly I would not go back and fix something. There are a lot of things I've written in the past I do no longer agree with. But at that time, it was OK. That twenty-nine-year-old writer, or however old I was at that time, had a right to write that. It stimulated dialogue then.

K.I. So one always has to see your writing in the context and in the time it was written.

C.M. Sure, in the ideal world. But it is not an ideal world, and therefore many critics often don't look at my work that way. People don't even pay attention to copyrights sometimes. I can give you an example on the issue of identity politics because *This Bridge Called My Back* is so strongly an advocate of identity politics, and I think there are a lot of weaknesses in identity politics from my perspective now. Sometimes I feel like *Bridge* too easily lent itself to making it seem as if, if you were lesbian of color, for example, given all these multiple oppressions that you have, you were somehow more revolutionary than somebody else— which is not true. The ideology—each of those identities compiled representing truth—is a very revolutionary position but not necessarily the individual itself. You can have a totally reactionary lesbian of color. And yet people took the book so literally on many levels; some people still do.

So, you know, had I rewritten it, then I would have qualified things more because I work smarter now, hopefully. But you can't. So people are going to do what they're going to do.

K.I. Have you ever thought about publishing a revised edition of *This Bridge Called My Back* or editing another volume?

C.M. I don't want to do that. *Bridge* came out of pure need. At the time we worked on it, we didn't even think that it was going to be published. Both of us—Gloria Anzaldúa and myself—were virtually unpublished writers. Most of the women in that book, with the exception of Pat Parker, Audre Lorde, and Barbara Smith, were unpublished writers as well. So everything started just out of pure hunger. We needed to know that there was some place in the world—and this place was at least between the covers of this book—where being a lesbian of color was not a contradiction in terms. It was given validity. Not just validity—it also had a vision attached to it. I always believe that the book did so well because the motivation of the book was very pure. So the only time I would do another book like that would be when the circumstances were such that I was called to do that. This means that politically the times were such that I had an insight about what we needed and what really had to be written. It would have to be the same kind of situation. But that doesn't exist. I never felt the same motivation in terms of collective voices. I've only felt it with regard to my own personal work, but certainly not to collect work by other writers. Not that I would never do that again, maybe sometime in the future. But right now I don't really feel the strong motivation I need to put out the energy that something like that requires.

K.I. What is most important for you at the moment? Is it theater? Or is it educating younger Chicana writers to get into that area and to teach them how to be successful in that genre?

C.M. I wouldn't say it is exclusively theater. For me the most important thing really is to continue to get better, to write better and better. I just want to write better and better and better and better and better. And that may mean different genres; that may not mean exclusively theater. I feel kind of disheartened with theater right now. I am working on a longer work now, the novels. This genre is determined a lot by my own kind of evolution as a writer. My bottom line is always that I want to get better and better and better, which means keeping an open heart and an open mind.

And I love teaching. That doesn't mean just teaching theater. I love teaching people to be artists, and that can be as actresses, as creative writers, that can be as *teatrista* [special-effects person], that can be a lot of things. I like teaching at the university setting as well as in the community. As long as I am doing that, for now there is a sense of sanity in my work.

K.I. Speaking of teaching, in particular teaching young children and kids, one genre that seems to be very popular among Chicano and Chicana writers at the moment is children's books. Gary Soto and Pat Mora do it; even Gloria Anzaldúa published two children's books not long ago. Have you ever thought about writing a children's book yourself?

C.M. Yes, just because I have a kid now. I mean, the youngest children I teach are high school kids. I just do best with college age and people past puberty. I like to teach adults, too. In terms of doing a children's book, I mean, just by raising my child, there is so much to make stories about all the time. So there is always the possibility. Especially if I get broke, that's an easy way to make money. They are really fabulous, so yes, that's a possibility. I would just do it because it would be fun. But there is not so much motivation for me to do it. There are people who teach young people, really little kids. They are so good at it, so they should do it. I think I am a good mum, but I am not about teaching little kids. My sister is wonderful at it. She just loves small children and has spent her life doing that. She has the patience that I would never have. So I know my limitations on that level. I have one kid and that is enough.

K.I. How important is your family to you?

C.M. My family is very important to me. But I keep them separate from my own professional life. I have a very good family. They really love me. Like any young writer, I had to go through a lot of stuff in order to separate the fibers that have formed me. But now as a forty-four-year-old woman, I certainly see my parents less now as my parents and more as human beings with their own faults and their own beauty. And I feel a sense of peace about that. I consider myself very lucky to have such a large family and such an extended sense of what love is. That has nothing to do with how good you are professionally, how much money you make, and any of that. It's just about basic blood and loyalty, and that is very strong in my family, also rituals around family and rituals of spirituality. There are a lot of things you have to learn, but there is a real base of strong values that I reinforce to my child now as well. So I am blessed in that sense.

к.ı. Before finishing the interview, I would like to ask you about the goals you might have set for yourself as a person and a writer for the present and future.

c.m. I want to be a better and better and better writer, raise my child with love, be a good lover to my partner, to make family and to make art as well as I can do it, and as honestly as I can do it. That's it.

NOTE

1. Catherine Wiley, "Performance Review of *Shadow of a Man* by Cherríe Moraga," *Theatre Journal* 47/3 (Oct. 1995): 412–414.

BIBLIOGRAPHY

Poetry and Prose

1983 *Loving in the War Years: Lo Que Nunca Pasó por Sus Labios.* Boston: South End Press.
1993 *The Last Generation: Poetry and Prose.* Boston: South End Press.
1998 *Waiting in the Wings: Portrait of a Queer Motherhood.* Ithaca, N.Y.: Firebrand.

Plays

1985 "La Extranjera." Unpublished play.
1986 *Giving Up the Ghost: Teatro in Two Acts.* Los Angeles: West End Press.
1993 *Three Plays: Giving Up the Ghost, Shadow of a Man, Heroes and Saints.* Albuquerque: West End Press.
1996 "Watsonville: Some Place Not Here." First produced at Brava Theater Center, San Francisco, May 29–June 30, 1996. Not yet published.
2001 *The Hungry Woman: A Mexican Medea and the Heart of the Earth.* Albuquerque: University of New Mexico Press.

Coedited Volumes

1983 With Gloria Anzaldúa. *This Bridge Called My Back: Writings by Radical Women of Color.* New York: Kitchen Table, Women of Color Press.
      With Alma Gomez and Mariana Rommo-Carmona. *Cuentos: Stories by Latinas.* New York: Kitchen Table, Women of Color Press.
1988 With Ana Castillo. *Esta Puente, Mi Espalda: Voces de Mujeres Tercermundistas en los Estados Unidos.* ısm Press. Revised, bilingual edition of *This Bridge Called My Back.*

1991   With Norma Alarcón and Ana Castillo. *The Sexuality of Latinas.* Berkeley: Third Woman Press.

1993   With Ruth Forman. *We Are the Young Magicians.* Barnard New Women Poets' Series. Boston: Beacon Press.

1994   With Elba R. Sánchez and Francisco C. Alarcón. *Lenguas Sueltas—Poems: Anthology of Seventeen Chicano Latino Poets.*

Mary Helen Ponce

Author and University Instructor

"I prefer books to people, . . . [and] I am convinced that words can be used to color the world."

HOLLYWOOD, CALIFORNIA, FEBRUARY 10, 1997

CALIFORNIAN FICTION WRITER Mary Helen Ponce deals in her work with issues of everyday life in Mexican communities of the present and past, as well as with such topics as feminism, education, religion, and the effects of socialization. She pays particular attention to Pacoima, a neighborhood in the Los Angeles area where she grew up.

Ponce has published one short story collection, *Taking Control* (1987); a novel, *The Wedding* (1989); and her childhood autobiography, *Hoyt Street* (1993), which has also been published in a Spanish version, *Calle Hoyt* (1995). Her short stories, essays, and articles have appeared in several English- and Spanish-language journals, magazines, and collections in the United States and Mexico.

Mary Helen Ponce was born on January 24, 1938, in the San Fernando Valley in southern California and grew up among first- and second-generation Mexicans. She has six older sisters as well as three older brothers and a younger one. After high school Ponce, just seventeen, got married and had her first child. A few years later she and her husband divorced, and she had to support her child as a single parent. She eventually remarried and had three more children, and for several years she was a mother and suburban housewife or "house frau," as she calls herself. After earning a B.A. and an M.A. in Mexican American studies at California State University at Northridge, Ponce won a Danforth Fellowship to enroll in the UCLA history program. After her efforts to develop an interdisciplinary Ph.D. program combining history and literature at UCLA didn't work out, Ponce left California and went to the University of

New Mexico at Albuquerque (UNM). In 1995 she was awarded a Ph.D. in American studies after completing a dissertation on the life and works of the pioneer Hispanic New Mexican Fabiola Cabeza de Baca, who had lived at the turn of the century. Ponce then returned to southern California, and she now lives by herself in the Los Angeles area, where she splits her time between creative writing, free-lance writing for the *Los Angeles Times*, and teaching university classes, including remedial studies, English, literature, women's studies, and a course she created, "Chicano Literature from a Historical Perspective."

Two characteristics of Ponce's writing are her verbalization of unspoken questions and interjection of humor when least expected. Memory is also a key element for Ponce to explore, allowing her to combine both of her great loves: writing and history. In *Taking Control* Ponce portrays exploited Mexican Americans who are finally able to improve their situation, become independent, and take control of their lives. This outcome contrasts markedly with the experience of the characters in *The Wedding*, Ponce's first novel, which is written in a mixture of Spanish, English, and the author's personal version of the vernacular Caló. Doing so, Ponce tries to give the reader a glimpse of the reality of barrio subgroups and, above all, of the inferior position of women, particularly as seen in the situation of the protagonist, Blanca Muñoz. Blanca is a young working-class woman and high school dropout. In a self-deceiving manner, she determines to make her wedding the fulfillment of all her dreams and the climax of her life. Clichés, old-fashioned concepts, stereotypes, rituals, and traditions are key elements in Ponce's stories about the experience of young Mexican Americans growing up in southern California in the 1950s. Critics were initially divided over whether *The Wedding* should be seen as merely an uncritical presentation of stereotypes, or a way to correct stereotypes by making people aware of them.

Having realized that everyday events were worth writing about and that the stories of her own life were, in their own way, "history," Ponce wrote *Hoyt Street*, published in English in 1993 and in Spanish in 1995. Ponce's autobiography is set in Pacoima, a little town north of Los Angeles, and recalls her childhood experiences there in the 1940s and 1950s. *Hoyt Street* was very well received by readers and critics alike.

Ponce started writing for the *Los Angeles Times* in the mid-1990s, but a writing grant has recently allowed her to concentrate fully on her creative writing. She is working on four books, including her second collection of short stories and a fictive piece on the life of Fabiola Cabeza de Baca. Besides her strong interest in pioneer Mexican, Hispanic, and Mexican American women, Ponce will continue to concentrate on women's issues, particularly the concerns of minority women in the United States and throughout the world.

KARIN IKAS Could you tell us a bit more about yourself, your family background, your education, how you were raised?

MARY HELEN PONCE I had a very, very nice and happy childhood in southern California. Like many women of my generation, I married very young. I got divorced and had a son from that marriage. Then I was a working mother for a few years before I married again. My second marriage is my first marriage, really, because the other one was not. I had three children from this marriage. Altogether I have four children now, one daughter and three sons. For many years I was a homemaker. And I always read and read and read. It was always a lot of college material I read, although I couldn't attend a college when I was growing up as there were no programs and no colleges nearby.

Then in the seventies, at the times of the Chicano movement, my nephews were in college, and they finally motivated me to think about going to college again, as they kept saying, "Aunt, you are always reading. You should go to college!" So when my youngest child started kindergarten, I applied for college and was accepted at California State University at Northridge. First I was there just for fun. But then I decided to go for a degree. During the following four years I had to be a kind of supermom as I had to do everything on my own: send the kids up to school, dash up to college, then later on dash out of class, pick up the little one, and go home, where my middle one was already waiting. I was housewife, mother, and student at the same time, and so my life changed quite a bit. However, my children's life didn't, and that was very important to me. I always wanted them to have a home, to have hot meals and everything. You know, my generation, which is the fifties, was very much into homemaking, and I did this for a long time. Even today, when I write, I still find myself doing other things, domestic things like sewing, arranging flowers, pictures, and doing gardening. Like I said, I changed, but my environment didn't. My relatives and friends always knew that I read a lot, and my father was very proud of me, as he was himself an enthusiastic reader. Of course, some other people thought I might be crazy, and I remember someone asking me, "What are you planning to do?" And I just answered, "Well, educate myself and best educate my children."

In 1978 I graduated with a B.A. in Chicano studies and anthropology, and I had a great party and was very happy. Then I went to graduate school, as I didn't want to work just with a B.A. Additionally, as my son was still very young at that time, working on my master's gave me the possibility to work and study more at home and also take care of him instead of working most of the time outside the home. And as I was socialized to be at home, be a homemaker, I really liked it in a way, too. In 1980 I graduated in the same department at California State University at Northridge. This time I did a lot of work in women's studies. Back then women's studies was just beginning to approach the disciplines in the eighties. I minored in women's studies. I never took a creative writing class although I was always writing short stories.

My autobiography, *Hoyt Street,* was first just a collection of short stories as well, and actually even started as a research paper for a folklore seminar for which I had to study three generations of my family and how they observed Easter. While collecting specifics about Easter traditions in particular, I got more and more interested in other events, cultural elements, et cetera, that shaped daily life for the people in my hometown back then as well. So finally it turned out to be that I was writing a kind of social history of my childhood, my family, and friends based on all the stories I had collected, but also very much based on my own memory. I wrote about what I recalled and what others had told me. *Hoyt Street* is written out of memory, and not according to facts I could have researched on Pacoima's history.

I collect stories and write in my head. That is why I do not have to plot things. However, now and then I put together little anecdotes from my children, funny things they did in school for example.

So I was always reading and writing—reading because books somehow have been my friends more than people. I prefer books to people, honestly. It is not that I do not like people, but I get a lot from books.

K.I. What were your favorite books and authors back then?

M.H.P. As a teenager my favorite books were *Lorna Doone, Wuthering Heights, Rebecca,* and *Jane Eyre.* My favorite author was Daphne du Maurier, who wrote of the English moors, but I read a lot of other European and American literature as well. When I went to college, I then discovered all the Mexican, Latin American, and Spanish literature. Of the Mexican and Latin American writers, I like Elena Garro, Elena Poniatowska, Rosario Castellanos, the poets Homero Ardijiz, Jaime Sabines, and the Peruvian writer Ciro Alegría.

Also I like the Egyptian writers like Naguib Mahfouz, for example. Of the European writers I read Leo Tolstoy, Vladimir Nabokov, Graham Greene, just to name a few, and, of course, feminist writers like Simone de Beauvoir. I love Tennyson's "Charge of the Light Brigade" and if I tackle poetry, I will try for epic poems.

I am also familiar with the works of Nadine Gordimer and several American writers like Jane Smiley and Peter Taylor, who is one of my favorite narrators. Also I like Robert Frost, Emily Dickinson, and Ralph Waldo Emerson.

So, that is how I got my education. I just read a lot.

K.I. Why did you become a prose writer?

M.H.P. I like words, many words, and that is why I have always been a prose writer. I enjoy poems as well, but I don't feel comfortable writing them. You have so many restrictions in poetry, and I don't like that. Additionally, I hate lyric verse, and I am not so much into handling meter so far. However, lyricism in literature is nevertheless quite important to me. I think through the good use of metaphors, new words, sounds, inflections, you are able to create a particular emotional tone of a literary piece that transcends the mundane, and that's what lyricism is to me. Of course, it is not easy to achieve, but I am working on it in my works. To me good writing means good word usage, no matter whether it is in prose, poetry, or drama. So, once again, I love words, and I love to use them. However, I think I just like too many words for poetry, and that is why I prefer prose. At home I have a lot of dictionaries. I like to look up new words, check for additional meanings of old words. A friend even bought me *A Superior Person's Use of English*, and it is hilarious. I am convinced that words can be used to color the world. That is something I learned from my father. He was very fond of reading as well, and he even taught himself to read both Spanish and English. I think of him a lot when I write.

My love for words and good language is one reason why I miss teaching, too. When I teach, I am always reaching for the best level of language. I want to be an instructor who uses a language students can learn from and aspire to.

K.I. Could you tell a bit more about your career as writer and teacher?

M.H.P. In 1980 I got a job as a health educator. It was another one of the many part-time jobs I had in between when the kids were out of school. Just for the whim, I then applied to the University of California at Los Angeles's history program. And, surprisingly enough, after having had an interview on the phone, I was accepted; actually I had even won the very prestigious Dorothy Danforth Fellowship. For the following two years I was in that program, and I loved it. However, I wanted to write historical fiction, and I could not get a program together in that area. I talked to two professors in the English department who would work for me, but no one in history, as they have a very traditional program. Maybe if I had had a mentor, somebody to work with, it would have been easier to work something out. But there was no one there to support my efforts.

Actually, I have always been alone. That is just something I am, a loner, at least up to a certain degree. I have always worked alone as there were hardly any women in my age group to be found at universities. They didn't even go to colleges to begin with. None of them was writing research papers, and so there was nobody to whom I could talk. And even today I am still very isolated.

At UCLA I did a lot of research on my own as well. However, after having been there for two years, then I still couldn't get my Ph.D. program together. I mean, I still couldn't get ready for the seminars or start writing my dissertation as there was nothing there that really appealed to me. One day my UCLA adviser said to me, "Mary Helen, go where the program is. There is a discipline called American civilization/American studies. Look into it." This was in 1987. In between I taught literature and poetry at Cal State Northridge. I taught there with my old professors, which was a lot of fun. However, I kept in mind what my UCLA adviser had told me: "I think what you need is American studies." As I did not have a clear picture of what American studies was, I researched it. I went to the library, where I found just two books on American studies. That shows you how new American studies was at that time. By reading the two books, I realized that American studies seemed to be so collective, it was everywhere, multidisciplinary. So I researched all the programs in American studies nationwide. There was one in California. As I preferred to stay in California, I tried this one first, but I couldn't even get ahold of the professors, and there were just two of them for the whole program anyway. The next programs were in New Mexico, Pennsylvania, and New York. New Mexico had a good program, good instructors, and scholars there, as I read a lot of the dissertations put out at that time by women there and I liked what I saw. Besides, it was not that far away. By then my children were more or less on their own and were out of the home. So I decided to go and get my Ph.D. at the University of New Mexico at Albuquerque. I was there for four years. In 1991 I came to the University of California at Santa Barbara (UCSB) to do the dissertation fellowship. At that time my younger son was a student at UCLA, and my daughter went to New York to work with Sony, Inc. She had attended UCSB before but left in her third year to form a rock band. She is a publicist now. My older sons were more or less settled. So things seemed to be settled in that context, and it was now time for me to find out what I wanted. I just refused to think that it was too late for me because I followed what was out there, like the writing and all these things. And I felt that I had something to say. Therefore, I began to publish very, very quickly, and it was in 1981 that my first piece was published. It was a short story entitled "The Dress." It appeared in *El Popo,* the CSUN Chicano studies student newspaper, in May 1981.

So I am a latecomer in many ways. At that time anyone else, like a lot of the writers I knew, my friends, for example, had already been writing, and some had even published as well. So I worked hard and published very quickly, too. I felt that it was important as I was writing history in a sense and doing a kind of historical reconstruction by my writing, I would say. My autobiography, *Hoyt Street,* is a good example for that way of writing, I think.

However, I had written short stories already before that. So I put them together into a short story collection entitled *Taking Control.* Arte Público Press accepted it very quickly for publication in 1987. Then two years later *The Wedding,* my first novel, was published. *The Wedding* came very quickly, and I wrote it very differently from how it finally was published. But I am going to tell you more about that later on.

After *The Wedding* I published a monograph entitled "The Life and Works of Five Hispanic New Mexican Women Writers" for the Center of Regional Studies at the University of New Mexico at Albuquerque. It was part of the grant. Next came the working paper, the monograph of *Hoyt Street,* in 1993. Then there was my dissertation, which is about the biography of Fabiola Cabeza de Baca, a pioneer Hispanic woman writer from New Mexico who was born in 1894. Then, later in 1993 the hardcover edition of *Hoyt Street* was published. The paperback edition followed in 1995. The same year I finished the translation of *Hoyt Street* into Spanish, and Anchor/Doubleday published it under the title *Calle Hoyt* in 1995.

K.I. One piece you published is quite different from all the publications you just mentioned. It is more of a sociocultural study, entitled "Latinas and Breast Cancer." I believe that this essay is the result of your working experience at a cancer clinic in Los Angeles, correct?

M.H.P. Yes, you are right. I worked for ten months as a health educator for the White Memorial Medical Center Cancer Clinic in Los Angeles. The article you are referring to is part of that experience there. It deals with all the cultural elements and traditions that are often responsible that so few Latinas do not go to have a breast examination at all. The essay was published in 1982. Not long ago I have written another article on that issue. It is entitled "Cultural Schizophrenia among Latinas." It has just been accepted for publication by *Saludos* magazine and will be published in the August 1997 issue. So as you can see, I still deviate in my writing.

K.I. What is your focus in writing at the moment?

M.H.P. Part is, of course, this somehow sociocultural writing, like the articles we just talked about. "Cultural Schizophrenia among Latinas," for example, is about successful Latina women who are still entrapped in that schizophrenia of being split between a very successful professional life and a very nonemancipated life at home. For example, they come home and then they have to do all of the home work on their own, like taking out the garbage and doing the cooking, as their husbands tell them that this is simply their job as women and wives. And they simply accept that. In this essay I talk about how dangerous this schizophrenia, this state of being split, is, and how nobody talks about it and just follows the old traditional customs instead.

Also I wrote articles for the *Los Angeles Times,* and I loved it. But then I stopped doing that for a while because I was constantly turning around for new topics and getting into that whole thing with time pressures, et cetera. To give you an example: One day I heard about a daughter of a friend of mine who was insulted at school. The parents were both professionals, and I immediately felt that these things could happen to my kids and me as well. So I wanted to write an article about the whole incident, but I didn't have time to think about it, polish it and so on. The story had to be written and published right away to keep it interesting for people, like it is with all daily news. So I was beginning to see that I was getting more and more into those intense moments with all that pressure of deadlines, et cetera, and I realized that this is what journalism actually is. Therefore, I now try not to get too much involved in journalism. However, I just completed an article on Latina gangs in Echo Park, California. It is mostly a rebuttal about how others write of Latina gangs from L.A. suburbs and give negative images. I criticize that and ask, "Why are there hardly any positive images of Latinas and Latinos?"

K.I. What is your working day like?

M.H.P. At the moment I write from 5 A.M. to 8 A.M. or 9 A.M. Then I jog or walk. Afterwards I do some other stuff and later on go back to writing. Also, I read several hours each day, in particular different newspapers as well as articles and information provided by the Internet.

Right now I am writing full-time as I am on a kind of self-imposed sabbatical. Before, I was at California State University at Long Beach, where I was recruited. However, I finished school and teaching in June 1996 and decided to take some time off. I might teach again in fall 1997. But until then I use the time off to clear up all the stories and books I have or am writing on. Also there was a lot of other stuff to do, like visiting my children and so on. Actually, since January 28, 1997, I am now approaching my writing as a job. I am a working writer, a full-time writer now until September 1997 or so. I do some other things, like giving lectures every now and then, too.

My lectures are on autobiography. I have even given lectures and presentations in Mexico City at El Colegio de México and at UNAM. One of the presentations I gave at UNAM was on Chicana literary history. It was later published in a book called *La Forma de Nuestras Voces*. It is a sort of bibliographic essay. I am very proud of it, anyway, as I translated it into Spanish myself, which was pretty difficult. Of course, they later changed a few things before publication, but more or less it was OK. I already got some experience in doing translations as I had translated some other texts before. And besides writing, I still do translations every now and then.

I just finished a new short story collection, and I am about to send that off. As soon as I get that done—and I gave myself for that till the end of February 1997—I am going to concentrate on a new piece.

K.I. What kind of writer are you? Do you revise a lot, for example?

M.H.P. I am very critical of my work, and yes, I do revise a lot. For example, I print out my manuscript after maybe the third revision. And I am still doing revisions later on.

In fact, I just finished the last revision of my new novella entitled "Passion for Jürgen," which takes place in Hamburg, Germany. The protagonist is Raymond, a Mexican American soldier stationed in Hamburg after World War II. He meets and marries Astrid, a young German woman, there. Astrid is a burn victim of British bombs. Raymond returns with her to the U.S. Much later Jürgen, Astrid's brother who is soon to enter medical school, visits them in the U.S. There he falls in love with Maren, Raymond's younger sister. However, Jürgen leaves Maren in order to marry a different woman back home in Germany. Maren has a breakdown then, of course. Years later Maren and Jürgen meet again. I like the tone of this work, but it is also tragic. Mostly I wanted to show the joy and pain of first love as the girl, Maren, is just fifteen, and Jürgen is about twenty. Then there is Jürgen's sister, Astrid, who is still suffering from burns. Here I wanted to show that young Germans also suffered a lot in the Third Reich and in World War II.

K.I. Before we started the interview you already told me that you are very interested in intercultural and cross-cultural aspects. What do you associate with intercultural understanding?

M.H.P. I associate with intercultural understanding the question of women, as this is a worldwide issue. Just think about female mutilation and all other forms of brutality, violence, and discrimination women have to suffer all over the world. One problem here is also that we are always looking at gross examples of oppression elsewhere, and we don't pay enough attention to all forms of oppressions we have already here in the United States. There is so much here in our society that has to be converted as well. And I think the Old World culture is still alive and well in many cultures. I call this cultural schizophrenia. We think we are so advanced. Yet if you can't change the world, it is always easy to go out and just preach a change. But real change has to start on a personal level. You have to start at home, in your family. So intercultural understanding for me is not investigating others but trying to be aware of the things that happen around yourself and in your life. In a broader context this also affects other people, other women in particular.

I am especially interested in the situation of other women. I read a lot about it. In all that literature and the articles you can see the oppression of women on all levels and throughout history. So the book I started not long ago will be a kind of historical fiction with regard to that. It is about the pioneering women who arrived in Alta California in 1775, the very first group who came. The majority of these women were married, some pregnant; one died, and others gave birth to their kids along the road. I did a seminar and a study on that. I am particularly interested in their motives: "Why did they do it?" Well, but on the other hand: "Why shouldn't they have done it?" as there were no prospects for them in Mexico anyway. Some of them were widows, so they had no one to wait there for them.

Because of my studies in anthropology I find it very, very, very difficult to write a story on an event without bringing in the social, historical, and the political. I have a tendency to look at everything holistically, like one does in anthropology. I see myself more and more as an anthropologist who writes fiction, because I am always interested in the way cultures interact.

K.I. Is your novel *The Wedding* a kind of fictionalized and maybe somehow an even satirical sociological study in that context?

M.H.P. A wedding is a whole world in itself. It is not just the wedding ceremony itself. There is so much more involved with it. Ramón Gutiérrez, who writes about marriage patterns in New Mexico in the seventeenth century, once said that "marriage is one of the institutions through which you can see so much, like property rights, the world of women, gender issues in general." So I think a wedding, in general, is a social history as well.

With regard to my novel *The Wedding*, it is a bit different, of course. In that novel I blend humor, irony, and love. It is a love story in a way, although sometimes a bit strange and exaggerated.

When I was at uc Santa Barbara, one of the instructors once asked me to come to talk to the class and also to listen to the reports students did on *The Wedding*. I went in there, and I could not believe how the students interpreted the novel. For example, they were saying that the novel is about gangs, alcohol, fights, and so on. So when it was my turn to speak, I told them, "You know, I keep thinking you read the wrong book." Then I kept talking to tell them that for me *The Wedding* is a love story. At that time, for a woman, a wedding implied a fundamental change towards respectability; it changed her status. It is also associated with love, happiness, new beginnings, and a rite of passage. The students were just listening to what I was saying, but nobody asked questions. Thus I think I was beyond them.

When I began to write *The Wedding*, I was experimenting at the beginning by trying to write a story from the retrospective. First I wanted to start the story with the death of a person looking back. Then I thought about writing something that had to do with a seamstress who sold dresses, also wedding dresses. And that's when I came across the whole thing with weddings and all that is associated with it, like the bride, the groom, the family, the job, every kind of wedding preparation, all the excitement around it, and so on.

But let me say that *The Wedding* is not autobiographical at all. I did not have weddings, and the weddings I attended were totally different from the one in the novel. The wedding ceremony described in that novel is more like how weddings seemed to be like in my sister's generation, which is some time after World War II, like in the 1950s or 1960s. However, I do not refer to a specific year. I remember one year when I was a kid and there were a lot of weddings and excitement going on, partly due to the soldiers that had returned from the war then, and maybe that influenced me a bit in writing that novel.

The purpose of *The Wedding* is that I wanted to call attention to how few possibilities there were for women of my sister's generation. Actually, that is what the whole book is primarily about. The novel is, if you think about the time frame, timeless, as there is not a particular time explicitly stated. It is critical with regard to the priest, for example, as he is a racist, like several priests were at that time and still are. Then one important element is the issue of women bonding, the social prestige that goes along with the wedding, the dresses, and all that a wedding really means, especially for someone like Blanca, who had nothing else really.

K.I. Speaking about the protagonist, Blanca—some critics have blamed you for giving a too negative and stereotypical picture of her. Why did you portray her as a kind of weak, subordinate, naive, suffering, and poorly educated woman who tries to escape into her dream world of soap operas, fashion, and beauty advertisements and so on instead of trying to change and improve her own situation?

M.H.P. I portrayed Blanca that way because there were a lot of women around that time who were to some extent just like her: all these girls who were high school dropouts, who were kept home from school or who were put back at school as the teacher felt they had bad English, and all those things. I felt very depressed by that, and that is why I wanted to write about them and not about women like my sisters who were intelligent, pretty, and very ambitious although they were not college educated either. The girls portrayed in *The Wedding* were pretty and intelligent as well. It's just that for some, there was nothing to aspire to but to get married. It was a different class. Everything always has to do with class somehow. Therefore, it is hard to say I am not writing about class at all. I am just not writing about my own class in *The Wedding*. However, the class issue is there, of course. Also, it is important to me to make [people] aware of all those stereotypes, internalized role models, clichés, and discriminations by portraying them in the novel so that people actually start thinking about them.

K.I. It sounds like reconstructing stereotypes in order to deconstruct them.

M.H.P. Yes, that is exactly what it is. When I created the protagonist Blanca in *The Wedding*, it was important to me that she had to be true to what I saw and experienced myself at that time. I mean, today Blanca might be one of the women who had become a bank president maybe, but not at her time in the fifties. This would not have worked according to what life and reality was like for women like her in my hometown Pacoima then.

K.I. There is a successful businesswoman in *The Wedding* anyway: Goldie Salomon, the owner of the bridal shop. However, she is from a different class and ethnic group, as she is of Jewish background. Do you use another stereotype here?

M.H.P. As I already said, the things I portray are more or less based on what I was told, saw, or remembered about the situation in Pacoima at the time I was growing up there. Of course, some things are imaginary as well. The name Goldie Salomon itself is already a kind of telling name. It shows you right away that the bridal shop owner, an Anglo woman, is of Jewish background. Also, it becomes quite evident in the story that she is very successful in her business. So that is a reference to the Jewish question, and the fact that they owned a lot of stores back then but were also considered as rip-offs. Another statement I make, that actually goes along with that somehow, is that the priest is very racist. However, he is not racist against Jews but only against Mexicans.

K.I. It seems that you are very much influenced by your environment, the area where you grew up, and the place you live, California. Would you agree with that?

M.H.P. Yes, of course. I am a Californian writer, and I am a very conscious regionalist. By that I mean that I am very conscious about how regions work into my work. The regional influence is just always there for me, whether I want it or not. Therefore, natural elements like the landscape, mountains, pine trees, and the Californian blue sky, for example, can always be found in my writing. The only typical Californian natural element I am not so much interested in is the ocean. I prefer more the interior landscape. I am much more fond of hiking than of walking along the beach. Anyway, I am strongly influenced by nature. That is why some critics, like Francisco Lomelí, have called me a naturalist. I am very conscious of the things that impact me, and as it is, I transport them into my protagonists.

Another major influence on me was the fact that I grew up in the shadows of Hollywood. When we saw a movie, the next day all us kids were having fun by trying to imitate some of the actors and actresses, wearing Maybelline makeup, et cetera. The whole notion of beauty and glamour was very important. And as it was in the postwar era, there seemed to be an even stronger urge and need for all that glamour. Very popular at that time, for example, were falsies, which meant stuffed bras, then tiny waists, wearing lots of makeup, and of course the colonial-style wedding dresses, the Scarlett O'Hara ones, were the hit of the day. That is why Blanca is wearing one herself in *The Wedding*. In my family my brother's wife had such a wedding dress at her wedding, too. So I was quite familiar with all that. Another thing is that brand names and products were and are still very important in California. And if you think about *The Wedding*, you can find many brand names in there, too.

So with regard to all that glamour and show, *The Wedding* is a kind of female *La Bamba* to me. Therefore, I would like to see it turned into a movie one day. In 1990, when I was at the University of New Mexico, I had already written a play based on this novel. It is entitled *Blanca's Wedding*, and it was almost staged by a theater group in Mesilla, New Mexico. The theater group was called Desert Playwrights. When I showed them *Blanca's Wedding*, they were very interested. Also, they told me that I have a very good ear for dialogue. Anyway, unfortunately at that time I didn't have enough time to revise the play according to the Desert Playwrights' specifications. However, I hope to get that done in the near future and then get it either performed, maybe even broadcasted, as I am about to think about a screenplay version, too. Actually, *Blanca's Wedding* comes close to a musical version of the novel *The Wedding* already. A musical would fit perfectly with the Californian culture portrayed by that piece. You know, there is all that Hollywood-influenced glamour, that car culture of zooming back and forth the freeways, the zoot suit era, importance of fashion, music, and, of course, there were also gang riots. All these things were a kind of substitute for the lack of education and so on. I hope that one day there will be a movie based on *The Wedding*. I don't want to be a producer myself, and I don't have much interest in screenwriting as well, but maybe someone else is going to do it.

K.I. What about the language you use in *The Wedding*? The vernacular language elements you include in the novel don't seem to fit exactly with the existing Caló.

M.H.P. You are right. It does not fit exactly as I just made it up. I created my own version of Caló, so to speak. I have been criticized for that quite a lot. But when I wrote the novel, there was just no language variety that seemed to fit with what I remembered how people were talking like in the fifties in Pacoima. Of course, there was English and Spanish and then Spanglish, as this mixture between English and Spanish was called. Caló was primarily the spoken language people identified with, in particular in the barrio. That Caló was the language that seemed to fit best for the characters of my novel. But at that time I could not find any dictionaries, grammar books, linguistic studies, et cetera, on Caló. So I had nothing to go by. It was very difficult for me to use that language for the novel because of that. In order to get a better hold of the language, I therefore watched movies that took place in a Latino cultural setting around that time. In these movies I often came across all those expressions like *chicks, bato, ese*. Other words I use are *nuttin* [nothing], *knock the chet outta her* [knock the shit out of her], *sumtin* [something], *jerk, okie dokie, don't cha*.

So to say it again, it is Caló what I use, but it is my kind of Caló. Actually, I don't know if I had consulted a Caló dictionary or grammar book—in case there would have been one there—at all. I didn't feel that I needed to. Also, I didn't write in Spanish as I was writing for an English-speaking audience primarily. And another thing is that I don't believe in sticking Spanish into my stories just because it is fashionable for Chicana writers or in order to show people that I know some Spanish as well, or a Spanish-speaking writer writes the book. I completely refuse that. What is important to me is that everything fits, the language as well. I don't use the vernacular language for all parts of the novel either because it does not fit with everything. So my language and sometimes the language mixture I use have to come naturally. It is a natural flow. I don't believe in sticking in words artificially.

K.I. How would you describe your ties with Mexico?

M.H.P. I don't have any strong roots down there in Mexico as my parents and family never went back to Mexico. Also, I didn't have any grandparents there whom I might remember. To me Mexico was an unknown country. Of course, I read a lot about Mexico, and I was always very fascinated by that country. And I am very fond of Mexican authors.

But, personally, I never had any family ties. That's why I had no firsthand experience in that sense with Mexico, Mexican family life, traditions, and so on.

K.I. But there are still elements of Mexican culture in your writing, right?

M.H.P. Yes, quite a lot. The music, the language, the food, religion—especially Catholicism—are areas that are very much influenced by Mexico and Mexican culture for me, whereas a characteristic like individualism I associate in particular with Anglo-American society. Mexicans and Mexican Americans to me have a better understanding of other cultures as well. All this can be seen in my writing. And I don't see myself wanting to write from the Anglo-American experience. It doesn't motivate me, as I associate that too much with vision, egoism, selfishness, not caring about each other, and things like that. That is not what I grew up with and how I felt. And I cannot write what I don't feel.

One thing that is very important for me is bread. I am a bread eater, and I write a lot about bread in my work. For me bread is a metaphor of home. My mother made homemade egg bread. Each time I smell *pan*, I think of home. In addition, I agree with a friend of mine who once told me, "You know the world is divided into two parts, those who have bread and those who don't have bread." Bread is universal. We all eat bread, and it can be found everywhere. Therefore, I researched bread. I read a lot about it, and I refer to it in many of my stories. This also comes together with my strong affinity for nature I already told you about at the beginning.

K.I. You are working on a new short story collection right now. Can you tell us a bit more about the focus of the stories?

M.H.P. At the moment I'm working on a book of essays called *Writing California*, which includes my articles published in the *L.A. Times* and other magazines. Also I work on the short story collection you just mentioned. So far I don't have a name for this new collection yet. Right now I call it just "second collection." I hope that I have it published next year, that is, in 1998. The stories in this forthcoming collection are more global than in the first one. This new book is divided into two parts: the first one deals more with the past, and the other one is more contemporary.

The first section, for example, begins with "Los Tísicos," a story that takes place in New Mexico in the 1930s and 1940s. Its prevailing theme is death and illness, in particular tuberculosis. The protagonist is a young girl. Then, after the scholarly work I did on the New Mexican pioneer woman Fabiola Cabeza de Baca, I wanted to write a fictional piece to see if I could capture her in fiction as well and make her come alive. So I wrote the short story "The American Way." It is a fictional account of one day in the life of Fabiola Cabeza de Baca. Also it is an effort to somehow supplement my research work on her. "The American Way" is already included in a book called *Confluencia*. It is going to be published by a woman at Hispanic studies, Northern Colorado University, Greeley. Another story in the first part of my forthcoming short story collection is entitled "Enero." *Enero* is the Spanish word for January, and it refers to the month I was born. I have written that story for my mother. I try to recapture her life and all the problems and pain she had to face and endure. "Enero" is being published in *Breves*, a journal in Paris, France, too. It is one of my better narratives.

Then the contemporary part of this new collection is included here. It is entitled "Chasing Nina Flor," a story about a married couple. Actually, this story is one of those that take place in my marriage, although I don't give any real specifics about my private life really. "Baja Shoes" deals with the impact of the U.S. on Mexican American and Mexican culture. It shows all the cultural conflicts (Mexican/Mexican American/Anglo-American) a Mexican American family has to face while going out camping with the kids to Baja California, Mexico. Although I don't want to be too didactic in that story, I deal with all these U.S.-Mexico border-crossing issues and the way they influence different aspects of daily life. Actually, "Baja Shoes" is a kind of continuation of "The Campout," a short story that deals with the same issues and which is part of my first short story collection, *Taking Control*.

The last section of the book then is more feminist. Also, I try to emphasize values like honesty, directness, reliability, and strength, and so on here. The story "Just Dessert" in that part is about divorce, feeling deserted, re-dating, and all these things. The title is a play on words. Another story is "Sisters." It is about a sister-sister relationship and about how a woman tries to get together with her sister, tries to be honest and direct. So it is about how relatives debate directness. As I like to be strong, one of my favorite stories is the one entitled "Real Man." It deals with strength in women and the fact that women who are too strong, too healthy, and too big intimidate most men. So I write here about a woman who is quite big and strong, stronger than a lot of men are. She works out a lot and she beats everybody running against her. Although men like strong women up to a certain degree, they are completely frightened by too much female strength and power. But that doesn't matter to the female protagonist of the story that much. What is more important is that she likes herself and that she is very comfortable with herself. Another story is called "The Enemy Camp," and it takes place in an academic setting. It deals with the relationship between straight women and lesbian women, homophobia, et cetera. It shows how very quickly the whole issue of being gay or heterosexual divides us. It is about a feminist writing group that splits after a while into two groups, as heterosexual women seem to be petrified to sit with lesbians, talk to them, and so on. But it shouldn't be that way because we are all feminists and should be supportive of other women, show solidarity, et cetera. In order to initiate a change, we thus have to ask ourselves, "Why do we split?" and "What can we do about it?" By the way, "The Enemy Camp" is based on a personal experience I once had when I was in New Mexico a couple of years ago. While being at the University of New Mexico at Albuquerque I met a student in class who was lesbian. She told me a lot about all the prejudices and the differences she has to face every day. One day she came up to me and said, "You know, Mary Helen, I think the enemy camp is within us all and you should write about all these issues to make them more aware." What struck me most about all that was the expression or quotation "enemy camp," which stayed with me. So I looked it up in the dictionary. I learned that Miguel de Cervantes first used this term in order to refer to all of these internalized ways of behavior and thinking that are most difficult to overcome. In my story I use this quotation in the preface. Then I apply it in particular to women, to the problems in their relationship with each other, to labeling and fear.

K.I. How is your relationship with Chicana lesbian writers? Do you feel that there are many differences between heterosexual and homosexual Chicana writers in general?

M.H.P. I include lesbian fiction when I teach. I use books by Cherríe Moraga and Gloria Anzaldúa like *This Bridge Called My Back* and the one edited by Carla Trujillo, entitled *Chicana Lesbians: The Girls Our Mothers Warned Us About,* for example. I teach them just as I do any other work. Some students feel uncomfortable about that, others don't. I believe that if this is what Chicanas are writing, I should call attention to it. I like students to respect all literature. They can critique it, but it always has to be within the context of the particular work. Very few students get personal, however. I think it is mostly the males who feel threatened.

There are some differences in lesbian writing, of course, like some subjects and themes in particular, but I wouldn't say that there are major differences.

K.I.   Do you have any affiliations with Anglo-American feminism? Are there some theories and writings that influenced you?

M.H.P.   I am totally out of that. I am not into anything because I am very isolated, and I am just into my writing. However, what is important to me is spirituality. In that context, the French Simone Weil, a communist, somehow influences me. Also I like Simone de Beauvoir.

With regard to all those labels and theories around, like deconstruction, et cetera, that are so popular at the moment—I have to say that I am more a constructionist than a deconstructionist. I prefer to stay at home and work on the construction of my work instead of getting involved in deconstruction. I don't want to peck myself, but nevertheless I am very supportive of women. Nowadays, people are very angry, but I am not. So sometimes I feel that I was born in the wrong century, as I am not futuristic at all. Instead, I look back because I would like to understand what happened to the women that came before me. The past is important to me. I believe that we learn from the past. I was born looking back; that is to say, that I have always liked history and what came before me.

K.I.   How does your strong interest in history affect your feeling about your roots, or nonroots, with Mexico, as you mentioned earlier that you can't think of any family ties with Mexico? Did you ever think about searching for your Mexican roots?

M.H.P.   I don't know my Mexican roots. I have researched my Mexican family history only to find that there is very little. People from the ranch—like my ancestors—did not always document their lives. I had no grandparents because my family never met or were looking for grandparents, uncles, aunts, or other family members who might be still in Mexico. Of course, I know my parents' history. I write about it in *Hoyt Street*. But what I mean is that I never had a close affiliation with Mexico except to the sixteenth of September, the Mexican Independence Day, when my father wrote poetry. But as there was not a lot of Mexican nationalism in my own family, there never is any of that in my writing as well. That's why my work doesn't have all the nationalism in there that many other Chicano and Chicana writers have, in particular the ones from Texas who live in the border zone.

K.I.   You already mentioned before that you consider yourself a "truly Californian writer." If you think about the Chicana and Chicano writers in Texas you just referred to, for example, how would you describe the regional differences between Chicana and Chicano writers in general?

M.H.P. A lot of the people from Texas are always looking over their shoulders. I don't say they are paranoid. However, my friend says that is pretty much what it is due to their growing up in places like El Paso, where there is that horrible discrimination and the strong daily police presence. I am from California. When I was growing up, minorities were a bit more accepted here. Of course, there was a lot of covert discrimination. Covert discrimination means, for example, that you are hired for the best positions, but once you are in, they put you in the back again to clean or sweep. But they couldn't keep us down. The best football players were all Chicanos. They were all my heroes, as I always liked football players. All the Mexican American girls I went to school with were a lot prettier than white girls. You know, I was pretty, and my girlfriends were pretty as well. So we had a lot of fun. I didn't feel as if I was missing anything. And the thing is, I never wanted to be white. To me it seems that many people stress too much issues such as "everybody should like me," "if you are smart, marry white," and stuff like that. I didn't cope with that. I am very self-assertive and self-sufficient. Although I married Mexican Americans both times, my marriages were quite white in many ways, like the way we think and the way our kids are. My children have a lot of different cultural influences. But that's how it is in California. In Texas it is different. I think you don't have such a variety of influences over there.

K.I. How about New Mexico? You lived there for quite a while when you worked on your Ph.D. at the University of New Mexico at Albuquerque.

M.H.P. Well, it was a culture shock for me to live there. People there don't think in terms of being Mexican American but Hispanic. And Hispanic means being Spanish-oriented. They look towards Iberian Spanish, but that's not what it is at all anymore. There is a lot of confusion and anger between Chicanos and Hispanics in New Mexico because Hispanics deny their Mexican connection. And actually a lot of my students in New Mexico were blond, blue-eyed, redhead. If they told me they were Spanish, I said "Fine" and left them as it didn't matter. However, if you say things like that in California or Texas, people want to lynch you as there is a lot of anger there that has to do with race and class. In Santa Fe, New Mexico, you can't tell the Hispanics from the Anglos. They all have blue eyes, blond hair, et cetera. And the Hispanic woman I wrote my dissertation on, Fabiola Cabeza de Baca, for example, is white and blue-eyed, too.

K.I. Fabiola Cabeza de Baca belonged to the landed gentry. She is from a completely different social class than the typical contemporary Chicano/a writers since the 1970s. They are of working-class background. So far there are not so many middle-class Chicano/a writers out there yet. Would you agree?

M.H.P. Yes, you are right, the Chicano and Chicana writer in general isn't of middle-class background. We are working class and working-class writers. However, the thing is that we don't always write on the working-class experience even if our roots will always stay with us somehow, of course.

In my reading I look for well-developed works. As an essayist I like Richard Rodríguez. He is very controversial. I also like Alfredo Vea Jr., an attorney by profession. He has written a narrative piece called *Maravilla*. At the moment I read a lot of autobiography. I like good, big, fat books. The last autobiography I read was by a woman from Romania, Queen Marie of Romania.

What I like about Chicana writers like Gloria Anzaldúa, Cherríe Moraga, and others is that they have very important things to say. They have a vision, a feminist vision. I get inspiration from their work even though I don't have a feminist vision myself. Instead, I am looking back. I am stuck. Ideally what I want to write about are pre-nineteenth-century women.

K.I. As you don't intend to promote a particular feminist vision by your writing, would you say that the genre of essay and critical writing is not that attractive for you?

M.H.P. I have written a bunch of essays. I might put them together one day to publish them in one collection. But usually I am not so much into writing critical essays myself. To me an essay is a very high form of writing, and I have very high standards myself. I don't write loosely, and I don't appreciate any writing that is that way. But that is me. Therefore, I prefer to wait for the critics to tell me. On the other hand, a lot of women writers want to create a new canon by writing differently from men. They don't want an introduction, transition, body, and theme. How that has worked, I don't know. I have other standards. As I read so much, I tend to look at works that flow. I like Joyce Carol Oates, for example.

However, her last book, titled *We Were the Mulvaneys,* disappointed me, as it is too disjointed. Some chapters are too long, others too short, and so on. At least the message of the book is still quite good.

K.I. You seem to be influenced by many different literatures. Also, you mentioned that you don't know much about your Mexican roots. Do you call yourself a Chicana writer at all then?

M.H.P. I am a Chicana writer. I am isolated just in terms of geography because of the place I live. Among Chicana writers I have many friends, like Silvia López-Medina, Roberta Fernández, Norma Cantú, and Sandra Cisneros. Helena María Viramontes, whom I knew ages ago, is a very good friend as well. Everybody, all my friends, are also colleagues. And then I have my "historical" or "homemaker" friends. They know nothing about literary criticism, but I really enjoy talking with them about domestic stuff like cooking, et cetera.

K.I. Is there a vivid correspondence and exchange of criticism and ideas about each other's writing among Chicana writers?

M.H.P. No, not at all. I have never been asked to give my comment on their works except one time. Helena María Viramontes and I had once an exchange. It was just a one-time exchange, and I don't even remember the subject. Otherwise, I prefer to work alone, which is not very good, I know. Therefore, right now I am considering thinking more about working together with others by getting more involved in editing work. Actually, two years ago I edited a collection of autobiographical pieces written by Virginia Dale, a friend of mine who lives in Santa Barbara. It is called *Never Marry in Morocco.* As I was the primary editor of that book, I had to decide how to put all the different pieces in a certain order. It turned out that I edited quite well. So this experience taught me that I could be an editor, too. I edited well, and I really liked it. But at the moment it takes too much time and energy away from my writing. Right now I prefer to concentrate more on my writing, as I want to be an even harder-working writer and a professional one.

However, when you write your own book, you have to do editorial work in a way as well. For example, in *Hoyt Street* all the pieces written had to do with Catholicism. So I divided the book into three parts that go along with that: the Age of Innocence, the Age of Reason—when you get your first communion—and then the Age of Knowledge.

K.I. You just mentioned Catholicism, the predominant religion among Mexicans and Mexican Americans. Are you Catholic as well? If not, how would you describe your religious belief?

M.H.P. I am a practicing Catholic. I pray a lot and the scriptures are very important to me. I was baptized and raised Catholic already. My children are Catholic as well. However, I don't share all the beliefs and postulates of the Catholic Church. For example, I am pro-abortion, but I also believe in the right to live.

K.I. How about female archetypes like La Llorona and the Virgin de Guadalupe?

M.H.P. I grew up with a literary tradition but not with a very eminent oral tradition. My parents were no storytellers at all. Of course, I was familiar with La Llorona, but she was not a very dominant figure for me. Neither was La Virgen de Guadalupe.

In our church the Virgen de Guadalupe is in many ways very Mexican. When I was growing up our priest was white. He even gave honors to the Virgin Mary, the Catholic European one who was white and had blue eyes. The Virgen de Guadalupe was nothing more than a head in a picture hidden somewhere in a corner of the church. Therefore, I grew more accustomed to the white Virgin Mary. I always grew up with the idea that the Virgen de Guadalupe was not that important, and that the only one we should really worship was the Virgin Mary. Furthermore, the Virgin Mary spoke English and I spoke English, too. So there was this connection in terms of language already there for me. I think that was also a way of socialization, to socialize people by language and religion. The priest was very progressive anyway.

No one in my family has ever had home altars. My father didn't like altars. As he read a lot, he knew the history of the *cristeros* in Mexico and so forth. Thus, I am very socialized in that context. However, I have a strong need to know my Mexican side, and I wish somehow my name had been María Elena. I think when they took away my name, they took a lot more.

K.I. Speaking about your name: There are different versions of how your name is written, like "Mary Helen" or "Merrihelen." Which one is correct?

M.H.P. Merrihelen Ponce Adame was my name for more than twenty years. While I was married, my married name was Adame. The first name in my birth certificate is María, but it is also María Helena. My pen name—childhood name—is Mary Helen. But I changed this to Merrihelen when I was in grammar school as there were too many Mary Helens there. At the time I started writing and publishing, my first name therefore was Merrihelen.

K.I. Do you have any plans for writing a children's book, like many Chicano/a writers do at the moment?

M.H.P. The protagonist in my book "Pioneering Women 1775" [not published] is a young girl twelve years old. I think I write particularly for adults, and that is why I never thought about writing a children's book.

K.I. What will be your priority in the future: teaching or writing? Do you intend to pursue your academic career, as you already have your Ph.D.?

M.H.P. Writing will be my priority in the future. I will teach just one or two classes a semester. It might seem to be a waste of my Ph.D. not to continue my academic career that strongly, but I don't see it that way, as I continue to give lectures every now and then. Everything is relative anyway. I have an essay coming out in *Women Studies Quarterly* next August–September. It is about why I write. Actually I published this essay elsewhere already, but it was not edited to my satisfaction at all. There was too much "I" in there. So I rewrote it. It is going to be included in the special issue of *Women Studies Quarterly* on Immigrant Women Writing. I am not an immigrant woman, of course. However, I write about the immigrant experience, and I was asked to contribute. So I went back to the already mentioned essay, rewrote and polished it, and handed it in for publication. But as I already said earlier in the interview, I am not so much into essay writing. I prefer to do a more comprehensive work, which I did then with *Hoyt Street*.

K.I. What kind of books can we expect from you in the near future?

M.H.P. Well, there are actually four books to come. First there is my dissertation about that nineteenth-century Hispanic woman writer Cabeza de Baca. It is to be published as a book entitled *The Life and Works of Fabiola Cabeza de Baca, 1894 to 1990*. Then I have a contract to write the biographies of other notable Mexican women writers of that time. Also to come is my second short story collection. In between, I write on a variety of subjects for the *L.A. Times*. I almost got a contract there in the editorial section a long time ago, but then right before that they fired about seven hundred workers and discontinued their Hispanic supplement.

I speak in particular to a Spanish-speaking public, which is very important to me. I would like to be a voice for Latinos, specifically for women in San Fernando Valley. But I also find that a lot of my work is universal. Like the piece I wrote on the environment and, in particular, on trees. Whether I will always primarily publish for a Spanish-speaking public is debatable. I have a lot of materials, and we will see what I am going to do with all that in the future.

K.I. How do you handle criticism?

M.H.P. Not being able to deal with criticism is what holds a lot of writers back. So I think it is very important to learn how to handle criticism. I have received very good reviews, so in many ways I am very spoiled. *Hoyt Street* got marvelous reviews, *The Wedding* got good reviews except for one, and *Taking Control* was received very well, too. I have consistently gotten very, very good reviews for all my work. But all that good criticism doesn't mean that I am not going to try even harder.

Except for the dissertation, I don't write much critical analysis, although everything—like discussions, et cetera—is a form of analysis. I teach literary theory as part of course work, but I am not all that interested in deconstruction, et cetera. I have read Hélène Cixous, and others. Also, I listen to editors. I am quite aware that there are always certain trends around among editors, publishers, and agents, but I don't write the Danielle Steel–type of women in the Chicano/a experience. I would never write that way. In Mexico my writing is considered very serious social history. It is very well accepted there. In France one of my short stories, "Enero," appeared in French in *Breves*, a journal published in Paris.

It is very nice to be contacted by people like the editors at Graywood Press. They read a lot of Chicano/a fiction. As they liked my work a lot, they called me, and all that shows me that craft is very important and is recognized in the end.

K.I. If you think about the publication of your books, were there many problems you had to face?

M.H.P. I never had any real problems with publishers. Well, except once, when I had some difficulties with the publisher I first had in mind for *Hoyt Street*. He wanted to split the book in two parts. I completely refused that. In the end, it turned out that I was right, of course. In order to avoid such things with the new publisher, I had to set a lot of conditions before I finally signed with UNM Press, which got *Hoyt Street* published then.

Additionally, I chose to participate in the translation of *Hoyt Street* into Spanish. However, had I known before how much work and time a translation like that would mean, I don't think I would have done it. But anyway, while teaching at UCLA I met Monica Maria Rubalcava, a student majoring in Spanish literature. She was 100 percent proficient in Span-

ish and English. I had her translate a short work of mine and also re-
quested the same of other people I was considering for doing the translation. Finally, I decided for Monica. I secured her contract with
Anchor/Doubleday to translate *Hoyt Street*. She did the initial or rough
draft of *Hoyt*. Then she and I worked together. I reread and revised the
manuscript four times altogether. It took all my summer in 1994, but I
wanted the translation to be perfect as well. Finally, in 1995 the Spanish
edition, entitled *Calle Hoyt: Recuerdos de una Juventud Chicana,* was published by Anchor/Doubleday.

Speaking about *Hoyt Street*, I would like to come back to what I have
already mentioned before; namely, that I do believe it is craft that in the
end will stand out. *Hoyt Street* is a very well-crafted book. Each single
story in there is very polished. All the good reviews I got for that book
seem to prove me right in that, too.

K.I. In *The Wedding* a lot of the characters have telling names. Do you
often choose names on purpose for your stories?

M.H.P. I have many stories in which I chose the characters' name on
purpose. Just think about the protagonist in *The Wedding*, for example.
Her name is Blanca, and that stands for "bleached," "white and pure," of
course. Other telling names I have in *The Wedding* are: Cricket, El Pan
Tostado, Porky—as I use the name for an overweight twelve-year-old
girl who likes nothing better than to eat—Lucy, which stands for "light,"
you know, like "Lucy in the sky," and several others I can't think of right
now. Then there is the protagonist in "The Permanent." Her name is
Altagracia, which stands for "high grace." In "Enero," one female character I call Constancia, and she is meant to represent the type of woman
that is a constant mother. So the name always carries with it a certain
message or a certain image that fits with the way the individual character behaves or looks.

K.I. What about your story "El Marxista," in which you portray a self-
ish, egoistic, and hypocritical Marxist? Is it based on a real experience?

M.H.P. Yes, it is based on an event that actually happened. A friend of
mine once had a similar encounter with a hypocritical Marxist politi-
cian. And I wrote the story similar to what she had told me about that
experience.

By the way, people really seem to love the "El Marxista" story. They
told me so quite often. All the college professors like that story as well.
Some even said to me, "That's exactly how it is in reality." Right now, a
friend of mine is even writing a screenplay based on "El Marxista."

K.I. One final question: If you had to describe yourself in just one sentence, what would you say?

M.H.P. I was born a writer.

BIBLIOGRAPHY

Books

Fiction

1987 *Taking Control.* Houston: Arte Público.

1989 *The Wedding.* Houston: Arte Público.

1993 *Hoyt Street: An Autobiography.* Albuquerque: University of New Mexico Press.

1995 *Hoyt Street: Memories of a Chicana Childhood.* Paperback. New York: Anchor Books.

Calle Hoyt: Recuerdos de una Juventud Chicana. New York: Anchor/Double-day.

Nonfiction

1992 "The Lives and Works of Five Hispanic New Mexican Women Writers, 1878–1991." Working Paper #119. Albuquerque: Southwest Hispanic Research Institute, University of New Mexico.

1995 "Escritoras Chicanas: Una Perspectiva Historica-Literaria (1936–1993)." In *Las Formas de Nuestras Voces: Chicana and Mexicana Writers in Mexico,* ed. Claire Joysmith. Mexico City: UNAM.

"The Life and Works of Fabiola Cabeza de Baca, New Mexican Hispanic Writer, 1894–1990: A Contextual Biography." Ph.D. diss., Albuquerque, University of New Mexico.

Short Stories/Articles/Essays

Fiction

1982/ "La Despedida," "Las Guisas," and "Los Vatos." In *Maize: Chicano Studies*
1983   *Anthology* (San Diego: University of California Press) 1/6 (fall–winter).

1983 "Cuando la Lia Got Engaged." In *Third Woman* 2/1 (1984): 53–56.

"The Funeral of Daniel Torres." In *Chismearte* (Los Angeles Latino Writers Association) (June).

"Los Piojos." In *Miniondas* (San Antonio, Texas), Oct. 7. Also published in *La Opinión* (Los Angeles), Sept. 16, and in *La Semana* (El Paso) Sept. 16.

1984 "Chochis and the Movies at Sanfer." In *Southern California Anthology* (UCLA) 1\1 (Dec.).

"Cuando Ibamos a la Nuez," "Los Piojos." In *Fem: Revista Cultural Feminista* (June–July).

"La Doctora Barr," "Los Piojos," "How I Changed the War and Won the Game." In *Woman of Her Word: Hispanic Women Write.* Houston: Revista Chicano-Riqueña.

1985 "Good Friday" and "Los Calzones de la Piña." In *Hispanic Link* (Washington, D.C.) (April).

"Holy Week." In *Nuestro Magazine* (Washington, D.C.).

"La Semana Santa." In *Fem: Revista Cultural Feminista* (Mexico City). Also in *La Opinión* (Los Angeles).

"My Boyfriend Lupe F." In *Nuestro Magazine* (Washington, D.C.) (June–July).

1986 "El Color Rojo" and "Remendar." In *Fem: Revista Cultural Feminista* (Mexico City).

"Los Tísicos." In *Southwest Tales in Memory of Tomás Rivera: A Contemporary Fiction Collection.* San Diego: Maize Press.

"Los Tísicos." In *Fem: Revista Cultural Feminista* (Mexico City) (April).

1987 "Las Animas." In *La Opinión* (Los Angeles) (Jan.).

1988 "Sandy." In *Saguaro: A Literary Journal* (University of Arizona) (winter).

"Los Calzones de la Piña." In *Las Mujeres Hablan.* Albuquerque: El Norte Publications/University of New Mexico Press.

"Chochis and the Movies at Sanfer." In *California Childhood: Recollections and Stories of the Golden State,* ed. Gary Soto. Berkeley: Creative Arts Book Company.

"The Funeral of Daniel Torres." In *Americas Review,* "U.S. Hispanic Autobiography" 16/3–4. Houston: Arte Público.

1989 "Rose." In *Phoebe: An Interdisciplinary Journal of Feminist Scholarship, Theory, and Aesthetics* (SUNY College, Oneonta, New York) (October).

"Los Tísicos." In *Confluencia: Revista Hispanica de Cultura y Literatura* 6/1 (fall) (University of Northern Colorado, Greeley).

1990 "Enero." In *Graywolf Annual,* vol. 7, *Stories from the American Mosaic.* St. Paul: Graywolf Press.

"How I Changed the War and Won the Game." In *Mexican American Literature,* ed. Charles Tatum. Chicago: Harcourt Brace Jovanovich.

"El Mes de Mayo." In *Fem: Revista Cultural Feminista* (Mexico City) (October).

"Mending" and "The Color Red." In *Frontiers: A Journal of Women Studies* 11, "Las Chicanas."

1992 "Blizzard." In *Iguana Dreams: Anthology of Hispanic American Writers,* ed. V. Suarez. New York: Houghton Mifflin.

"The Marijuana Party." In *Mirrors Beneath the Earth: Short Fiction by Chicano Writers,* ed. Ray González. Willimantic, Conn.: Curbstone Press.

1993 "Campesinas," "Onions," "Grandma's Apron." In *Aztlán: Journal of Chicano Studies* 20/1–2 (Chicano Studies Research Center, UCLA).

"Concha." In *Growing Up Chicano: An Anthology,* ed. Tiffany Ana López. New York: William Morrow.

"On Writing: An Essay." In *New Chicana/Chicano Writing,* vol. 3, ed. Charles Tatum. Tucson: University of Arizona Press.

1994 "Green, or Red?" In *In Other Words: Literature by Latinas of the United States,* ed. Roberta Fernández. Houston: University of New Mexico Press.

1995 "The American Way." In *Confluencia: Revista Hispanica de Cultura y Literatura* (University of Northern Colorado, Greeley) 10/2 (spring). Ed. Alfonso Rodríguez, Department of Hispanic Studies.

"Just Dessert." In *Latina: Women's Voices from the Borderlands,* ed. Lillian Castillo Speed. New York: Simon and Schuster.

"Mandy." In *Where Coyotes Howl and Wind Blows Free: Growing Up in the West,* ed. Alexandra R. Haslam and Gerald W. Haslam. Reno: University of Nevada Press.

1998 "A Passion for Jürgen." In *Anglistik* 912 (September): 21–45.

Nonfiction

1983 "The Honeymoon Is Over." In *Daily Bruin* (Los Angeles, UCLA) (January).

"Juan Gómez Quinones: Scholar and Poet." In *Caminos* (Los Angeles) (June).

1984 "Profile of Dr. Shirlene Soto, Vice Provost: California State University at Northridge." In *Caminos* (Los Angeles) (June).

"Wedding in Loreto." In *Caminos* (Los Angeles) (Dec.).

1992 "Rosemary Catacalos, Southwest Poet: A Literary Biography." In *Dictionary of Literary Biographies: Chicano Writers,* 2d series, ed. Francisco A. Lomelí and Carl S. Shirley. Chicago: Gale Research.

1995 "Learning About Police Harassment—Firsthand." *Los Angeles Times,* Oct. 22.

"Third World Conditions in Backyard." *Los Angeles Times,* Nov. 14.

1996 "A Cure for What Ails You, Sprouting in the Backyard." *Los Angeles Times,* Jan. 14.

"Old vs. New History." *Los Angeles Times,* Mar. 10.

"Stress of Being Poor Takes Its Toll." *Los Angeles Times,* May 26.

1997 "Cultural Schizophrenia Among Chicanas." In *Saludos Hispanos* (Aug.)

"Essay: On Language." In *Women Studies Quarterly* (fall).

"Mothers Day Revisited." In *Hispanic Magazine* (May).

"Women and Sports: A Healthy Mix." *Los Angeles Times,* May 26.

ACHILLES STUDIO

Estela Portillo-Trambley

Playwright, Fiction Writer, Poet, and Actress

"Writing is still my journey of self-discovery."

EL PASO, TEXAS, FEBRUARY 14 AND 28, 1997

Estela Portillo-Trambley died in December 1998. Her papers have become part of the Nettie Lee Benson Latin American Collection at the University of Texas at Austin. This appears to be one of the last in-depth interviews conducted with Portillo-Trambley, a pioneer of Chicana literature, and I am very grateful to her daughter Bethany Portillo-Trambley for granting permission to publish it. I hope the publication of this illuminating interview, along with the list of Portillo-Trambley's work, will contribute to keeping alive the memory of this gifted writer, playwright, actress, and teacher, and honor her groundbreaking work in the fields of Chicano/a literature, theater, culture, and the arts.

ESTELA PORTILLO-TRAMBLEY, a native of El Paso, Texas, was the first Chicana to publish a book of short stories (*Rain of Scorpions and Other Writings*, 1977) and the first to write and perform a musical comedy (*Sun Images*, 1976). A distinguished Chicana playwright, fiction writer, and poet, Portillo-Trambley has had several other works published, including the plays *The Day of the Swallows* (1971) and *Sor Juana and Other Plays* (1983), the musicals *Morality Play* (1974) and *Sun Images* (1976), the novel *Trini* (1986), and a collection of haiku, *Impressions of a Chicana* (1974). In 1983 a radio adaptation of her short story "The Burning" was produced at a Western Public Radio workshop. At the time of the interview, Portillo-Trambley was finishing her second novel and also working on a new collection of short stories and a one-woman theatrical piece.

Estela Portillo-Trambley was born on January 16, 1936, to Frank (a diesel mechanic) and Delfina Portillo. In 1953 she married Robert D. Trambley, who was in the automobile business. They have five children and several grandchildren and live in El Paso, Texas. Portillo-Trambley graduated from the University of Texas at El Paso in 1957 with a B.A. in English. After having worked for several years as a high school English teacher in El Paso (1957–1964) and as chair of the English department at El Paso Technical Institute (1964–1970), she went back to UT El Paso and earned an M.A. in English in 1977. A former resident dramatist, teacher, and theater director of Community College in El Paso (1970–1975), she has also been a hostess for several radio and TV shows, including the talk show *Estela Says* on Radio KIZZ (1969–1970) and the cultural show *Cumbre* on KROD-TV (1971–1972). Since 1979 she has been affiliated with the Department of Special Services at El Paso Public Schools.

In her work, Portillo-Trambley examines the quest for self-determination of women and Chicanos in societies that assign them to subservient roles. She then puts the Chicano/a experience in a broader, international context. As Thomas Vallejos discusses in "Mestizaje: The Transformations of Ancient Indian Religious Thought in Contemporary Chicano Fiction," Portillo-Trambley's writing and her belief that the human sprit is more powerful than its environment goes back to ancient Nahuatl cosmology.[1] In that context Portillo-Trambley emphasizes the importance of nature and the need for an international, cross-cultural, and nonpolitical humanism, a vital and human experience that everyone, whatever ethnicity or gender, can relate to. Therefore, she considers her work to be written not just for a Chicano/a audience or for readers within the Americas, but for people from all over the world.

KARIN IKAS Looking back to how everything started when you were born in El Paso and raised by your grandparents, what were the cultural, societal and personal factors that somehow influenced you most to become the person you are right now?

ESTELA PORTILLO-TRAMBLEY I grew up in a Mexican culture, middle class, where the fabric of my life was threaded in the traditions of church rituals, a happy extended family, and people open and affectionate and very disorganized. I was raised by grandparents who adored me, spoiled me outrageously, and gave me a love for reading and music. In Mexico, my *abuelita* [grandmother] Mama Chita had been the harpist for the Chihuahua Symphony Orchestra. I was highly introspective and preferred reading to playing with friends. My grandparents had three small grocery stores in the barrio. Presidio life with all its laughter and tears was part of the common pattern in my life. I was not really of the barrio, but the barrio was an important part of my life. Spanish was my first language; English was the language of my reading world. This was the world I lived in—an idealistic world, an unreal world that filled my senses with hopes, with joy and identification. My experiences were not a part of a struggling world, the isolation of racism that ran rampant outside the barrio in a white world. If that had touched me, I would have been a different writer, probably a better writer.

K.I. Do you feel comfortable with terms like "Hispanic," "Chicana," "Mexican American," or "Latina"? How would you describe yourself?

E.P.T. I feel comfortable with any of the labels—"Hispanic," "Chicana," "Mexican American," and "Latina." I am all of them: Deep in my psyche I am no different than any American—I have a greater command of their language than they do. I am a composite of all the heroines in the books I've read—legendary, mythological, fictional ones. I wonder if I am real? I want to be!

K.I. How are your feelings about Texas, California, New Mexico, and the U.S. in general? Do you feel there is a big difference between Chicanos and Chicanas from Texas, California, or New Mexico?

E.P.T. My feeling for Texas is like this: I like the mountains of vegetation, the sunsets, and the overall good weather. I like New Mexico as well. There white audiences go to Spanish plays and enjoy them. People in New Mexico are great on culture, and they feel their history. In California I have lectured in almost every university. I taught at the University of California at Riverside for one semester; as a guest writer I was farmed out to UCLA, Stanford, et cetera, for readings, workshops, and lectures. I was a visiting playwright at Claremont College for six weeks. I held a presidential chair in creative writing at UC Davis in 1995. Many universities have put on my plays, and I always attend these performances. California is *my state*. I love the people, the atmosphere, the university life. It's like a seen heaven! I would like to live in California if most of my family were not in El Paso!

K.I. What about the Chicana writers in these places?

E.P.T. I think all Chicana writers, no matter in which state they live, have a common focus on the exploitation of women, their struggle for emergence as a whole woman, emancipation, and the problem of loneliness.

K.I. In an interview with Juan Bruce-Novoa in 1980,[2] you mentioned that at that time you were still searching for your role as a writer vis-à-vis the Chicano Movement. How do you feel about the Chicano Movement and your role in the movement, and in Chicana and Chicano literature right now, seventeen years later?

E.P.T. I am still searching for my role as a writer, not so much vis-à-vis in the Chicano Movement, but as a woman writer for all audiences. I've always been at the peripheries of the Chicano Movement because the Chicano world does not consider me Chicana enough. They, however, respect me as a writer. As a writer in my latest work, I seem to be getting out of the Chicano experiences, but never out of my "Indian-ness." The gods of Mexico are part, in most part, of my foundation.

K.I. Being the first Chicana to publish a book of short stories [*Rain of Scorpions and Other Writings*] in 1976 and the first to write a musical comedy [*Morality Play*, 1974], you are a pioneer of modern Chicana literature. In the 1980s and 1990s more and more Chicana writers appeared on the literary scene.

Do you feel there might be a "generational gap" between the earlier Chicana writers like yourself, who started in the 1970s, and the younger generation of Chicana writers, like Roberta Fernández, Demetria Martínez, Helena María Viramontes?

E.P.T. There is no "generational gap." I tend to be very universal in my writing and belong to all time.

K.I. Do you think that nowadays Chicanas, more and more, dare to set the rules and limits for how much male behavior and vision will impact their lives? Have women therefore reached the stage you asked for in 1979: "Not to fight machismo but to transcend it"?[3]

E.P.T. I just finished telling you I was timely! But today the abhorrence of machismo is felt not only by strong women, but also by *intelligent, secure* males.

K.I. Although your work—in particular, *Rain of Scorpions and Other Writings*—is often studied with regard to how you portray and develop female characters, your work seems to convey less an exclusively female message but a quest for a new transcendental humanism, one that transgresses borders and celebrates a mystical union between human beings and nature. Would you agree with that—in particular with regard to your novel *Trini* and the new and revised edition of *Rain of Scorpions and Other Writings* (now *Rain of Scorpions and Other Stories*, 1992)?

E.P.T. You've got it! By the way, don't refer to the first *Rain of Scorpions*! Use the second. It is so much better.

K.I. How much are you influenced in your writing by Native American culture and spirituality?

E.P.T. It is the most important influence—because it is part of nature. Furthermore, the Toltec philosophy that goes back to the eighth century is as beautiful as the Greeks'. Our association with respect for nature is the very best in every human being.

K.I. The new edition, *Rain of Scorpions and Other Stories*, differs significantly from the first or original edition, *Rain of Scorpions and Other Writings*, from 1975. It contains just five of the ten stories of the original version, and even these have been revised, and are joined by four new stories. The 1992 version seems to be more about a new vision than a new edition. Would you agree with that? And if so, could you be a bit more specific about this new vision?

Also, what was your motivation for rewriting instead of publishing a completely new short story collection?

And finally, what were your reasons for not including the stories "The Trees," "Pilgrimage," "Duende," "Recast," and "The Secret Room" in the 1992 edition?

E.P.T. I have grown in my humanitarianism and that is reflected in the new edition, titled *Rain of Scorpions and Other Stories*. The vision is the same, but now it is clear and more real.

I owed the first *Rain* a rewrite. My philosophy of a good writer is: "Good writing is rewriting!" I have learned to write by trial and error (the first *Rain*). I believe writing is a skill, not a God-given talent. We improve as human beings, improve in our wisdom, and improve as writers. I am not the writer of 1979.

I did not include the other stories because they needed too much work. "The Trees" was awful. It had a novel plot (a whole book) contrary to the development of a short story. Whenever I spoke of it to university audiences, I always warned that "The Trees" is the way *not* to write a short story.

K.I. What is the ultimate message you want to communicate to the reader of your work? How did that change—in particular, with regard to the first and the revised editions of the *Rain of Scorpions* short story collections?

E.P.T. The second *Rain of Scorpions* is more accepting of people and situations. It does not pontificate like the first *Rain*. I hope that I've improved as a writer, not to communicate a message, but to speak "life"!

K.I. In the past you have been accused by some critics of overloading your stories in order to "preach" to the reader about your beliefs; for example, about your belief in a general concept of wholeness, which you describe in the title story of *Rain of Scorpions* as the "Full Circle of all things." How do you feel about that criticism? Does a writer sometimes have to be a preacher?

E.P.T. The critics were right! I pontificated! No, we do not preach in fiction. It is a cardinal sin! I had to live in reality to be humble. But the "Full Circle of all things" is not preaching. It is the vision of Indian philosophy, and the truth about men's actions in the realm of nature.

K.I. Your writing is very international in the sense that you deal with a wide range of different countries, cultures, and ethnic groups: France ["The Paris Gown"], Spain ["Duende"], Germany ["The Secret Room" and "If It Weren't for the Honeysuckle"], Mexico [*Trini*], the gypsy culture ["Duende"], and of course Native American, Chicana/o, and Anglo-American culture and life.

What do you therefore associate with terms like "intercultural understanding," "multiculturalism," and "internationalism," and how do you feel about the concept of the world as a "global village"?

E.P.T. All these terms and concepts touch on the "sameness" in all beings. Barriers are odious and against nature.

K.I. How important is traveling to you, and how does it affect your writing?

E.P.T. My travels have always been tied to my writings: "Transfusions for the imagination."

K.I. Do you think tourism can enhance a global mutual understanding, or does it just foster stereotypes?

E.P.T. Tourism fosters stereotypes. Tourists are mostly *not* enlightened people—middle-class mindlessness! They do more harm than good.

K.I. What about the role of literature in that context? Do you feel that literature can promote a nonbiased coming together of different cultures and people? Can it therefore enhance a deeper understanding across various borders: cultural, ethnic, racial, class, and sexual?

E.P.T. Good literature can promote a coming together of different cultures. But it is a slow process, and words seldom move mountains.

K.I. Speaking about borders and border crossing: What do you think about Gloria Anzaldúa's work *Borderlands/La Frontera*? Do you agree with her vision of a new mestiza consciousness? Does the new Chicana live in several "in betweens," or Borderlands, as Anzaldúa sees it?

E.P.T. Sounds great, but I have not had the pleasure of reading *Border-lands* yet.

K.I. What is your interest in writing right now? Do you pursue certain themes? Certain projects? Certain genres? What about your future plans?

E.P.T. My latest novel, "Masihani," develops a new theory of the origin of the folktale La Llorona because all books written on La Llorona so far are not sufficiently researched. I researched my book in all Mexican Indian lore. I found the origin of the folktale in tenth-century Toltec mythology. All stories of La Llorona never place her tale before the fifteenth century. Her story—part mythology, part fiction—takes place in the three Heavens of the Toltecs. It is her tragic love for the Prince of Darkness, Tezcathipocol, which makes the nature god turn away from her. The only human she is ever able to tell her story is a professor of folklore from a university in Abedea, Texas. That's why he becomes a protagonist in my sequel to "Masihani," called "Ghost Dancing in Abedea." Currently, I am in the midst of this novel. Meantime I have rewritten all the plays in my anthology *Sor Juana and Other Plays*. In addition, I have rewritten *Days of the Swallows*, and I have converted the play *Sor Juana* into one of monologues for a one-woman show. My daughter, an actress, performs it in universities in Colorado, New Mexico, and Texas. Also my play *Sun Images* has been rewritten, four times, with less plot. It is called *Los Amores de Don Estufas*.

K.I. What happened to your novels *La Luz* and *Woman of the Earth* that had been in progress in 1980? Did you ever publish them?

E.P.T. *La Luz* and *Woman of the Earth* became one novel titled *Trini*. Bilingual Press published it in 1986.

K.I. Besides the new and revised edition of *Rain of Scorpions and Other Stories* in 1993, you haven't published a book for years. Why is that so?

E.P.T. I have published short stories in seventeen American short story anthologies. Right now I am looking for an American publisher for "Masihani" and "Ghost Dancing in Abedea." I am also writing a new short story collection called "La Posada del Rey."

K.I. Are you planning on rewriting some of your other works, too? If that is the case, then what is going to be different in these revised editions?

E.P.T. The stories left out from the first *Rain* will be meticulously rewritten and be part of the new short story collection "La Posada del Rey."

K.I. In the already mentioned interview with Juan Bruce-Novoa you describe Chicano literature's distinctive perspective on life, and the effects of Chicano literature on literature in general as follows: "The Chicano can cement tradition to changing trends; a restructuring toward universality; the new American, the cosmic man."[4]

Can you tell us a bit more about this "new American, the cosmic man"?

E.P.T. This was a nice idealistic dream of long ago. It is not going to happen. These days I refuse to deal with idealism. There is enough good happening in the real struggle in an America still blinded by racism.

K.I. Would you like to say something on your person or on your work that we haven't touched upon yet?

E.P.T. I think I've said too much in the world and not done enough. My happiest involvement is with my six children and seven grandchildren. They fill my life. Reading and writing are luxuries to me now. But writing is still my journey of self-discovery.

NOTES

1. Thomas Vallejos, "Mestizaje: The Transformations of Ancient Indian Religious Thought in Contemporary Chicano Fiction." Ph.D. diss., 1980. DAI 41.4A:1602.

2. Juan Bruce-Novoa, "Estela Portillo-Trambley," in *Chicano Authors: Inquiry by Interview* (Austin: University of Texas Press, 1980), pp. 163–181.

3. Estela Portillo-Trambley in a video interview with Professor Francisco Lomelí at the University of California at Santa Barbara, 1979.

4. Bruce-Novoa, "Estela Portillo-Trambley," p. 176.

BIBLIOGRAPHY

For a comprehensive bibliography, see Patricia Hopkins, "Bibliography of Works by and about Estela Portillo-Trambley," in *Rain of Scorpions and Other Stories*, pp. 171–175.

Plays

1971 *The Day of the Swallows.* First published in *El Grito* 4/3 (spring 1971): 4–47.
1974 *Morality Play* (three-act musical). First produced in El Paso at Chamizal

National Theatre. Excerpt from *Morality Play* in *Chicanas en la Literatura y el Arte*. Special issue of *El Grito* 7/1 (Sept. 1973): 5–6.

1975 *El Hombre Cósmico*. [The Cosmic Man.] First produced at Chamizal National Theatre in 1975. Unpublished.

1976 *Sun Images* (musical). First produced at Chamizal National Theatre. Published in Kanellos, Nicolás, and Huerta (eds.), *Nuevos Pasos: Chicano and Puerto Rican Drama*. Special issue of *Revista Chicano-Riqueña* 7/1 (winter 1979): 19–42.

1983 *Sor Juana and Other Plays*. Ypsilanti, Mich.: Bilingual Press. In addition to *Sor Juana*, this collection includes the plays *Puente Negro, Autumn Gold*, and *Black Light*.

Prose

1975 *Rain of Scorpions and Other Writings*. Berkeley, Calif.: Tonatiuh International.

1986 *Trini*. Binghamton, N.Y.: Bilingual Press.

1993 *Rain of Scorpions and Other Stories*. Tempe, Ariz.: Bilingual Press.

Editor

1973 *Mujeres en Arte y Literatura*. Berkeley, Calif.: Quinto Sol.

Forthcoming

"Ghost Dancing in Abedea."

"Masihani."

"La Posada del Rey," a collection of short stories.

K ARIN IKAS is a postdoctoral fellow and lecturer at the University of Würzburg, Germany, in the Department of Cultures, Languages, and Literatures of English Speaking Countries. She holds an interim diploma (similar to a bachelor of arts degree) and a master of arts degree (1996) in English literature and linguistics, and German linguistics from the University of Würzburg. In 1999 she was awarded a doctor of philosophy degree with overall excellence (summa cum laude) in English and American literatures and cultural studies from the University of Würzburg; her doctoral thesis is titled "Die zeitgenössische Chicana-Literatur: Eine interkulturelle Untersuchung" [Modern Chicana-Literature: An Intercultural Analysis] (Heidelberg: C. Winter, 2000).

Ikas has participated in the Quarter-Study Program of the State University of New York College at Oneonta, and has been awarded several prestigious scholarships, including the one-year undergraduate exchange scholarship for the University of Texas at Austin; the 1996-DAAD (the German Academic Exchange Service) graduate scholarship for the United States to conduct extensive research on Chicano/a studies and literature at the University of New Mexico at Albuquerque, the University of California at Berkeley, and the University of California at Santa Barbara; the renowned KAS (Konrad-Adenauer Foundation) scholarship for outstanding graduate students and dissertation fellows (1997–1999); and the HSP III postdoctoral scholarship.

Ikas is a member of MLA, ANGLISTIK (German Scholars of English Association), the German Association for American Studies, the Bavarian American Academy, DHV (Association of German Universities), and

the DAAD-Alumnis. Her publications include articles on Chicana literature, feminism, cultural studies, and a collection of short stories for high
school students, *Mexican American Stories* (München: Langenscheidt-
Longman, 2001). In addition, she is coeditor (with Francisco A. Lomelí,
UC Santa Barbara) of *U.S. Latino Literatures and Cultures: Transnational Perspectives* (Heidelberg: C. Winter, 2000). She has participated in several
national and international conferences where she presented papers in
English, including, among others, conferences in Frankfurt, Germany;
Shreveport, Louisiana, U.S.A.; Pamplona and Malaga, Spain; and Bris-
bane and Adelaide, Australia. She is particularly interested in ethnic literatures, the international reception of Chicano/a literature, and the
intersection of Chicano/a studies, feminist studies, and cultural studies.
Her new research projects also involve studies of female writers, particularly playwrights of the 1860s to the 1930s, war and gender, and modern
drama of the English-speaking world.

INDEX

Page numbers in **boldface** refer to illustrations

Homophobia: and lesbians, 153, 192
Huerta, Dolores, 23
Huitzilopochtli, 14
Human rights activism: Martínez
and, 113, 115

Ibarbourou, Juana de, 70, 79
Infante, Pedro, 60
Identity: ideas of, xiv; role of art and
literature in, xiv, xv; female, 37
INS (Immigration and Naturalization
Service), 119–20
INTAR (Hispanic-American Arts Cen-
ter, N.Y.), 154
Intercultural: situation, 8; under-
standing, 8, 58, 120, 139–40, 184,
210
Internal exiles: Chicanas as, 21
Ishtar (goddess), 39, 43, 122

Jews: as Chicana ancestors, 60, 114,
122; as fictional characters, 187

Kahlo, Frida, 140
Kitchen Table: Women of Color
Press, 154
Koning-Martinez, Tessa, 97, 110n. 7
Kristeva, Julia, xiv
Kundera, Milan, 121

Language. See Spanish language
Latina: as self-definition, 51, 207;
experience, 107; perceptions of, 96,
99, 101–2, 146, 183; sensibility, 107;
voice, 136
Latin American Theatre Artists, 155
Latina/os: identity of, 133; as consumers, 100; as writers, 145
Latina Theatre Lab, xv, 5–6, 92,
96–108 passim, 164. See also Lujan,
Jamie
Latino Arts Center (San Jose, Calif.),
13

Lesbian, 19, 153, 158, 192; and lesbian-
ism, 155, 158; of color, 169. See also
Queer
Literature: globalization of, 124
Llorona, La, 6, 9, 12, 13, 17, 23, 73, 101,
140–41, 166, 197, 211
Lomelí, Francisco, xv, 19, 188
López, Josefina, xv–xi, 20, 164
López-Medina, Silvia, 196
Lorca, Federico García, 51, 70, 83, 135
Lorde, Audre, 159, 169
Lugones, María, 15
Lujan, Jamie, 90: interview, 91–111; on
acting, 94–96; background of,
91–94; on being Chicana, 92–93, 98;
on Chicano theater, 97, 103–5; and
Latina Theater Lab, 96–97, 98, 104,
105, 106–7; on stereotyping, 96, 97,
99–101;
—works of, 110–11; The Immaculate
Conception, 100–103, 104, 105;
"¿¡Qué Nueves!?" 98–100

Machismo, 60, 103, 208
Madre de los Desaparecidos, 121–22
Malinche, La, 23, 39, 77–79, 100, 101,
123, 140–41
Mango (press and literary magazine),
28
Marimacha, 18, 19. See also Movimiento Macha, El
Márquez, Gabriel García, 51
Márquez, Teresa, 123
Marriage: as an institution, 185
Martínez, Demetria, 112, 135; interview, 113–25; background of, 113,
114–15; on Chicana/o literature,
124; on crossing cultural borders,
119, 120; and Sanctuary Movement,
113–14, 119–20, 124; and Spanish
language, 115, 118, 123; on spirituality, 122, 124; on writing, 116–18, 121,
123–24

Guadalupe, 1, 17, 23, 39, 79, 92, 100, 101, 122, 140–41, 197
Virgin Mary, 15, 197
Virgin-whore mythology: in Chicano culture, 100

Wagner, Richard, 70
Walker, Alice, 31, 135, 159. *See also* African American
Weil, Simone, 193
White Buffalo Woman, 17
Winfrey, Oprah, 140
Wolfe, Thomas, 51
Women: place of, in major religions, 15, 16, 38; oppression of, 28; and political activism, 118–19; as writers, 19, 195, 208. *See also* Women-of-color
Women-of-color: and feminism, xviii, 5, 158, 161

Women Writers' Union, 4
Working Women's Festival (San Francisco, Calif.), 106
Wong, Nellie, 4
Woo, Merlie, 4
WORD FOR WORD THEATRE CO., 91, 106
Writers: people of color as, 134; role of, 117, 121, 208
Writing: approaches to, 7; as healing ritual, 71, 116, 167; process of, 69–70

Yamayá (female deity), 17, 39. *See also* Spirituality
Yarbro-Bejarano, Yvonne, xiv, 166

Zamora, Bernice, 32, 80, 86
Zamora, Daisy, 117